Wendy Wasserstein

MICHIGAN MODERN DRAMATISTS
Enoch Brater, Series Editor

Michigan Modern Dramatists offers the theatergoer concise, accessible, and indispensable guides to the works of individual playwrights, as interpreted by today's leading drama critics.

TITLES IN THE SERIES
Edward Albee by Toby Zinman
Suzan-Lori Parks by Deborah R. Geis
Harold Pinter: The Theatre of Power by Robert Gordon
Paula Vogel by Joanna Mansbridge
Wendy Wasserstein by Jill Dolan

Wendy Wasserstein

Jill Dolan

UNIVERSITY OF MICHIGAN PRESS
ANN ARBOR

Published in the United States of America by the
University of Michigan Press
Printed and bound by CPI Group (UK) Ltd, Croydon, CR0 4YY

2020   2019   2018   2017   4   3   2   1

A CIP catalog record for this book is available from the British Library.

Library of Congress Cataloging-in-Publication data has been applied for.

ISBN 978-0-472-07362-7 (hardcover : alk. paper)
ISBN 978-0-472-05362-9 (paper : alk. paper)
ISBN 978-0-472-12313-1 (e-book)

Acknowledgments

This book became one of those emblematic projects in the life of a scholar, the kind that gets snagged on the shoals of career and geographical transitions that force it to wallow and flounder, because you just can't give it the time it deserves. In 2006 editor LeAnn Fields generously suggested I write a book about Wendy Wasserstein for Michigan's Modern Dramatists series. She thought it would be a neat trick for a feminist critic who'd been mostly sour about the playwright's work to write a full-length consideration of her plays. In part because her death had already prompted me to rethink Wasserstein's opus, I agreed, signed the contract, started working, and soon found my life uprooted by a move from the University of Texas at Austin to Princeton University. I returned to Wasserstein often in the years that followed but could not find sustained time to do the project justice. I hope I have finally been able to do that here.

Over its long gestation, numerous friends and colleagues provided incalculable support, advice, and insights. Michael Cadden and Bob Sandberg, my Princeton Theater Program colleagues, both went to the Yale School of Drama with Wasserstein and knew her well. Michael introduced me to others, including playwright Christopher Durang, who spoke with me by phone. Bob shared with me an unpublished version of Wasserstein's first play, *Any Woman Can't*, which he directed at Yale, and recollected for me how the process and the production were received.

Katie Welsh, the ace research assistant and 2015 Princeton graduate I've shared with Stacy Wolf over the years, helped me finish the book over several summers, collecting reviews, fact checking, and drafting paragraphs that compiled her research. I honestly could not have completed this book without her eye for detail, her magnanimous assistance, her excellent writing and research skills, and her supportive good humor. My colleagues and friends Wendy Belcher, Judith Hamera, and Tamsen Wolff read a draft of the introduction, offering me a deadline that jump-started the end of the writing process and sharing insightful suggestions for how to organize the book's opening salvos about Wasserstein's life. Tamsen's essay in the *Chron-*

icle of Higher Education on the occasion of Wasserstein's death remains one of the best short-form analyses of the playwright's work. Emily Mann—the director, playwright, and long-time artistic director of Princeton's McCarter Theatre—reminded me again and again of the value of Wasserstein's plays, even as Emily's diverged politically and formally from the commercial comedies that made Wasserstein famous. Emily's artistic generosity is, I hope, a model for what I intend as my own critical generosity here.

Stacy Wolf patiently lived with me and with Wendy over this project's many years, persuading me that I could indeed finish the book before my life took yet another turn in directions that would take me farther from this material. Her emotional support, intellectual engagement, and keen editorial eye make everything possible and, somehow, pleasurable.

I'd like to thank Catherine Schuler and David Saltz, and the anonymous reviewer they solicited, for their editorial work on my essay "Feminist Performance Criticism and the Popular: Reviewing Wendy Wasserstein," *Theatre Journal* 60.3 (October 2008): 433–57, which became, in a profound revision, the basis for this book's introduction.

Contents

Preface: The Context

This book offers a critical analysis of Wendy Wasserstein's major plays. When I became a feminist theater and performance critic and theorist in the early 1980s, feminist theater and performance studies privileged collective theater work and radical strategies that saw theater as an agent of social change. Feminist theater theorists then eschewed the kind of playwriting that Wasserstein's exemplified: realism of the "dramedy" style, written by a single playwright with a singular voice. Many feminist theorists even encouraged artists to overthrow exactly these conventions, to explode realism and what they saw as other outmoded styles and genres, and urged playwrights toward the collective devising that British playwrights like Caryl Churchill pioneered and to which feminist groups like At the Foot of the Mountain and the Women's Experimental Theatre aspired. For many feminist performance theorists in the 1980s, a study of a single playwright smacked of liberal, accommodationist critical practices. And we'd have none of it.

I was a part of that movement thirty-five years ago, a fellow (or sister) traveler with critical firebrands who took no prisoners as they blazed new ways of thinking about the political potential of performance for women, people of color, lesbians and gay men, and those whose identities crossed these and other categories. A lot of excellent critical and artistic work derived from those commitments, and our conversations and debates urged audiences and critics to think seriously about performance subcultures that might otherwise never have been written into history.

But meanwhile, playwrights committed to working within conventional forms often infuse them with radical politics. And the theater "industry"—whether on Broadway, in the regional theaters, in college and university theaters, or in community, amateur theaters—continued to perpetuate itself and its practices. The business as usual that many feminist theorists in the eighties disparaged as liberal, assimilationist modes of production continued to dominate the mainstream scene. Women fared no better there than ever; the number of female playwrights produced on Broadway, as only one index, remained stagnant year after year.

But in the early eighties, collectives reigned in the imaginations of feminist performance theorists like myself, as we read poststructuralist theory that proclaimed the "death of the author" in ways useful to women who had too long been taught only the history of plays written by men. Those ideas fueled a generation or more of theater and performance critics and artists committed to social change, encouraging them to think differently about form and structure, spectatorship and reception. Those ideas reimagined theater's potential to change how people see, think, and act toward one another in the larger human landscape.

At the same time, however, women continued studying to be authors and aspired to be playwrights whose voices would contribute to the narratives theater tells to enhance our understanding of contemporary, historical, and future cultures. Thanks in part to the work of the feminist movement inside the academy and out, more women entered MFA playwriting, directing, and design programs, which by the 1980s had proliferated across the American academy. By the early 1990s, pioneering women like Emily Mann, Timothy Near, Martha Lavey, and Irene Lewis had taken the helm of resident theaters like McCarter in New Jersey, the San Jose Repertory Theatre in California, Steppenwolf in Chicago, and Center Stage in Baltimore, embarking on twenty-plus-year-long careers that helped to shape the professional theater as we know it today. These women followed in the footsteps of Zelda Fichandler, who helped found the regional theater movement when she established Arena Stage in Washington, DC, in the 1950s. These women used their platforms, insights, and talents to advocate for new voices and styles. And although they're all white women of a certain generation, these female artistic directors produced work by women and men of color, LGBT people, and international playwrights to create a more diverse tapestry of the interwoven identities, stories, and styles of theater practice.

The last twenty years, as a result, established a new generation of theater artists who deserve sustained, focused, critical and scholarly notice. This generation's women playwrights, especially, produce work of stylistic and thematic variety, cross-cutting forms, structures, and ideas in often thrilling ways. The Michigan Modern Dramatists series already includes monographs on Paula Vogel and

Suzan-Lori Parks. I can imagine reading others about towering figures like María Irene Fornés and Lorraine Hansberry, as well as Annie Baker, Kirsten Greenidge, Sarah Ruhl, Tanya Barfield, Amy Herzog, Quiara Alegría Hudes, Julia Cho, Anne Washburn, Lydia Diamond, Halley Feiffer, Lynn Nottage, Lisa Loomer, Madeleine George, Tanya Saracho, Kia Corthron, Danai Gurira, Lisa Kron, and many, many more women playwrights who have all produced bodies of work that could sustain a critical investigation like the one I've written about Wendy Wasserstein here.

This is the historical and contemporary context in which I offer this critical engagement with Wendy Wasserstein's most significant plays. My goal has not been to avoid a feminist engagement with modes and sites of production, or the intimate exchange between form and content, or the examination of cultural context and reception as ways to understand a playwright's work within a historical moment. Those theoretical tropes let me look closely at the specific interpretive project Wasserstein's plays provide. Wasserstein, like so many of the women characters she created for our consideration, couldn't do it all. I don't position her in the pages that follow as a theater revolutionary such as, for only one example, the late Judith Malina, whose career with the Living Theatre collective ran parallel in history to Wasserstein's, if in a different world of theater making and political commitments. But in her own sphere, as a woman with aspirations to the mainstream imagination and the cultural forum of Broadway and the regional theaters, Wasserstein offered quite a lot. And her legacy continues.

I hope this book will provide a model for other feminist engagements with theater, ones that speak to students and teachers, scholars and artists, critics and spectators with ideas about how and why plays like Wasserstein's continue to matter in American culture. Our work investigating and intervening in the politics of performance continues.

—Jill Dolan
Princeton, New Jersey

CHAPTER ONE

Wendy Wasserstein:
A Feminist Reconsideration

Wendy Wasserstein's status as a canonical female American play-wright remains intact, years after her untimely death from cancer in 2006 at the age of fifty-five. Born in 1950, Wasserstein lived through the contemporary feminist era in the United States, when much attention was paid to women's equality across society and culture. When she began her education as a playwright at the Yale School of Drama in 1973, she was one of very few women accepted into the prestigious graduate program. When she died thirty-three years later, she was one of very few women whose plays were regularly produced on Broadway and acclaimed with prizes like the Pulitzer or a Tony Award. Wasserstein's exceptionalism continues. Although her oeuvre is limited—she wrote six significant plays, a novel, a children's book, and two collections of essays, as well as numerous articles and interviews over the years—a close examination of her plays reveals quite a lot not just about her talent and prescience as a playwright but about American culture over her lifetime. Wasserstein's plays and their critical reception also illuminate how the theater industry views work by women and women's continued marginalization in the years since Wasserstein died.

Wasserstein's plays remain popular choices for regional and New York theater production. *The Heidi Chronicles* (1989), *The Sisters Rosensweig* (1992), and her final play, *Third* (2005), especially, are often remounted at theaters around the country, and since her death, her early play *Uncommon Women and Others* (1977), too, has been frequently revived. In this book I'll consider what Wasserstein offers

American artists and audiences that allow her plays to be so often produced when so many other women playwrights still can't achieve a toehold on the mountain of public esteem. Obviously, her race and her class privilege provided connections that positioned her to garner public approval. But her plays' familiar themes and genres—mostly comedies or witty, thoughtful, topical dramas—also let them assimilate easily and profitably into the mainstream of popular theater. Wasserstein's work is also important because, chronologically, she is a second-wave, baby-boom feminist, but her aspirations were fulfilled within sanctioned culture, rather than a more experimental or politically radical gendered subculture. And her plays mostly espouse a modern, younger generation's feminist cultural critique, which presumes a complacency about capitalism and the status quo that second-wave feminism once eschewed.

Wasserstein's contributions to public debate about women's lives and her achievements as a contemporary American woman playwright make her an important cultural figure, and her status as a beloved friend, daughter, sister, and mother garners her memory much public affection when her plays are produced. The details of Wasserstein's life spin a good yarn and, in fact, the playwright was known for incorporating autobiographical details and portraits of friends and family in her plays. Many profiles of Wasserstein depict a woman insecure with her own power, who undercut her cultural authority by speaking in a high, squeaky, girlish voice embellished with a giggle. Her mother, Lola, was a domineering woman, an artistically inclined free spirit who nonetheless denigrated her daughter's accomplishments, persistently badgered her about her weight, and criticized her single lifestyle with surprising venom. In 1999 Wasserstein gave birth to her own child, Lucy Jane, after years of fertility treatments and a pregnancy complicated by pre-eclampsia that left her on bed rest. Lucy Jane's father has never been publicly identified.

Aside from these fascinating biographical details, Wasserstein's pioneering work as a playwright deserves more extensive analysis.[1] This book considers Wasserstein's plays through a feminist critical lens. Her work and its public reception changed with the fortunes of feminism, and her life as a playwright parallels the growth of American feminism's second wave in the late 1960s through the 1970s. Her plays, in fact, offer one of the few popular—if partial—histories of the movement's progress and its effects on the daily lives of a certain segment of America's women.[2] Whether or not her plays specifically narrated feminist history, as did her Pulitzer Prize- and Tony Award-winning play *The Heidi Chronicles* and her very last play, *Third*, Wasserstein's oeuvre always depicted women characters whose sense of themselves was determined by shifting social expectations, public politics they were required to work through on the microlevel of very personal choices. Whether debating marriage to a man in *Isn't It Romantic* (1981) or a position in the president's cabinet in *An American Daughter* (1997), Wasserstein's heroines inevitably hold their personal choices accountable to the vagaries of a social movement and the backlash against it that shifted across her thirty-year career.

My own critical project focuses on several questions. What do Wasserstein's plays and career suggest about the last forty years of U.S. feminism? How does her journey through the most powerful echelons of American theater provide a role model—or, on the other hand, a cautionary tale—for artists who might follow? What can we glean from reading her most significant plays with an eye toward the venues in which they were produced, the directors who mounted them, and the designers who helped bring them to life? What's revealed by studying the critical response to Wasserstein, as her plays remained for so long among the few titles by women admitted into the canon of American comedy and drama?

Wasserstein's success on Broadway especially prompts analysis because visibility in commercial, mainstream, popular forums is crucial for women theater artists. As critic Laurin Porter comments, "While popular success is obviously not a reliable index of artistic merit or a worthy objective in and of itself, it is one measure of a work's potential for making an impact. At the very least, it speaks to the possibility of reaching an audience."[3] In other words, a successful run does not automatically mean quality product. *The Book of Mormon*, for instance, which premiered in 2011 as a wildly popular musical created by the television writers who produce the *South Park* series, is seen by some scholars as a lackluster example of American musical theater. But in 2016 it remained one of the most difficult Broadway tickets to secure. And it boasts execrable race and gender politics. Feminist critics continually lambast mainstream commercial and regional nonprofit theater for its persistent gender inequities, as well as for continuing to marginalize playwrights of color.[4] But those critiques don't thwart its financial success.

Wasserstein's career remains ripe for analysis because all these many years into the project of U.S. feminist performance criticism and theory, American women—whether white, straight, lesbian, and/or of color—still have not achieved the visibility and access that feminist arts advocacy might have predicted. Susan Jonas and Suzanne Bennett, in their landmark *Report on the Status of Women: A Limited Engagement!*, prepared for the New York State Council on the Arts in 2002, note that the situation for women playwrights and directors has remained virtually the same over the last almost thirty years.[5] That report is still the only one to publish hard data on the number of women playwrights and directors working in the field. Princeton economics major Emily Glassberg Sands, in 2009, wrote her senior thesis on bias against women playwrights, using the play submission process to demonstrate how male playwrights fare better than their female peers, even under the scrutiny of women artistic directors. Sands's controversial work was widely discussed, but little changed in its wake.[6] In 2016 the Wellesley Center for Women published a report based on research from 2013–14, commissioned by Carey Perloff, the long-term artistic director of the American Conservatory Theater in San Francisco, and Ellen Richard, the theater's former executive director, that studied the gender and race distribution of artistic directors in American resident theaters. Their results, too, showed a shameful hiring pattern in which white men far outnumber women and people of color and those who are both.[7]

Other activist projects on behalf of theater women continue to proliferate. The organization 50/50 in 2020 was established in 2010 by Susan Jonas, Melody Brooks of New Perspectives Theatre, and Julie Crosby, who was then the artistic director of the Women's Project and Productions Theatre, to continue public agitation.[8] The Lilly Awards, named after playwright Lillian Hellman and established by playwrights Julie Jordan, Marsha Norman, and Theresa Rebeck in 2010, produce a gala affair every year that calls attention to notable women theater artists and occasionally the men who support them.[9] An ad hoc group called The Kilroys took to the blogosphere in 2013 to produce a curated list of plays by women that activists could access whenever they were told there are no "good" women writers, a plaint still resorted to frequently when artistic directors are confronted about gender inequality at their theaters.[10] The New York–based League of Professional Theatre Women programs public events, and the Women and Theatre Program of the Association for Theatre in Higher Education holds an annual conference for feminist theater scholars and artists, where it also gives out the distinguished Jane Chambers Playwriting award to a student and a professional each year.[11] In other words, gender, sexuality, and race continue to be salient factors in artists' opportunities to work in American theater. And critical questions about what work by marginalized playwrights means, does, and effects in American culture continue to vex theater artists, critics, and spectators.

This ongoing debate about women in theater makes a study of Wendy Wasserstein's plays timely and relevant. Although she was much beloved as a person and popular as an artist, her career and her life exemplified the complications of being a white, upper-middle-class female playwright in the last decades of the twentieth century. Wasserstein lent herself to contradictory interpretations. When she died from lymphoma, very few of even her closest friends knew the fifty-five-year-old playwright had been ill. At her death, her daughter, Lucy Jane, was seven years old; even Wasserstein's intimates had no idea who had fathered the child she bore as a single parent when she was forty-eight years old. Likewise, while critics and theater industry leaders thought they could easily peg the playwright's work to the genre of witty, popular comedy, her last two plays—*An American Daughter* and *Third*—although funny, seriously and poignantly inquired into the status of professional women and their differential treatment in American life.

Her plays were always wry and comic, but Wasserstein yearned for the gravitas that critics felt mostly escaped her talents. And although many commentators dubbed her a feminist playwright, many feminist critics found her work too liberal and accommodationist to be claimed for a radical political movement. Wasserstein contributed to the contradictions apparent in her life and work, since she was utterly private but professionally powerful in public, where she often projected the ingratiating personal qualities of a much younger, less wise or worldly woman.

Wasserstein acknowledged these disparities and, in fact, sometimes appeared in control of her persona's effects. She told interviewer Esther Cohen in 1988, just as *The Heidi Chronicles* was poised for success, "I giggle a little too much. But yes, I think [that humor is important in my relationships with people] because one, it makes one entertaining, two, it deflects, and also it's a way of commenting on things. . . . And it sort of pricks a hole in things, too, keeps things in line. And then also it helps you deal with things which are overwhelmingly tragic."[12] She appreciated that her plays allowed her to "divide yourself into a lot of characters and hide yourself in different places" and admitted to Cohen that "I am shy."[13] Carrie Richman, who worked as Wasserstein's assistant while she was writing *The Sisters Rosensweig* (1992), emphasizes that the playwright was a warm, generous person eager to take care of Richman, who had just graduated from college, even though Richman was working for her. Richman recalls that although Wasserstein was always "humble and tentative . . . and very funny and very disparaging of her own process," she was also joyful about theater and "felt that being a woman in American theatre was a responsibility."[14]

Wendy Wasserstein had the right pedigree to assume her leadership role. She was born in 1950 to an immigrant Jewish family made good. Her grandfather emigrated from Poland and worked in Yiddish theater, which gave her mother, Lola, an eccentric dancer, an opportunity to have dinner with the famous performer Molly Picon. This sort of status and access to the rich and famous became customary for Wasserstein, although her work satirized them even as she often dined with them. Wasserstein's father, Morris, was a successful textile manufacturer (he invented velveteen) who moved his family fairly early in her life from Brooklyn to Manhattan's Upper East Side. Her siblings became financiers and entrepreneurs. Wasserstein's brother, Bruce, chaired a powerful investment-banking firm and owned *New York Magazine* (he, too, died young, at sixty-one, in 2009, and left a fortune estimated at $2 billion). Wasserstein's two sisters were also securely upper middle class. Georgette Wasserstein Levis (who died in 2014) ran the Wilburton Inn in Vermont and inspired the character Gorgeous in *The Sisters Rosensweig*. Sandra Wasserstein Meyer (who died in 1998) was one of the very first women to succeed in the top ranks of international business, first as a marketer for General Foods and later in positions with American Express and Citicorp.

The Wasserstein family, despite their assimilation into particularly American notions of economic success, also kept secrets in ways that perhaps underlined their shtetl roots. Wasserstein was already an adult when she learned that her older sister, Sandra, actually had a different father. Their mother, Lola, had first been married to George Wasserstein; when he died young of a burst appendix, she married his brother, Morris, but failed to tell Wendy, Georgette, and Bruce about her first husband. In addition, Wendy had another sibling named Abner, also George's son, who was institutionalized as a child because he had epilepsy and emotional challenges. Although Lola and Morris (his uncle) visited Abner throughout their lives, to his siblings he was a shadowy, unknown figure. These family secrets suggest that Wendy came by her own reticence honestly.

Wasserstein was educated at the elite, all-girls Calhoun School on Manhattan's Upper West Side. She went to college at Mount Holyoke, graduated in 1971 with a BA in history, and received an MA in creative writing in 1973 from City College of the City University of New York, where she worked with novelist Joseph Heller and playwright Israel Horovitz. She attended Yale for a masters of fine arts in drama, after a brief debate about whether she'd pursue the arts or go to law school. When she was accepted into the School of Drama, she was one of the very few women playwrights in the program. Her exceptionalism—less generously described as her outsiderness—became significant to her work and her life.

She used humor to deflect and to defend herself from lifelong comments about her gender and her weight. Her mother was one of her worst critics; Lola withheld her approval from Wendy, even after she began to receive the most acclaimed awards in the theater industry, including the Pulitzer Prize for Drama and a Tony Award for *The Heidi Chronicles*. In Lola's strict cosmology, marrying and having children topped any kind of creative work. In a much-quoted phrase, Lola told her daughter, "Your sister-in-law is pregnant and that means more to me than a million dollars or any play."[15] According to Julie Salamon's biography, Wasserstein's mother lived by "the upwardly mobile Jewish mother's motto: 'You can never be too rich or too thin.'"[16] Given that Wasserstein was rarely thin and never quite rich, although her writing eventually allowed her to make a comfortable living, Lola's disapproval haunted.

Wasserstein, in fact, seemed to use her appearance to undercut conventional expectations. In feature stories before her death and in obituaries after, she is often described as unkempt or disheveled, approachable, sometimes ebullient, and often sweet, but never as sophisticated or chic. In an otherwise admiring *New Yorker* profile in 1997, before *An American Daughter* opened on Broadway, writer Nancy Franklin remarks, "Wasserstein, at the age of forty-six, has a bohemian, graduate-student look even when she's wearing tailored clothes. She could be said to resemble the character Janie Blumberg, the budding writer in her 1981 play, *Isn't It Romantic*: 'Her appearance is a little kooky, a little sweet, a little unconfident—all of which some might call creative or even witty.'"[17]

Many of Wasserstein's characters are actually stand-ins for herself and her friends or family, which became her trademark way of populating her plays. Salamon says, "At City College, she began to work on the approach that would become her signature—mingling memory, observation, reality, and fiction. The 'Cuisinart method,' Bruce [her brother] called it. 'She had perfect-pitch memory for conversations, but then she'd put them in the Cuisinart and they'd come out in random ways,' he said."[18] Numerous family members and friends apparently blanched when they recognized themselves (and sometimes their words) in her plays. Wasserstein insisted she took poetic license and told those she hurt that her characters were really all different versions of herself. But her ability to use what she observed among her intimates became, perhaps, a kind of comeuppance for how she felt herself judged against conventional standards of female beauty and accomplishment that her own work often railed against.

Wasserstein's willingness to critique impossible social standards for women struck an obvious chord with her spectators. As she became well known, people would talk to Wasserstein on the street. The playwright William Finn, who was one of Wasserstein's good friends, told Salamon, "When we walked down the street, all these sixty-five-year-old Jewish ladies would come up to Wendy and she would talk to them. . . . They'd talk about their husbands and their daughters, and when they left, I'd ask her who was that, and she'd say, 'I have no idea.' This went on constantly. People embraced her as if she were going to explain their lives to them."[19] And for a certain strata of American women, Wasserstein did just that.

Wasserstein was admitted to Yale on the strength of *Any Woman Can't*, a play she wrote in response to David Reuben's *Any Woman Can!*, a 1971 pop psychology guide to what he saw as women's sexual and personal fulfillment, published as a follow-up to his enormously influential *Everything You Wanted to Know about Sex (But Were*

Afraid to Ask) (1969).[20] The play was produced in 1973 at Playwrights Horizons in New York, which was an incubator for Wasserstein's work throughout her career. Playwright Christopher Durang, who became her lifelong intimate, read *Any Woman Can't* before Wasserstein arrived at the Drama School and remembers it as a funny play about the difficulties of dating. He recalls that when he met Wasserstein, she seemed grouchy, which prompted him to remark, "You must be very smart to be bored so quickly." A variation on the line was later immortalized in *The Heidi Chronicles*, when Peter Patrone meets Heidi Holland at a high school dance where she's reading *Death Be Not Proud* and comments, "You look so bored you must be very bright."[21]

Aside from the friendships she made at Yale, her MFA program was difficult (she called it "the Yale School of Trauma").[22] The school's director, the famed theater critic Robert Brustein, never liked Wasserstein's work. He admonished her for being a lightweight, comic writer and overlooked her presence at the Drama School when he later reported his years there in his own memoirs. Apparently, only when her last play, *Third*, was produced did Brustein give Wasserstein his approbation, which she accepted with grace but reserve. That critics like Brustein didn't take her seriously upset Wasserstein throughout her career. On the other hand, she was determined from the start to rectify what she felt were the gender inequalities in her chosen field. When Wasserstein began at Yale in the early 1970s, feminism was just beginning to percolate through American culture. *Uncommon Women and Others* (1975), which she wrote as her Yale masters' thesis, is a loosely autobiographical comedy that traces a group of five women friends reuniting six years after their college graduation to reminisce about their days together at one of the seven sister schools. Wasserstein used the play to rehearse her own experiences as an undergraduate at Mount Holyoke, but she said she wrote it so that she could see people like herself onstage—a theme that echoed throughout her career. She reported that she very much wanted to see an all-women curtain call on a stage at Yale and relates a typical response: "What I'll never forget about *Uncommon Women* was, there was an after-play discussion . . . and the dramaturg raised his hand and said, 'I can't get into this—it's about girls.' And this was . . . 1976. And I said to him, 'Well, you know, I've spent my life getting into *Hamlet* and *Lawrence of Arabia*, so why don't you just try it?'"[23] In graduate school, professors required her to see and read plays in which women were evil influences on the male heroes; she determined early in her career to reverse that gendered presumption.

Wasserstein's plays often outlined women's issues that were just breaking into public view. *Uncommon Women and Others* remains one of the first protofeminist realist plays, and *Isn't It Romantic*, a too-often-ignored early play, addresses heterosexual romance and marriage with dry-eyed pragmatism. Wasserstein was among the first popular playwrights to engage the terms of feminist debate. Given what was then a range of new professional choices, how would women like her characters manage to juggle romance, family, a career, and politics and gain the esteem of their peers? How would they "have it all," the theme of the zeitgeist that critics see as fundamental to Wasserstein's work, even as she resented that women were forced to confront these questions in ways that men escaped?[24] As Franklin suggests, "Wasserstein's characters have a lot of questions about identity and self-determination, questions that women used to ask silently, if at all: What should my life be like? What if I do this? If I do this, can I still have that? What do I want? And do I really want it, or am I just supposed to want it? And if I don't want it, what do I do then?"[25] These unresolved questions and her ongoing ambivalence about women's place in the world attracted audiences to Wasserstein's plays. People saw themselves and their own doubts in her work, and economically comfortable, white, heterosexual women especially presumed an empathetic airing of their personal and political grievances when they came to see her productions.

But with *The Heidi Chronicles*, her 1989 Broadway debut play, Wasserstein stepped into a fault line of opposing sides in a cultural debate about feminism. *Heidi* is the fulcrum work in her oeuvre, in which the feminist art professor Heidi Holland ventriloquizes Wasserstein's ambivalence about how feminist activism had and hadn't served women by the end of the 1980s. The play perhaps most fiercely stages Wasserstein's accusation that second-wave feminism didn't fulfill the promises with which it enticed women to challenge their personal and political status quos.[26] Because it was the first play by a woman to openly criticize feminism from a Broadway stage, *Heidi* became a lightning rod. This, after all, wasn't Marsha Norman's *'night, Mother* or Beth Henley's *Crimes of the Heart*, the only two plays by women to have won the Pulitzer Prize for Drama in the decade before. Not insignificantly, *'night, Mother* narrates a young woman's decision to (successfully) commit suicide and *Crimes of the Heart* is a Southern gothic comedy about three sisters in a beleaguered family. *Heidi*, by contrast, depicts a consciousness-raising group and a demonstration for women in art and illustrates the casual sexism of men who presume to speak for women. The play also addresses the HIV/AIDS pandemic in the context of Heidi's personal and professional choices. And in Heidi's speech to an audience of women at her high school alma mater, she confesses bitter resentment at what she sees as the false promise of feminist community.

Although the character's choice to adopt a baby at the end of the play and to defer her hope for a feminist future to her daughter's generation set some feminists' teeth on edge, *The Heidi Chronicles'* story about contemporary history made it relevant to debates about feminism happening well beyond Times Square. In her post-*Heidi* plays, Wasserstein continued to track her understanding of the feminist conundrum across several different milieus. She mixed the complexities of Jewish identity with gender exploration in *The Sisters Rosensweig*, a critically acclaimed, frequently produced family saga notable as one of the few plays in which Wasserstein makes the aspirations of and relationships among Jewish American women central to the plot's unfolding. In *An American Daughter*, her incisive, fictionalized account of a Zoe Baird/Kimba Wood/Lani Guinier–style woman's sabotaged nomination for high public office, Wasserstein staged a play of ideas in which gender inequities and the wildly different expectations of feminist generations drive a plot that offers an astute critique of Bill Clinton–era gender betrayals. Her final play, *Third*, is a morality tale that addresses the dogmatism of identity politics in the United States by challenging the values of a second-wave feminist professor caught in the web of her own suddenly parochial beliefs.

Whatever their content, Wasserstein asserted that the fact that her plays were produced at all was a political, feminist gesture. She said, "My work is often thought of as lightweight commercial comedy, and I have always thought, No, you don't understand: this is a political act. *The Sisters Rosensweig* had the biggest advance in Broadway history, therefore nobody's going to turn down a play on Broadway because a woman wrote it or because it's about women."[27] Wasserstein was hopeful about breaking the historical pattern that kept women playwrights invisible, but the important moment that *The Sisters Rosensweig*'s large advance represented faded from memory and, years after her death, little has actually changed for women playwrights who would like to see their work on Broadway.[28] Wasserstein pioneered gender equity in a mainstream forum that continues to be closed to real, lasting progress for women artists. She single-mindedly kept women at the center of her work and insisted that people reckon with the particularities of their lives. When she observed the rampant sexism at Yale during her graduate program, critic Christopher Bigsby says, "She decided to write a play in which all the characters were women, a play whose politics lay essentially in that gesture. As she has said, 'It's political because it's a matter of saying, "You must hear this." You can hear it in an entertaining fashion, and you can hear it from real people, but you must know and examine the problems these women face.'"[29]

The women about whom she wrote were predominantly white, economically comfortable, well-educated, and heterosexual, and many women just like her characters composed the audiences for her plays. Wasserstein was always perceptive about and generous with her audiences. She told interviewer David Savran, "Even when I was young, when I did *Uncommon Women* I thought, I want to put the people who come to my plays up on the stage. Same thing for *The Sisters Rosensweig*. I thought, If the Gorgeouses of life are the matinee ladies, let them see themselves on stage. Why do they have to sit there and see themselves as the wife who's a jerk and getting divorced?"[30] She wrote, too, for professional women "roughly my age," "because those people often keep culture alive."[31]

Always a deft humorist, Wasserstein's Jewish ethnic roots and native New Yorker sensibilities lent her work the wit and pungency of Neil Simon, George Kaufman, and Moss Hart, as well as the intellectual and emotional depth of Arthur Miller.[32] Her plays plumbed the contradictions and consternations of women trying to maintain professional careers as well as rich personal lives. As critic Jan Balakian notes, "Wasserstein is always interested in the traps of being an intelligent, well-educated woman."[33] Like Miller's, her work focuses on domestic situations that resound with telling social detail and poses ethical issues peculiarly American in their concern with the struggle between the individual and her community, between those who would do a modicum of good in the world and the forces that conspire to impede their idealism.

And like those four white, male, Jewish playwrights, Wasserstein's plays for the most part rely on the ethnic cultural knowledge that came from the playwright's ancestry as the child of Jewish immigrants. Her profound sense of outsiderness—often analyzed through her feminist politics—evolved as much from her Jewishness as her gender, and her concern for what it means to be part of any tribe recurs in her plays. Wasserstein is known for her comedies, but laced throughout her work is a rich vein of concern over the state of American democracy and the place of women as major players in its progress. As her career moved forward, her trepidations mirrored the situation of U.S. feminism, shifting focus from the more local, personal analysis of women's domestic lives to pose larger questions about people's relationships to political power and decisions with international resonance. Her plays opened up thematically as her worldview expanded; she insisted in numerous interviews that she wrote "plays of ideas," even if they were funny. She told *The New Yorker*'s Franklin, "In some ways, I wish I *could* write a farce. . . . People say, 'She's commercial,' or 'Her plays are just like Neil Simon's.' I like Neil Simon. I think he's a real craftsman. But then you think, no, *The Heidi Chronicles* is about the women's movement. This man is not obsessed with what I'm obsessed with."[34]

Wasserstein's connections as a Yale graduate and the progeny of a reputable New York family no doubt assisted her career as one of the only female playwrights to regularly see her work produced on Broadway and remounted at the most prominent regional theaters in the United States. Her first two plays immediately captured public attention. *Uncommon Women* was produced at the Phoenix Theatre in New York, presented on television by the PBS *Great Performances* series (1978), and later revived by Second Stage Theatre (1994). In 1981 *Isn't It Romantic* premiered at the Phoenix and was then revised and remounted in 1983 at Playwrights Horizons. That production established her relationship with André Bishop, Gerald Gutierrez, and Daniel Sullivan, prominent men of the theater who would go on to champion or direct the rest of her plays. Sullivan, for example, lent Wasserstein the cachet of a prestigious regional theater in which to hone her work. While he was the artistic director of the Seattle

Repertory Theatre, several of her plays premiered there. Sullivan followed each production to New York, helming the Broadway productions of *The Heidi Chronicles*, *The Sisters Rosensweig*, and *An American Daughter*. Sullivan also directed Wasserstein's final play, *Third*, at the Lincoln Center Theater.

Wasserstein wrote the characters she never got to otherwise see at the theater, just as feminist theater makers of the same era used collective methods to stage stories of women who were invisible in cultural representations. As feminist historian Charlotte Canning suggests, "[The] primary motivation [of the feminist theater groups of the 1970s] was to create performance they were not seeing."[35] Critic Charles Isherwood likewise reports in the obituary he wrote for the playwright that Wasserstein "recalled attending Broadway plays as a young woman and being struck by the absence of people like herself onstage: 'I remember going to them and thinking, I really like this, but where are the girls?'"[36]

Although Wasserstein expressed her politics in a more conventional theater form, her work ran parallel to the same feminist movement that gave birth to theater collectives like It's All Right to Be a Woman Theater, or Split Britches, or At the Foot of the Mountain Theatre in Minneapolis. Wasserstein's career arced from 1973 to 2005, a thirty-year period that was formative for the second and third waves of American feminism and that saw many theater women enter the field with new artistic visions. The feminist theater highlights of the period are notable and would no doubt have influenced Wasserstein's worldview, given that she always lived in New York and was an avid theatergoer from the time she was a child. Although I haven't seen documents that prove whether Wasserstein saw any of this work, these productions and performances were part of the zeitgeist that she soaked up and that no doubt fueled her own work. For example, Lily Tomlin's remarkable *Search for Signs of Intelligent Life in the Universe* premiered on Broadway in 1985, a virtuosic solo performance written by Jane Wagner that narrated the history of the feminist movement and celebrated Geraldine Ferraro's historic 1984 nomination for the U.S. vice presidency on Walter Mondale's presidential ticket. At that point, Wasserstein had written and produced *Isn't It Romantic* and was working on *The Heidi Chronicles*. In performance spaces in downtown Manhattan, Peggy Shaw, Lois Weaver, and Deb Margolin performed their feminist visions as the Split

Britches trio and expanded artists' and audiences' notion of what could be done with performance address and reception. In the 1980s and 1990s the Five Lesbian Brothers launched their own brand of satirical feminist comedy, which was mostly written by Lisa Kron, whose own Jewish sensibility remains so evident and operative in her plays and solo shows. And Margolin began her career as a solo artist, premiering at New York's Jewish Museum in 1996 her performance *O Wholly Night and Other Jewish Solecisms*, in which she treads some of the same comic but rueful territory about Jewish femininity and ethnicity that Wasserstein's plays detail in formally different but thematically similar ways.

In the same era, Eve Ensler's *The Vagina Monologues* premiered at the HERE Arts Center in 1996 before moving uptown to the off-Broadway Westside Theatre for a long, heralded run. If she saw it, Wasserstein might have wondered what the fuss was about, as critics and audiences celebrated Ensler's daring for peppering the word *vagina* throughout her vivid solo investigation of female sexuality. After all, Wasserstein's characters openly explored clitoral orgasms and tasted their menstrual blood in *Uncommon Women and Others* more than twenty years before Ensler's play seemed so daring. Kathy Najimy and Mo Gaffney presented *Parallel Lives* in The Kathy and Mo Show in the mid-1980s, in which they performed their own parodies of feminist practices off Broadway, which propelled both women into careers in television and film concurrent with Wasserstein's success on Broadway. And Whoopi Goldberg, at about the same time, began as a solo performer with a vivid critique of the systemic social connections between race, class, and gender. Her first solo performance, *The Spook Show*, premiered in 1984; it moved to Broadway with Mike Nichols's help and was retitled *Whoopi Goldberg*.[37]

Likewise, Beth Henley's Pulitzer Prize for Drama for *Crimes of the Heart* in 1981 and Marsha Norman's for *'night, Mother* in 1983 also reflected female-gendered perspectives on cultural mores and norms. Both plays have also been criticized by feminists. *Crimes*, for instance, is a comedy in which three sisters suffer under the thumb of their ailing father and their backwoods neighbors, relying on stereotypes about female rebellion and southern culture to score its humor. Some feminists excoriated *'night, Mother* for telling the story of a young woman determined to kill herself because her life hadn't turned out the way she expected. Feminist critics observed that the play's inexorable progress toward the woman's death denies her power and agency.[38] But at least Norman's and Henley's plays were written by and about women. Before their selection in the 1980s, no woman had been awarded the Pulitzer Prize for Drama since Mary Chase won for *Harvey* in 1945.

In a 1997 interview, Wasserstein told scholar David Savran, in response to a question about whether she saw herself as part of a community of women writers who came of age in the 1970s, "Eighties, too. In the mid-eighties three women won the Pulitzer Prize. I thought, that would be an interesting book if somebody wrote about me and Marsha [Norman] and Beth [Henley]. . . . I admire Paula Vogel's work. I was once on a panel with Paula and María Irene Fornés. It was kind of great, because I thought the three of us were wildly different people. But there's an intelligence and a caring there."[39] Regardless of how you parse their different interpretations of feminism, Wasserstein's preoccupations echoed with those of other women in theater working at the same time.

Wasserstein brought certain gendered actions, objects, and issues to the stage that were notable in their time and place. For instance, in 1977, just as the women's movement caught public attention, a character in *Uncommon Women and Others* makes "Rorschach tests with her menstrual blood to summon back Edvard Munch" and delivers a frank monologue about penises.[40] Another character sits onstage "filling a diaphragm with Orthocreme" (32), a spermicidal contraceptive. These characters might have been wearing Villager sweaters and Bass Weejuns—the sartorial accessories of the moment for white, upper-middle-class women—but Wasserstein caught the zeitgeist in the stage business she wrote for them and in the cultural references she littered throughout the play, which both place it in history and give it topical weight.

Wasserstein also shifted the typical American dramaturgical emphasis from fathers and sons to mothers and daughters in all of her plays, viewing gender as a site of solidarity as well as oppression. She also took careful if satirical note of the differences between and among women, writing Jewish women characters full of complex desires and histories and comparing them to their gentile counterparts, affectionately tweaking the noses of both groups. She focused on mother-daughter relationships not as an essentialist paradigm of cozy mutual narcissism but as a battleground of values and generations. In *Isn't It Romantic*, the mothers are much more progressive than their daughters. Janie Blumberg's mother carries an attaché case loaded with exercise equipment and wears a cape with a tie-dyed leotard underneath (not unlike Wasserstein's mother, Lola). She is a dancer and encourages her daughter to follow her highly performative artistic spirit. This struggle between the artistic and the professional, between the outlaw and the insider, echoes throughout Wasserstein's work, as she continued to mull women's options.

Along with their detailed engagement with mothers and daughters and feminist generations, Wasserstein's plays engage the vicissitudes of relationships among women. While all of her heroines are resolutely, normatively heterosexual, *Isn't It Romantic* also proposes that it's unconscionable for women to prioritize relationships with men over their friendships with one another, another tension to which Wasserstein's subsequent plays return. The men in *Isn't It Romantic* suffocate the women, but somehow, social expectation dictates the women should marry them regardless. That Janie, Wasserstein's heroine in the play, dumps her man instead of wedding him is something of a radical act. Wasserstein uses the play to ask why women always capitulate to socially dictated demands that they grow up to marry and have kids. She urgently questions how heterosexual women can redefine their relationships with one another so that they'll be considered "grown up" without men.

Many of her heroines, however, wonder how they can mark their passage through their lives without these conventional milestones. Wasserstein often tracks her characters at transitional moments, when they wonder whether or not they're "in life" now. As Heidi tells Scoop in *The Heidi Chronicles*, "Scoop, we're out of school. We're in life. You don't have to grade everything."[41] Yet because she can't quite understand what being "in life" means for a woman whose fulfilled ambitions are bittersweet because she doesn't have an appropriate male partner, a typical Wasserstein gesture is to pass the future on to the next generation, to the daughters that Wasserstein assumes all women should want to have. Daughters are not debatable in her cosmology, even as husbands become increasingly disposable. By *Third*, the main character's husband is referred to but never seen, while her daughter is a fully fleshed out character who helps to drive the plot.[42] This is clearly an autobiographical element in Wasserstein's work.

But as critic Robert Vorlicky says in his discussion of *The Heidi Chronicles*, remarking on Heidi's sudden choice at the play's end to adopt a child, "My concern is that very complicated choices are often represented in commercial theatre as being too easily realized."[43] The adoption in *The Heidi Chronicles* happens magically, with no reference to the economic or emotional costs of Heidi's choice. As Gayle Austin said in her review of the Broadway production, "The realism it employs makes invisible the real difficulties a woman in Heidi's position encounters, such as the costs of the transactions in the play."[44] Wasserstein might have challenged women who betrayed their female friends for men, but she proposed sometimes too-facile solutions to the problem of how single women might nonetheless constitute families.[45]

Yet realism also allowed Wasserstein to reach larger audiences, nimbly employing its accessibility and transparency, its ability to provoke identification and catharsis, to reel spectators into her stories and align them sympathetically with her female heroines. Realism fulfilled Wasserstein's intentions as a playwright. While feminist critics like Austin, Vorlicky, and others might cringe at the form's superficial resolutions, its inability to offer apt solutions to social problems, and its preservation of the status quo, Wasserstein used it to bring women's lives into public view. Her plays address the complications of the contemporary moment from the perspective of women whose voices are typically silenced in public debate—even when their lives center the storm of media scrutiny and disapprobation, as she illustrates persuasively in *An American Daughter*. That Wasserstein made such characters available to public examination, identification, and empathy on Broadway was a liberal feminist achievement in the debate about the status of women in American democracy.

The most effective gesture in Wasserstein's plays is the often repeated stage direction instructing women characters to exit the stage arm in arm. This insistent demonstration of camaraderie and affection strikes me as moving and hopeful each time I read it, regardless of what the rest of the plot might dictate for these determining, foundational female friendships. In some ways, these embodied gestures communicate more about Wasserstein's commitment to women than some of her dialogue. Those women exiting arm in arm become larger than themselves, significant of something hopeful and hopefully predictive about the potential for women's solidarity to change themselves and their world. She often uses the gesture to bridge the public and the private, since in many of her plays, Wasserstein clarifies that for women, despite what might be our desires otherwise, no separation holds between the two.

In *An American Daughter*, for example, feminist generations clash openly around this question and precipitate the main character's public disgrace. Lyssa Dent Hughes, who has been nominated to be surgeon general by a president reminiscent of Bill Clinton, is a second-wave feminist long committed to women's health. But the media use the matter of an unanswered jury summons to torpedo Lyssa's nomination, and a younger, third-wave feminist journalist who goes by the gender-neutral, patrician name Quincy Quince plays a key part in Lyssa's undoing. The play sorts out women's very different relationships to the project of feminism and demonstrates once again how smart, capable women are routinely kept from important centers of power. Wasserstein criticizes the media scrutiny that makes public life personal rather than political in exactly the wrong way, by perverting the old feminist adage "the personal is the political."

If more plays written by and about more and different kinds of women were produced and publicly discussed, Wasserstein's wouldn't continue to bear the burden of representation.[46] As she said in response to the feminist critique of *Heidi*, "One woman . . . can't write that one play, that one movie. You can't put that kind of weight on something. . . . Suddenly you become a spokesperson, and finally you want to say, 'Honey, thank God there's a play about a gay fantasia on Broadway. And maybe next season, there'll be three more, and you'll like the next one.' I felt that very much about *Heidi*."[47] Likewise, the answer to the problem of women's unequal representation in American theater isn't to dismiss Wendy Wasserstein but to advocate for more visibility and serious consideration for more women playwrights. I hope my discussion of Wasserstein's plays in the pages that follow will contribute to that conversation.

My investigation of Wasserstein's opus moves chronologically through her life and work. Each chapter focuses on an important play, from *Uncommon Women and Others* through *Third*. Each discussion considers the play's themes, style, structure, and reception and tries to place it within the historical moment in which it was created, received, and many times, remounted for subsequent productions. Wasserstein, in fact, remains an important cultural icon because her plays are so frequently performed, whether in regional, community, and university theaters around the country or on Broadway. One of my motivating questions concerns the durability of her work; are her plays remounted because they're so accessible, sometimes easy soundbites into large and complicated social questions? Are they often produced because they have good roles for women? Because they tick the box "female playwright" in a regional theater season in an era in which social attention to diversity requires a gesture toward gender equity? Although when her plays premiered, many (male) critics found them "lite" and topical and read them as peculiarly disposable, Wasserstein's work has in fact proved lasting within certain strata of American culture.

Although I proceed chronologically through the plays, their thematic preoccupations echo across the thirty-odd years of Wasserstein's career, and her stylistic choices remain durable. The lives of her heroines tend to mirror her own; they age as she does and reflect the governing, gendered preoccupations of women of her race, ethnicity, generation, and socioeconomic status. The women of *Uncommon Women and Others*, for instance, are about to graduate from college, separately and collectively anxious about how they'll steer the course of their lives. Wasserstein wrote the play when she was in graduate school, not far removed from her characters' concerns, and equally unsure about what her next move would be and how she would find both personal and professional fulfillment. Janie Blumberg, in *Isn't It Romantic*, has moved to New York City to find her way but gets caught in conflicting social messages about whether women should have career or domestic aspirations, since having both then seemed impossible.

Heidi Holland, of *The Heidi Chronicles*, is approaching middle age, just as Wasserstein was when she wrote the play (at thirty-eight years of age), secure in a visible career but dissatisfied with how her choices have been delimited by social convention. *The Sisters Rosensweig*, too, across generations of women in a Jewish family not unlike Wasserstein's own, charts their different choices and ponders what they might have done, had history and culture provided them alternative ways of crafting a life, despite what were by then significant social gains for white, upper-class, well-educated women like themselves. *An American Daughter*, in fact, puts one such accomplished woman squarely in the public sphere, to examine how even wealthy, well-connected, and privileged women suffer the consequences of gendered political histories that circumscribe their future potential. And in *Third*, the final play of Wasserstein's career and the one that completes my analysis here, a women's studies professor at a liberal arts college reexamines her life when, as her father suffers dementia and her husband moves into retirement, she understands that she's become unwittingly entrenched in her own dogma.

Through these narratives, Wasserstein managed to trace the shifting gendered mores of American society across thirty years of contemporary history. She became a cultural chronicler, considering the political through the personal choices of women very much like herself. Her characters' relationships are formative, crucibles for growth and choice as well as disappointment. Although they aren't the fiercely radical, collectively committed feminists who formed activist groups in New York in the 1970s and 1980s when Wasserstein began her own career, her characters are women whose friendships with one another become foundational and predictive. Their choices offer a window into those of women like them, however particularized by race, ethnicity, class, and educational status.

Likewise, Wasserstein's trademark theatrical practices resonate through each of the titles I consider here. Although their narratives concern mostly private lives, public culture is always present, often through a disembodied authoritative voice. In *Uncommon Women* the voice of the college (male at the beginning, female at the end) frames each scene, positioning the coeds in time and place and pinpointing the political ironies they face. *Isn't It Romantic* accomplishes similar commentary with the voices on Janie's answering machine, which begin each scene. *The Heidi Chronicles* uses period music to similar effect, employing popular songs to remind spectators of particular moments in history, often with more sentimental than political results. *The Sisters Rosensweig*'s narrative is framed by its references to Chekhov in plot and tone, and *An American Daughter* and *Third* use media voices diegetically to underline their characters' places in history. Throughout her career, Wasserstein's trademark devices lent her work its style and tone.

Across the six plays I consider here, Wasserstein enumerates her concern for women. When does a woman's life start? How might it happily and productively proceed and eventually end? What can her women hope to achieve, given the constraints of how their gender (and race and class and sexuality) is perceived in their given cultural moments? What's the most honorable way to live one's life, given certain kinds of privilege and possibility? Wasserstein's work was remarkably consistent in style, tone, and theme, but her women characters grew along with her—and alongside the American cultural moments she chronicled.

CHAPTER TWO

Uncommon Women and Others

This chapter analyzes *Uncommon Women and Others*, in which Wasserstein sets the stage for themes that echo throughout her career, sketching a group of women characters about to graduate from one of the Seven Sister colleges just as feminist concerns began to make the teas and niceties of their sheltered existence anachronistic. The five women Wasserstein draws so presciently range from Kate, the accomplished, capable if confused young woman who eventually becomes a lawyer, to Rita, the liberated free spirit who intends to become an artist but succeeds only in forever deferring the spectacular creative success she envisions for herself and her friends.

Setting the play against the doctrine of discipline and "Gracious Living" inculcated by women's colleges in the fifties and sixties, Wasserstein demonstrates how her own generation of white, upper-middle-class women was caught in conflicting expectations of conventional marriage and motherhood versus meaningful public work and ambitious professional careers. The play is observant and bittersweet, funny and poignant, and its thematic concerns and realist, comic theatrical choices became paradigmatic of Wasserstein's style. The women's friendships, always vexed by concerns over their relationships with men and their ambivalence about their lives, appear throughout Wasserstein's oeuvre and now, ironically, reflect even more contemporary twenty-first century preoccupations. Yet thinking about the play in its own historical setting is a potent reminder of how radical were its concerns and its contents when it was first produced.

Wasserstein wrote *Uncommon Women and Others* as her MFA thesis play at Yale, where she was among the very few women enrolled in the distinguished playwriting program. She is often quoted as saying that the play was prompted by her desire to see an all-women curtain call and by her exposure to Jacobean plays in which men would be poisoned when they kissed the skulls of dead women. In her typically witty but incisive way, Wasserstein noticed first that the so-called universal experience of men in classic drama she was taught at Yale had no place for women and, second, that even in contemporary theater, women's experiences were nowhere to be seen. Her work cut out for her, Wasserstein proceeded to mine her own life and the lives of her friends to rethink the representation of women on the American stage.

Uncommon Women was first produced professionally in 1977 at New York's Phoenix Theatre. Cast with a number of women who'd studied acting at Yale—several of whom went on to become the most famous performers of their generation, including Meryl Streep (who replaced Glenn Close from the original cast), Swoosie Kurtz, and Jill Eikenberry—the play uses a flashback structure to consider the lives of friends at Mount Holyoke on the eve of their college graduation in 1972. Gathering in a Manhattan restaurant in 1978, five friends reminisce about their last days at college, just as feminism was beginning to shift the dynamics and the import of what it meant to attend an all-women's school. As the women arrive with a rather forced excitement and sentiment about seeing one another again, it's clear that their meeting provides an opportunity to measure where they thought they'd be six years ago against what they've so far attained.

Flashing back to the dorm rooms in which the women first established their relationships, Wasserstein creates a hothouse, women-centered environment in which her heroines are pulled by the conflicting demands of a college established to breed women for lives of community service and marriage and a transformation in American culture that promises them much more. Smart, mostly well-off, talented, and socially attuned, Kate, Muffet, Holly, Rita, and Leilah are Mount Holyoke seniors reacting in very different ways to the unfolding of their lives. Their choices seem at once dictated by common understandings of what it means to be women of their position and privilege and by their sense that their options have been thrown open in unexpected and not entirely welcomed ways. Wasserstein describes each character in her notes before the play with humor and empathy. Clearly, she knows these women; as with all of her work, these are fictional characters steeped in the experiences and perspectives of herself and those she knows very well indeed.

Kate Quin is a lawyer who carries an attaché case that "alternately makes her feel like a successful grown-up, or handcuffed," Wasserstein quips, describing in a quick phrase the complications of being a professional woman.[1] Samantha Stewart, who married her college sweetheart (an actor named Robert), is "like a Shetland cable-knit sweater, a classic" (5). Holly Kaplan (Wasserstein's stand-in), is the Jewish girl among these WASPs from Mount Holyoke, although Wasserstein never explicitly names Holly's ethnic difference. Holly "has devised a strong moral code of warmth for those you love and wit for those you're scared of." She "saw the Radio City Easter Show in second grade and planned to convert" (5). Holly also has a weight problem, and of all these young women, is the least successful at either relationships with men or with a professional life. Muffet di Nicola and Rita Altabel are polar opposites, Muffet as straitlaced and WASPy as her name suggests and Rita as bohemian, imaginative, and nonconformist as the times permit. Although she won a Daughters of the Revolution scholarship to Mount Holyoke, Rita's politics borrow from the ecofriendliness, feminism, and hippiedom just then beginning to influence the zeitgeist.

Surrounding this satellite of close friends are Leilah, who competes with Kate to be the most intelligent, attractive, and protosuccessful; Susie Friend, the overachieving, oversocial, overenthusiastic booster who embodies the moral code of the school without ever resisting or questioning its tenets; and Carter, the rather odd, sometimes catatonic freshman whose presence allows Wasserstein's senior characters to "teach" her and the audience the ropes of what it means to be at Mount Holyoke in 1972. Reigning over these relationships is Mrs. Plumm, the dorm housemother who attempts to instill in her charges the values of the institution and of the era, even as the world shifts under her feet.

Superior to Mrs. Plumm is the disembodied voice of "the man," who delivers the wisdom of the Mount Holyoke catalog and rule book at the start of each flashback scene. That the man's voice is, by the end, replaced with a woman's voice illustrates the sea change that *Uncommon Women* traces, as the feminist movement and a general loosening of American mores upend all the certainties in the crucible of which Mount Holyoke's rituals and values were formed.

If "the man" begins as the unseen but omnipresent voice of institutional and social authority, the voice of "the woman" at the play's end is equally disquieting. This is liberation, but only of a sort, as Wasserstein suggests that although its gender might have changed, the disembodied presence of authority persists, in ways that her uncommon women try hard to fathom.

Reading or seeing *Uncommon Women* now makes it seem a history play, a snapshot of a time when feminism and the values of the New Left were just beginning to seep into American consciousness. But Wasserstein wrote the play in the mid- to late seventies, when the history she relates was still quite fresh. Her ability to see with a certain objectivity and perspective the very recent past (or present, as *An American Daughter* and *Third* demonstrated later in her career) marks Wasserstein's plays. She has an unerring ear for the key phrases and idiomatic language that marked a moment, as well as for the products, fashions, and fads that distinguished, in this case, 1972 from 1978. Wasserstein's ability to understand and illustrate culture through its trends was one of her gifts. Reading *Uncommon Women* reminds me that the brands that seemed important and desirable in 1972 now seem quaint, relics of an earlier moment not just in the history of feminism but in the history of American capitalism.

That is, Wasserstein's feel for the zeitgeist comes from her deft ability to sniff out its tastes and how they manifest in the things we buy and with which we adorn ourselves. The insufferable Susie Friend, then, doesn't just wear pink sweaters; she wears a pink *Villager* sweater and *Weejuns* ("of course," Wasserstein notes in her character description [6]), underlining the significance of the Villager clothing brand and Bass Weejun loafers as the mark of a particular kind of early seventies preppie. The brands recall a specific kind of character, forged through a relationship with consumerism and redolent of a specific place in the invisible but felt American class strata. These details enliven Wasserstein's plays, especially for readers and spectators for whom they ring with familiarity and nostalgia. Making these references legible for younger generations, however, could be a challenge in contemporary productions of *Uncommon Women* and could require a dramaturg's perseverance and perspicacity.[2]

The specificity of Wasserstein's references also marks her intelligence and her own cultural capital as a playwright. She passes on to her characters quick, witty references to the cognoscenti, artists and intellectuals and politicians of generations past that they name-drop as evidence of their (and Wasserstein's) superior education as well as their facility with low culture. In an exchange in *Uncommon Women*'s first scene, when the friends reestablish their relationships with one another and introduce themselves to the audience, Wasserstein writes,

> KATE: Muffet, I am a very important person now.
> MUFFET: Don't you still sneak trashy novels?
> HOLLY: I thought of you, Katie, when Jacqueline Susann died.
> SAMANTHA: Did you know she had a buttocks enhancement? Eva Le Gallienne told Robert when he was touring in *Cactus Flower*. . . .
> KATE: Who's Eva Le Gallienne?
> HOLLY: She wasn't our year. (8–9)

The scene is hilarious for spectators who understand the reference because it plays up a low-culture desire to participate in a trashy, soft-porn milieu in which Jacqueline Susann ruled as well as the high-culture knowledge of Eva Le Gallienne, the doyenne of American art theater during the Little Theatre Movement of the early twentieth century. Holly's remark that "she wasn't our year" speaks to an audience whom Wasserstein assumes will know Le Gallienne, letting spectators in on a joke that pokes good-natured fun at the insularity of these Mount Holyoke graduates.

Wasserstein's canny ability to pepper her plays with such high and low cultural references makes them very much a part of the historical moment they capture. In *Uncommon Women*, Villager sweaters, Bass Weejuns, Jacqueline Susann, and Eva Le Gallienne are mentioned in dialogue alongside Virginia's enabling husband Leonard Woolf, lesbian rock bands, the contraceptive Ortho-Crème, and Rorschach tests, as well as artists and authors such as Edvard Munch and Germaine Greer, singer-songwriters Judy Collins, James Taylor, and Leonard Cohen, the Dave Clark Five, and *Holiday* magazine.[3] These references become for Wasserstein a shorthand to her characters, a fast and easy way to indicate the things they care about and their ability to buy their place in, as well as to shape, American consumer culture.

Rita, for example, the most artistic of the women, wants to be a novelist and prepares to be inspired by living on the edge during her college years. She follows the instructions of Germaine Greer, who "says the test of a truly liberated woman is tasting her menstrual blood" (37). In a parody of extreme early feminist actions to defy patriarchy, Rita accepts every possible injunction to liberate herself. But when she goes on job interviews at the publishing houses into which Seven Sister college graduates typically feed, the interviewer inquires if she has experience using a Xerox machine. Rita answers, "Yes. And I've tasted my menstrual blood" (60). As a young idealist, she refuses to "throw my imagination away. I *refuse* to live down to expectation" (60).

Yet despite her emboldened willingness to take life by the balls, as it were, Rita can't quite focus her rebellious energy. Her mantra throughout *Uncommon Women* is that she and her friends will be spectacular in the future. "If I can just hold out till I'm thirty, I'll be incredible," she says her last year in college; her line "When we're . . . *forty-five*, we can be pretty fucking amazing" (72, italics in original) ends the play. Her constant deferral of her own arrival in her life delivers Wasserstein's poignant observation of the confusions of a generation of women that was never quite taught how to get from there to here. Their own aspirations were roundly transformed by the differences between the world into which they graduated and the more insular milieu in which they were molded.

Because she is the play's resident feminist, Rita also introduces much of the ideology that swirled around college women who were nascent women's liberationists in the early seventies. In her analysis of the world, gender puts women at a distinct disadvantage. Although her perspective now might seem obvious—if not, to some people, "politically correct"—in 1977 when the play was first performed, Rita's remarks would have been radical and new. She tells her friends,

> This entire society is based on cocks. The *New York Times*, Walter Cronkite, all the buildings and roads, the cities, philosophy, government, history, religion, shopping malls—everything I can name is male. When I see things this way, it becomes obvious that it's very easy to feel alienated and alone for the simple reason that I've never been included 'cause I came into the world without a penis. (34)

Rita's friends, however, take her newly minted analysis with a grain of trademark Wasserstein salt. As Rita exits with her usual dramatic flourish, Holly says drily, "I think she's wrong about the shopping malls" (34). Later, when Kate interrupts the friends' study session to ask Holly if she ever had penis envy, Holly responds, "I remember having tonsillitis" (57). Wasserstein's humor both pokes fun at a society that diagnoses women as lacking in comparison to men and also describes how her characters must measure themselves against ideas newly circulating in a culture that touches them intimately. The point is made. These women gradually realize that while their school pumps them with bon mots about Gracious Living and receiving "MRS" degrees (which stand for the marriage certificates for which many of the characters openly prepare), the world outside Mount Holyoke roils with the uproar of a social movement that's discovering both women's inequality and their new potential in the same hurricane-force breath.

Each of the characters responds to these complications differently, allowing Wasserstein to paint a rainbow of choices for 1970s women without necessarily authorizing any one in particular. *Uncommon Women*, in fact, begins Wasserstein's evenhanded, career-long analysis of women's choices. She rarely comes down on one side or the other of debates about gender, women's roles, or their numerous options but prefers instead to chronicle the riptides of social movements that entrap her characters. Kate, for example, who's the most accomplished student and by 1978 has the most successful career (though Wasserstein reminds us that her attaché case is a ball and chain as much as a signal of her professional importance), worries about where her sympathies lie. She contemplates what all these changing social mores mean for her own life, monologuing while Carter, the enigmatic and withdrawn first-year student, pecks away at her typewriter on the floor. Kate muses, "But if I didn't fulfill obligations or weren't exemplary, then I really don't know what I'd do. I have a stake in all those Uncommon Women expectations. I know how to live up to them well" (56).

At the same time, Kate fears the predictability of her life as it's been so carefully planned. She tells the silent Carter, "I came in here because I just got into law school and I don't think I should go. I don't want my life simply to fall into place" (56). She's frightened by her success, but at the same time, Wasserstein clarifies that Kate's strength lies in her willingness to conform to the inevitability of a life's path for which she's been carefully groomed. Nascent feminism might make her wonder, surprised at her own unexpected ambivalence, but it does not deter her from a life of privilege and power that is already hers for the taking. The punchline of Kate's ruminative monologue comes when she finally focuses on Carter, whom she realizes has been typing "Now is the time for all good" twenty-five times as Kate rattled on. When Kate asks why she has been typing nonsense, Carter responds, "I am cramming for my typing test. I need fifty words per minute to get a good job when I get out of here" (57). You can almost hear the drums beat "ba-da-boom" at that line, punctuating the irony of Kate's self-obsessions, the final irrelevance of her self-absorbed, disingenuous debate with herself, as the just as intelligent but less financially privileged Carter, who wants to be a filmmaker, prepares herself for a career that will start in the typing pool, rather than at law school.

Because Carter says little throughout the play, Wasserstein fashions her as a projection screen on which the other characters examine their strengths and weaknesses. Carter is an artist who wants to make a film about Wittgenstein. This unlikely subject and genre fascinate her friends. In the character notes preceding the play, Wasserstein says Carter "may seem catatonic, but she has a rich inner life—though it is debatable whether she is a genius or just quiet. Carter is inner-directed" (6). Each of the other characters has a long monologue at some point in the play in which she expresses her fears and desires, her dreams and anxieties, all crisscrossed with ambivalence and ambiguity about the suddenly exploded social landscape. But the audience never hears what Carter really thinks, and neither do the other characters. Her silence gives her power and mystique, allowing her to be unknowable in a way that contrasts sharply with the other women's transparency. Carter serves as the play's hub, the quiet center around which the other characters wheel frantically.

Although none of the characters onstage in *Uncommon Women and Others* are male, the women refer to an offstage cast of men who wield a great deal of influence in their lives. Samantha's boyfriend-cum-fiancé Robert is an actor to whom Samantha always gives the last word. "Robert says I'm a closet wit," she reports (37); "Robert says that I never grew up into a woman" (54). Samantha is perfectly happy to contemplate a life beside a man she considers a genius, while she sees herself as "a little talented at a lot of things. That's why I want to be with Robert and all of you. I want to be with someone who makes a public statement" (54). Samantha funnels her own sense of self through her boyfriend's, seeing herself in the helpmeet role for which she's long been groomed.

Chip Knowles, the self-appointed women's studies professor at Mount Holyoke, tells Muffet that "women's history is relevant" and assigns Betty Friedan's *The Feminine Mystique* and Kate Millett's *Sexual Politics* to his students (24). Men are the vehicles of feminism for Wasserstein's women. Kate asks Leilah what she knows about clitoral orgasms, to which Leilah responds, "Well, my gentleman friend, Mr. Peterson, says they're better than others," deferring, as usual, to male expertise even on female sexual pleasure (31). Kate muses, "I wonder if I've had any," to which Leilah responds, "Kate, I'm sure you have. It's a fad" (31). Although something as cataclysmic to feminism as insisting on clitoral orgasms becomes part of Wasserstein's joke, she writes an undercurrent of wonder about whether or not women's rights are in fact a passing trend, which enhances her characters' confusion about their life choices.[4] Expressing her surprise at how much she likes her women's history course, Muffet wonders (like Kate, to the unresponsive but ever-present Carter), "Do you think women will lose their relevancy in five years? Like 'Car 54, Where Are You?,'" referring to a once-popular television series (24).

Even as I find myself laughing aloud at Wasserstein's sharp humor, I recognize the poignancy of her speculations about the vitality and longevity of a movement that took women seriously for the first time. Underneath the witticisms and jokes runs a current of anxiety, even panic, that these women pioneers face the moment of their own brief significance before they fade back into the woodwork of a male-dominated society. Wasserstein writes her characters on the cusp of a future they can neither imagine nor ignore, wondering which way and to whom they should turn as they contemplate their choices, while still controlled by male power.

In one scene, Leilah and Muffet talk about their futures, as Muffet broods that she's had a fight with her boyfriend. Muffet decides that the two women should go out together for the evening. In a trademark Wasserstein dramatic flourish, Muffet sets the scene for their evening: "I've always wanted to do this. We can go to a bar—not too sleazy, but also not a place where two nice girls usually go. And we'll sit alone, just you and I, with our two Brandy Alexanders, and we won't need any outside attention. We'll be two Uncommon Women, mysterious but proud" (50). Leilah says she'd like to do that, but immediately after their fantasy is spun, Muffet gets a phone call from her boyfriend and rushes off to spend the night with him instead.

These characters' choices aren't coincidental. Wasserstein uses similar scenes in many of her plays, from *Uncommon Women* to *Isn't It Romantic* and onward, to demonstrate that although women's friendships with one another are foundational, their relationships with men determine their lives. To her credit, Wasserstein draws this insight with irony and not a little rue. But throughout her plays, the pattern persists, suggesting that she can't see a way around the primacy of male relationships even in a world so thoroughly and delightfully homosocial as the one she draws for women. That sadness endures for Wasserstein and perhaps for other women. Even in 2011, the wildly successful popular film *Bridesmaids*, cowritten by Annie Mumolo and Kristen Wiig, draws its pathos from narrating the story of a woman whose best friend leaves her to marry a man. Likewise, the independent films *Frances Ha* (2013) and *Obvious Child* (2014) tread similar narrative territory, detailing more soberly how heterosexual marriage sadly curtails some women's intimacy with one another. That marriage and heterosexual relationships continue to interrupt female friendship and to derail women from their sustaining relationships with one another seems a persistent, if rather understated or unacknowledged, theme in stories about women.

In her own revealing monologue, Holly (Wasserstein's doppelgänger in *Uncommon Women*) speaks long distance to Dr. Mark Silverstein, a man she encountered very briefly while visiting a museum in Boston with Muffet. She seeks him out again with vague ideas about reconnecting, which are quickly dashed when he doesn't even remember her. But Wasserstein uses the conceit of the phone call to expose Holly's inner feelings, which reveal that she, too, is caught in the contradiction of loving her friends but assuming that she'll be legitimated only by a relationship with a man. Draped in a raccoon coat for comfort while she talks, she tells the unseen Dr. Silverstein, "Often I think I want a date or a relationship to be over so I can talk about it to Kate or Rita. I guess women are just not as scary as men and therefore they don't count as much" (63). Holly knows the importance of her women friends, and yet she can't disentangle herself from what feminist poet Adrienne Rich once called "compulsory heterosexuality."[5] Holly's monologue serves the same truth-telling function as Alan's phone call to his high school friend in Mark Crowley's famous gay play *Boys in the Band* (1968). The unexpected phone call to someone whose voice the audience and the other characters don't hear serves as a dramatic device that lets Wasserstein portray Holly's bittersweet self-knowledge, even though the moment speaks to an unfortunate, pathetic abjection. The monologue also presages Heidi Holland's famous "I feel stranded" speech in *The Heidi Chronicles* a decade later, in which Wasserstein uses a similar theatrical choice to let her heroine vocalize her fears, anxieties, and by the late 1980s, resentments about feminism.

But in 1977, in *Uncommon Women*, Holly's personal and political sadness is offset by the insistent cheerfulness of Mount Holyoke's mottos, delivered at the top of each scene by the "man's voice" and within the scenes from 1972 by the redoubtable Mrs. Plumm. The housemother's injunctions to Gracious Living and a bootstrap self-possession warn against the emotional self-indulgence the others' monologues betray. Mrs. Plumm tells the young women to take their feet off the furniture and bemoans Holly's choice to wear pants to the ritual teas that structure both the women's daily lives and their sense of themselves in the world (17). At the same time, a hint of resistance structures even Mrs. Plumm's remarks. During her annual Father-Daughter Weekend welcome, the housemother describes how she and her dear bird-watching friend Ada Grudder once bought a rifle to protect themselves on their excursions into the wild and how they "set up a firing range on Upper Lake, where we reenacted the Franco-Prussian War" (47). Describing her own encounter with social strictures, she admits, "For two years I received notes from home saying, 'Please marry Hoyt Plumm,' and 'Can't you teach bird-watching at the high school?' Finally, being a dutiful daughter, I did" (47). The wages of duty require self-sacrifice, no less in Mrs. Plumm than in this cohort of uncommon women, whether their commitment is to their fathers or to their alma mater.

The girls graduate at the play's end and Mrs. Plumm retires, but Wasserstein writes the housemother a farewell speech that demonstrates a resilience that perhaps surpasses that of her charges. Mrs. Plumm says, "The realm of choices can be overwhelming. However, those of you who have known me as the constant dutiful daughter of my alma mater, and my family, may be surprised to know that I do not fear these changes for my girls, nor for myself" (66–67). In fact, Mrs. Plumm plans to travel to Bolivia to bird-watch and has once again connected with her now and always "dear friend" Ada Grudder who, in her own life's adventure, now resides in India. Although she's been the source of the girls' derision through much of the play, Mrs. Plumm in many ways gets the upper hand by blazing off into a sunset bright with freedom and possibility, more sure in her ability to navigate than any of the young college graduates she wishes well.

In the play's last scene, the authoritative male voice that has dictated rules for the women to live by fades into a woman's voice that announces, "Women still encounter overwhelming obstacles to achievement and recognition despite gradual abolition of legal and political disabilities. Society has trained women from childhood to accept a limited sct of options and restricted levels of aspiration" (67–68). This female voiceover's more sober assessment of the uncommon women's situation echoes into Wasserstein's wistful ending, in which the friends—back in their present moment—ponder momentarily how they got from their Mount Holyoke graduation to lives in which choices have been made but ambivalences persist. Kate is, as predicted, a high-powered lawyer, but she wonders about the paths she might have taken or could still: "I wonder if I'll ever decide to have a child. I hardly think about it, and when I do I tell myself there's still a lot of time. I wonder what it's like when you stop thinking there's a lot of time left to make changes" (70). Muffet is surprised to be supporting herself, even at something she considers as undistinguished as hosting insurance seminars. Rita is supported by her husband's wealth but isn't writing the novel she's dreamed of publishing since college. She says resentfully, "If you spend your life proving yourself, then you just become a man, which is where the whole problem began, and continues. All I want is a room of my own so I can get into my writing" (66), she announces, echoing Virginia Woolf's famous admonishment that if women had rooms of their own they could produce lasting contributions to culture and the arts just like men. But in fact, Rita does have a room of her own by the play's end, and she still defers her commitment to her own work. Wasserstein complicates the outlook for women, suggesting that even honoring Woolf's plea that women have time and space for their own contributions might not facilitate the free expression and artistic production for which Rita longs.

No simple fixes appear on the winding road to personal fulfillment or social engagement. Holly admits that she hasn't "made any specific choices" in the last six years: "My parents used to call me three times a week at seven A.M. to ask me, 'Are you thin, are you married to a root-canal man, are *you* a root-canal man?' And I'd hang up and wonder how much longer I was going to be in 'transition.' I guess since college I've missed the comfort and acceptance I felt with all of you. And I thought you didn't need that anymore, so I didn't see you" (71, italics in original). Holly/Wendy speaks a certain truth that her friends, too, seem to feel. They were supposed to be amazing by the time they were thirty, but just before the turn of their forties, the friends remain perplexed and unsure about what they've done and where they're going, too embarrassed to even confide their ambivalences to one another. In subsequent decades, feminism would define their plight as the problem of communities of women. In the late seventies, although Wasserstein and her characters begin to diagnose the problem, the language and analysis necessary to forge a solution remain out of reach.

Despite Wasserstein's humor and insight, *Uncommon Women* ends on an unresolved, wistful note. Forever deferring their arrival at full bloom, Rita predicts "When we're . . . *forty-five*, we can be pretty fucking amazing" (72, italics in original) and "they exit with their arms around each other." This stage direction repeats an earlier note when, at the end of a scene between Rita and Samantha, Wasserstein instructs, "They start to giggle and exit with their arms around each other" (55). In the gesture of warmth and community that ends the play, Wasserstein demonstrates more hope than she does in written dialogue that's much more dubious about these characters' futures. The play's final image outlines a gesture of community that one wishes Wasserstein's future narratives would amplify. Despite the complexities of female friendship she's illustrated throughout, Wasserstein seems to linger on the possibility that with their arms around one another, these women will, together, be able to settle into clear and determined futures.

Even seen forty years later, that stage gesture would be moving and inspiring. *Uncommon Women* was one of the first plays to draw the complexities of the dawning feminist moment, albeit for women of a certain class, race, and sexuality who were privileged enough to grapple with choices rather than economic compulsion. With gestures and images that might now seem small and insignificant, Wasserstein represented aspects of women's lives that were as uncommon onstage as her characters were told they were in the world. In one scene, Rita and Leilah happen on Holly filling a diaphragm with Ortho-Crème, a contraceptive gel (32). This might have been the first time in American stage history that such stage business was written or enacted. Rita remarks, "Holly, you've got enough Orthocreme in there to sleep with the entire USS *Constitution*" (33), and Holly admits that she doesn't want to "bud" (33), a reference to pregnancy. The play takes place in 1972, before the passage of *Roe v. Wade* in 1973. Although Wasserstein doesn't mention abortion in the play, the historical context in which she places her characters would have meant that "budding" would lead to either unwanted pregnancy or a back-room, illegal abortion. Representing women experimenting with contraception, even in a comedy, was a rather radical act, one in which Wasserstein made the bold decision to make women's private intimacies very public. As Gail Ciociola writes, "The real history in Wasserstein's plays . . . is the private impact of the changing sociopolitical climate that the women's movement generates in individual women like the fictitious characters of her dramas."[6] Likewise, a scene in which Rita and Samantha play at being men embodies gender differences that at that point were not regularly performed in the mainstream theater where Wasserstein's work was produced:

> RITA *enters in a denim jacket and cap:* Hey, man, wanna go out and cruise for pussy? . . .
> SAMANTHA *puts a hairbrush in her mouth as if it were a pipe:* Can't we talk about soccer? Did you see Dartmouth take us? They had us in the hole.
> RITA: I'd sure like to get into a hole.
> SAMANTHA: Man, be polite.
> RITA *gives Samantha a light punch on the arm:* Fuck, man.
> SAMANTHA, *softly at first:* Shit, man. *Laughs hysterically.* . . . Won't you sit down? Can I get you a drink? Want to go out and buy Lacoste shirts and the State of Maine? (52–53)

After a few such exchanges, Samantha protests that she doesn't want to "play" anymore, which disappoints Rita, who enjoys the psychic drag of mocking male authority. While this scene, too, might seem benign after several generations of feminists poking fun at male privilege based on their anatomy, imagine what the scene might have meant when the play was first performed at Yale, for audiences filled with men who no doubt did buy Lacoste shirts and were wealthy enough to buy Maine.

And in another moment of feminist *gestus*, in which an action executed onstage becomes socially symbolic of the world beyond,[7] Wasserstein ends act 1 of *Uncommon Women* with her characters dancing together to the lyrics "If you want to be happy for the rest of your life, never make a pretty woman your wife" (41).[8] They dance and laugh, as Samantha mimics Robert's wretched movement style and Carter joins them, dancing like "a dying swan" in her arty, interpretive manner (42). Kate says, "Do you think Germaine Greer remembers the night she danced with her best friends in a women's dormitory at Cambridge?" (41), marking, in Wasserstein's deft, inimitable fashion, how the moment the characters enact will become iconic in their memories, referring, in fact, to how the same characters are at the very same moment, in the larger frame of the play, remembering back to that time of camaraderie and warmth and possibility that's already slipped out of reach though not out of mind.

Later in her career, Wasserstein would bring that same spirit of both celebration and elegy to the consciousness-raising scene in *The Heidi Chronicles*, when the women join one another to dance to Aretha Franklin's song "Respect," emblematizing the community and the abandonment of being among women friends in a ritual as iconic as it is fleeting in the context of an episodic play in which one historical period is quickly replaced by another. Wasserstein's ongoing ability to see women together singing and dancing, at least in the earlier part of her career, demonstrates her hopefulness about feminism and women's community.

Wasserstein's work evinced the tension between individual women's achievement and a more collective feminist movement throughout her career. At its best, the American feminist movement that came into focus shortly after *Uncommon Women and Others* was first performed foresaw a future of collective action, of women acting on behalf of one another and not just themselves, in ways that might translate into alliances of overlapping social justice movements organized around race, class, and sexuality. But Wasserstein was a conventionally trained playwright who structured her plays in punchy comic scenes—however episodic—that observe realist dramatic conventions that circumscribe their radical gestures. Spectators see her characters as "real," individual people; they speak to one another and not to the audience; their narratives have a beginning, middle, and end. While other feminist theater practitioners in the early seventies experimented with other forms—such as ritual, documentary theater, or Brechtian direct address—Wasserstein expressed her understandings of feminism from within mainstream theater forms and the society to which they spoke. She didn't propose solutions, but her witty, sharp insights brought the dilemmas that feminism made visible in American society to commercial theater audiences for the first time.

Reviews of the play's first professional production, at the Phoenix Theatre in 1977, mostly approved of Wasserstein's humor, while chiding her for a plot they found too spongey to hold heavy ideas. Critic Harold Clurman, writing in the *Nation*, remarked that her characters have a "special gift for epigrammatic (frequently funny) sallies in sophisticated slang."[9] Edmund Newton, in the *New York Post*, called Wasserstein a "young woman with a darting sense of the ridiculous, eyes which flicker mercilessly across a room and spy one absurd detail after another."[10] In the *Christian Science Monitor*, John Beaufort called the characters "glib with feminist newspeak, but their liberation seems to consist chiefly of exchanging new stereotypes for old."[11] Richard Eder, in the *New York Times*, called the play "exuberant to the point of coltishness."[12] Most of these male reviewers commented on the "female" nature of the content, especially the *Daily News* critic, Douglas Watt, who called the play "a succession of scenes joined on a string rather than a plot. But they are entertaining scenes and they somehow add up to a warm, witty and wise evening designed for females, in particular." Watt went on to describe the scenes as "hen sessions" and ended by admitting that "Miss Wasserstein has a way with words that should keep you happy, especially the women in the audience, all evening long."[13]

Considering that *Uncommon Women* was one of the first plays to mine this particular territory, the reviews are fairly generous. But it's also clear that these critics considered the play something of a trifle and the playwright young and green. None of them predicted Wasserstein's staying power, or that she would go on to become an artistic voice with which to reckon. On the other hand, their distinctly gendered response to her first play would persist in critics' reception of Wasserstein's work throughout her career.

CHAPTER THREE

Isn't It Romantic

Isn't It Romantic (1981, rev. 1983) focuses on a pair of postcollege-aged women about to make choices that will determine the rest of their lives. The play also illustrates Wasserstein's first use of ethnic humor, pitting the Jewish cadences of Janie Blumberg, her heroine, against the non-Jewish, WASPish standard of Harriet Cornwall, Janie's best friend, whose names couldn't capture more perfectly the differences between their social and cultural upbringings. Caught in the desire to "have it all," the governing mantra of 1980s mainstream feminism into which the 1970s version of *Uncommon Women and Others* had morphed, Janie and Harriet wrestle with conflicting needs and competing role models.

Janie's mother, Tasha (a character based on Wasserstein's mother, Lola), is an artist who wears a leotard and practices yoga and aerobics, in an example of Wasserstein's social prescience, since the play was written twenty years before the United States embraced the yoga craze. Harriet's mother, Lillian, is a businesswoman who worked outside the home while Harriet grew up. These four women's various relationships exemplify the web of possibilities in which upper-middle-class white women found themselves at the time, both ex-panding their horizons and trapped by social expectation. The play's frank view of heterosexual women's friendships, and their alliances with men over their allegiances to one another, make *Isn't It Romantic*—one of Wasserstein's least-produced titles—an important indictment of the impossible paradox of contemporary U.S. femi-nism. The play is perhaps Wasserstein's most explicitly feminist, as it leaves Janie ready to make a life alone, with a job, an apartment, and a commitment to making choices for herself on her own terms in her own time. Nonetheless, the play falls short of launching a broader feminist social critique. As in most of Wasserstein's work, her liberal attention to individual protagonists forecloses a more incisive study of the social structures within which their choices are made. But *Isn't It Romantic* delivers a poignant portrait of two upper-middle-class white women wending their way through their own, often new, possibilities.

Janie Blumberg extends the Holly Kaplan character from *Uncommon Women and Others* and becomes Wasserstein's stand-in for what is perhaps her most autobiographical play. Janie and Harriet, both native New Yorkers, have returned to the city to start their lives after graduating from college. Their years away have recalibrated their perspectives and left them at odds with their families. Janie's and Harriet's families derive from different immigrant experiences, and Wasserstein beautifully and humorously plays on the contrasts between those who trace their genealogies to the *Mayflower* and those who escaped the pogroms that rocked Russian shtetls in the late 1800s and early 1900s. That Janie and Harriet are close friends nonetheless allows Wasserstein to demonstrate the happy collision of cultures that distinguishes New York City.

In its 1981 premiere production at the Phoenix Theatre, which commissioned the play, Janie was played by Alma Cuervo, a staple performer in premieres of Wasserstein's productions, who had played Holly in *Uncommon Women.* Cuervo's self-described Spanish ethnicity must have represented Wasserstein's Jewishness, in a neat substitution of one racial difference for another in the face of WASP supremacy.[1] *Isn't It Romantic* shows off Wasserstein's familiarity with the rhythms and ethnic peculiarities of upper-middle-class Jewish culture. While Holly Kaplan's father in *Uncommon Women*, like Wasserstein's, invented velveteen and graciously donated two thousand slightly damaged ribbons for a Mount Holyoke affair, Janie Blumberg's father, Simon, is a stationery purveyor who would like nothing more than for his daughter to join his business. Simon is the "very sweet . . . though not chatty" counterpart to his wife (whom Wasserstein calls his "partner"), Tasha, Janie's dramatic, artistic, emotionally overwhelming mother.[2] She sweeps unannounced into Janie's apartment wearing a cape and carrying an attaché case that holds a Jazzercise tape (87), a towel (118), and a bag of string beans she eats for her snack (119). Under her cape, Tasha wears tie-dyed leotards, always ready for the dance classes she takes with much younger women who admire her energy and confide their problems and desires.

Tasha and Simon first announce themselves in the play by singing "Sunrise, Sunset" from the musical *Fiddler on the Roof* into Janie's answering machine, establishing both their ethnicity and their perpetual desire to see Janie married to a nice Jewish boy. Their overprotective ministrations to their prodigal daughter provide some of the play's most hilarious but perceptive humor. They always arrive at Janie's apartment unexpectedly, shocked that there's no doorman to greet them. They bring her the coffee and morning rolls on which Janie grew up, since her mother provided for her and Simon by ordering up, rather than cooking in, a particularly Upper East or Upper West Side New York way of nurturing. Wasserstein satirizes Janie's inability to cook a chicken as a result of her upbringing, but Tasha and Simon are unflappable with pride about how they eat. They also encourage Janie not to capitulate to conventions that insist she know how to make a chicken to be a proper woman. Her father kindly announces,

> And, Janie, from a man's point of view, the next time someone wants you to make him chicken, you tell him I was at your sister-in-law Christ's house the other day and she ordered up lamb chops from the Madison Delicatessen. How hard is it to cook lamb chops? You just stick them in the broiler. If Christ can order up lamb chops—and she's a girl from Nebraska—you don't have to make anybody chicken. Believe me, you were born to order up. (151)

As in all of Wasserstein's work, gender, class, and ethnicity mingle here to comic but astute effect. Janie's sister-in-law is actually named Chris, but because she's not Jewish, Tasha and Simon call her "Christ" (as in Jesus, a joke at which I can't help but laugh aloud each time I read the play, so typical is it of Jewish parents' suspicion of anyone not part of the "tribe"). In addition to Jewish pride, the statement also epitomizes a specifically New York sense of entitlement and ease, in which living with disposable income in the city allows you to behave in certain ways. But the scene also suggests that Janie should never capitulate to anyone's insistence that she be a conventional woman with appropriate cooking skills. Tasha provides a very different kind of role model. "I'm a modern woman too, you know," she asserts. "I'm an independent woman—a person in my own right" (150). Even though she ends her declaration by asking her husband to affirm it ("Am I right, Simon?"), Tasha's example is partly what confuses and consternates Janie, just as Harriet's mother, Lillian, has a life that inevitably influences her daughter's choices.

Once again trailblazing in her particular analysis of gender in drama, however, Wasserstein focused the play on the relationship between two best friends and their mothers (including one memorable scene in which Tasha and Lillian also have a conversation), making it unique in the early eighties off-Broadway theater scene. Janie and Harriet take up where the uncommon friends of Mount Holyoke left off, moving into the city to assume their lives and to make their numerous and confounding choices. Here, though, Harriet quickly finds a corporate job with Colgate-Palmolive, following Lillian's professional lead. Janie, the more artistic woman, wants to be a freelance writer, though one of her first efforts is rejected via the ubiquitous answering machine that plays the messages that open each scene, an establishing and framing device much like the voiceovers in *Uncommon Women and Others*. A voice announces, "Miss Bloomberg [mispronouncing Janie's last name]. This is Julie Stern at *Woman's Work* magazine. We read your portfolio. Our readers feel you haven't experienced enough women's pain to stimulate our market. Thank you" (86). Eventually Janie is hired by *Sesame Street*, the children's television program, where she begins working her way through the letters of the alphabet. That her big break comes on a children's show, however, also somewhat diminishes Janie's professional standing, even as it provides Wasserstein with many opportunities for humor.

Unlike the all-women environment of *Uncommon Women*, *Isn't It Romantic* includes men in its cast, whose effect on Janie's and Harriet's lives is vexed and determining. The unseen men of Wasserstein's earlier play all advanced opinions about their girlfriends in supercilious, superior ways. The men in *Isn't It Romantic* do the same, to even more deleterious effect, though they also become foils against which Janie and Harriet form themselves. Marty Sterling is a doctor—the Jewish mother's stereotypical dream catch for her daughter—who changed his name from Schlimovitz when he entered Harvard. When he and Janie begin to date, it's clear he's a prototypical Wasserstein male character with a tendency to tell women all about themselves. Because Janie is ambivalent, Marty makes all the decisions in their relationship, including renting an apartment in Brooklyn to which he wants them to move so that he can set up his practice. He calls Janie "Monkey," a term of endearment but also of diminishment, and he warns her that her burgeoning professional life as a writer shouldn't get in the way of their relationship. He shrugs, "You want to interview at 'Sesame Street,' fine. They do nice work. But don't let it take over your life. And don't let it take over our life. That's a real trap." Janie protests, "Marty, I haven't even interviewed there yet" (129). Marty's insufferable superiority controls and oppresses Janie, but his ability to make decisions obviously appeals to a young woman who can't quite navigate her own options. Eventually, Marty's distasteful preening and his fixed ideas about who wears the proverbial pants in the relationship make Janie balk. He insists that their relationship should be enough for her, but she says,

> JANIE: I guess to a man I love I want to feel not just that I can talk,
> but that you'll listen.
> MARTY: Do you think I don't listen to you?
> JANIE: You have all the answers before I ask the questions. (137)

This pattern of the controlling male who diagnoses his girlfriend before she even knows there's a problem recurs in Wasserstein's plays, starting with the offstage boyfriends of *Uncommon Women* and running through *The Heidi Chronicles*, epitomized in the pompous arrogance of Scoop Rosenbaum, for whom Marty Sterling is a clear prototype.

That Janie finally rejects Marty as a suitable mate is a hopeful choice, but his own ethnic predilections also allow Wasserstein to complicate the play's representations of gender conflicts with the complexities of ethnicity and class. Marty's family changed their last name "for the sake of the family and the business" (84), so that he could better assimilate to the high-WASP culture of the Ivy League. His restaurateur father owned Schlimovitz Kosher Dairy restaurants in Brooklyn before starting his successful chain of Sterling Tavernes. Janie calls Marty's father a genius: "Mr. Sterling, the little man who comes on television in a colonial suit and a Pilgrim hat to let you know he's giving away free popovers and all the shrimp you can eat at Ye Olde Salade and Relish Bar—that guy is Milty Schlimovitz, Marty Sterling's father" (84). Wasserstein deftly illustrates how underneath the fabricated homogeneity of white capitalism lies a Jewish immigrant making a fortune from constructing a fake history of founding "American" authenticity. In fact, Milty started out in show business, telling jokes at Grossinger's, the hub of Jewish ethnic humor in the Catskill Mountains of New York (97). Milty's son, Marty (who was born Murray), feels nostalgic for the old neighborhood from which his parents' generation has eagerly moved away. He thinks "Jewish families should have at least three children" because "it's a dying religion. Intermarriage, Ivy League colleges, the *New York Review of Books*" (97). He tells Janie he's "decided we should live in Flatbush or Brighton Beach, where people have real values":

> My father never sees those people anymore, the *alta kakas* [Yiddish for "old people"] in Brooklyn, the old men with the accents who sit in front of Hymie's Highway Delicatessen. I miss them. My father and mother never go to Miami anymore. They go to Palm Springs or Martinique with their friends from the Westchester Country Club. My father thought my brother was crazy when he named his son Schlomo. He kept asking my brother, "So what's his real name?" And my father will think I'm crazy when we move to Brooklyn. (110)

After a generation of financial success through assimilation, Marty and his brother hunger for the specificity of Brooklyn Jewish ethnic life. Wasserstein, whose own family moved from Brooklyn to Manhattan's Upper East Side, setting the example for her characters' move up the ladder of class privilege, uses the complexities of economics and ethnicity, of success and striving, to nuance their gender complications. Although ethnicity provides much of the play's humor—especially in Harriet's mispronunciations of Yiddish, like saying "nachos" for *"naches"* (143), the Yiddish word for good fortune—the debate over assimilation versus Jewish particularity also lays out the play's pathos.

Wasserstein uses Harriet as Janie's parallel, which enables her to describe how gender strife transcends ethnic difference. While Janie debates the relative merits of her relationship with Marty, Harriet takes up with Paul, a married man who is her boss's boss at work. Paul calls Harriet "Beauty," his pet name for her and every other woman with whom he comes in contact, an endearment nearly as insulting as "Monkey." Harriet complains, "The other day I was standing in front of your office . . . and you called your secretary

'Beauty,' you called whoever called you on the phone 'Beauty,' and I think you called the ninety-year-old messenger boy from Ogilvy and Mather 'Beauty'" (112). People are interchangeable for Paul, whose wife, the unseen Cathy, gives him an excuse to be emotionally and physically inaccessible. Harriet wonders if Cathy even exists, or if she's "an answering service [Paul] hired to call [him] three times a day" (112).

Despite his peripheral place in Harriet's life, Paul presumes to diagnose her problems just as Marty does Janie's. In parallel scenes in the center of the play, Wasserstein puts Marty and Janie on one side of the stage and Paul and Harriet on the other, illustrating how they confront the same problems, despite their ethnic differences. As Harriet complains about their relationship's constraints, Paul announces,

> I see what's going on here. It's the old "I'm afraid of turning thirty alone and I'm beginning to think about having a family." . . . I've been through this with a lot of women. You want a man who sees you as a potential mother, but also someone who isn't threatened by your success and is deeply interested in it. . . . But when you need him, he should drop whatever it is he's doing and be supportive. . . . The girls I date now—the ones like you, the MBAs from Harvard—they want me to be the wife. They want me to be the support system. Well, I can't do that. Harriet, I just wasn't told that's the way it was supposed to be. (112–13)

Men are allowed to reject new paradigms, while women in Wasserstein's cosmos struggle to find ways to transform themselves while still achieving the milestones of marriage and motherhood that have always been considered appropriate white middle-class women's goals, now burdened by the additional expectation of a successful and interesting career.

Isn't It Romantic articulates the stressful complication that *Uncommon Women and Others* had yet to name: how will women be able to "have it all"? By the time *Isn't It Romantic* was produced, mainstream media had reduced the radical feminist platform that reimagined kinship structures as well as gender roles to a question of material acquisitiveness and frank greed. Although the term is attributed to Helen Gurley Brown's 1982 book *Having It All: Love, Success, Sex, Money . . . Even If You're Starting with Nothing*, the *Cosmopolitan* magazine editor apparently hated the title and begged her editors to change it.[3] And yet once the book became a bestseller, Gurley Brown, like Wasserstein after her, was forever associated with a term that belittled her more complicated understanding of women's plight in a social structure designed to their disadvantage.

In *Isn't It Romantic*, Harriet asks her professionally successful mother, Lillian, "Mother, do you think it's possible to be married or live with a man, have a good relationship and children that you share equal responsibility for, build a career, and still read novels, play the piano, have women friends, and swim twice a week?" To which Lillian responds mordantly, "You mean what the women's magazines call 'having it all'? Harriet, that's just your generation's fantasy" (133). Lillian's assessment might be harsh, but she's very realistic about the limitations of the pipe dream about which Harriet wonders. Lillian remarks, "And you show me the wonderful man with whom you're going to have it all. You tell me how he feels when you take as many business trips as he does. You tell me who has to leave the office when the kid bumps his head on a radiator or slips on a milk carton. No, I don't think what you're talking about is possible" (134).[4] Lillian sacrificed pleasing her husband because she decided to prioritize her career and her child. Although Harriet might not appreciate her mother's choices, Lillian rebuffs her accusations: "Harriet, you can't blame everything on me. I wasn't home enough for you to blame everything on me" (132). In a smart twist, Wasserstein creates a woman of the previous generation who is clear-sighted about her own choices and sacrifices and very realistic about the even greater equity her daughter's generation expects.

Wasserstein's insightful analysis of a fraught situation continues to be relevant. In June 2012 the *Atlantic Monthly* published an essay by Anne-Marie Slaughter, former dean of the Woodrow Wilson School at Princeton University, which describes her decision to leave a distinguished position in then-President Obama's State Department because the demands of her family and her career couldn't be juggled.[5] Thirty years earlier, Wasserstein had participated in diagnosing a situation to which Slaughter still felt she had to capitulate. Slaughter suggests that in fact women are more concerned with their children's traumas, more beholden to their physical presence in their households, even when their husbands are temporarily willing to share fully in parenting responsibilities. Slaughter gives in to a refrain that by 2012 had become tired and worn, the plaint that highly privileged white women still can't achieve their highest career goals because family demands keep them tethered to more flexible, manageable professional routines.

Had she been alive to read it, I think Wasserstein would have made hay of Slaughter's essay in her inimitably witty, perspicacious way. For all her liberal individualism, Wasserstein was determined that her characters imagine their way out of the constraints of the marriage-children-career triad, revising their priorities and the energy with which they devoted themselves to each. In 1983 Wasserstein's characters are close enough to the renovating vision of early feminism that they can at least try to reimagine what family means. Reminiscing about growing up together, Harriet reminds Janie, "Remember when you and I would meet for dinner because Lil was at a meeting and Tasha only had brewer's yeast in the refrigerator? I always thought, Well, I do have a family. Janie's my family. In fact, that still helps a lot. I always assumed it was some sort of pact" (107). Inspired by protofeminist mothers making their own way through the conservative thicket of 1950s nuclear family politics, Harriet and Janie become one another's family.

But ironically, Wasserstein points out, with feminist politics ratifying other options for how to construct a satisfying life, Harriet finally capitulates to convention because she so fears turning into her mother. Lillian might be admirable at work; Harriet's boyfriend Paul, who once interviewed for a job with Lillian, says, "That woman has balls. Do you know what it took for a woman in her time to get as far as she did?" (100). But Lillian goes home to watch *The Rockford Files* reruns on television at night, ending her days alone. Harriet admires and wants to emulate her mother's resilience. She tells Janie,

> There's nothing wrong with being alone. . . . Maybe it's because I'm Lillian's daughter, but I never respected women who didn't learn to live alone and pay their own rent. Imagine spending your whole life pretending you aren't a person. To compromise at this point would be anti-feminist—well, anti-humanist—well, just not impressive. (104)

That Harriet moves down a chain of political positions to describe her stand—from "feminist" to merely "impressive"—presages her eventual capitulation to marriage and social convention.

Ultimately Harriet dumps her irritating and humiliating relationship with Paul but impulsively decides to marry Joel Stine, a man she's known for only two weeks before she makes her commitment. In a choice reminiscent of Muffet choosing her boyfriend over the adventurous evening she describes to Leilah in *Uncommon Women*, Harriet suddenly does an about-face and arranges a marriage for herself that happens faster than speed dating. Against Janie's distraught protestations, Harriet insists, "Marrying Joel is just a chance that came along. . . . Of course you should learn to live alone and pay your own rent, but I didn't realize what it would feel like for me when I became too good at it" (143). She tells Janie, "I love you. But you want us to stay girls together. I'm not a girl anymore. I'm almost thirty and I'm alone. . . . I lied to myself. It doesn't take any strength to be alone, Janie. It's much harder to be with someone else. I want to have children and get on with my life" (144). Janie is horrified by Harriet's reversal and describes how Harriet has in fact been buoyed by waves of social fashion:

> What do you do? Fall in with every current the tide pulls in? Women should live alone and find out what they can do, put off marriage, establish a vertical career track; so you do that for a while. Then you almost turn thirty and *Time Magazine* announces, "Guess what, girls? It's time to have it all." Jaclyn Smith is married and pregnant and playing Jacqueline Kennedy. Every other person who was analyzing stocks last year is analyzing layettes this year; so you do that. What *are* you doing, Harriet? Who the hell are you? (144–45, italics in the original)

But her friend's capitulation allows Janie to assert her own independence and determination. She says, "Harriet, you're getting married to someone you've been dating for two weeks. I am much more scared of being alone than you are. But I'm not going to turn someone into the answer for me" (145).

In this climactic exchange, Wasserstein carefully draws the fault lines in American feminism circa 1983. Janie and Harriet have in fact been family to one another; Harriet's decision to marry a man, any man, because she wants a more conventional family betrays her long relationship with her friend. Just as Muffet abandoned Leilah when Muffet's boyfriend called unexpectedly, Wasserstein suggests that women do this to one another all the time, in more and more profoundly intimate and violent ways. They deny their primary relationships with one another because social dictates persuade them that they're not full, self-actualized human beings until they've conformed to conventional determinations of what adulthood means—marriage and children, and with any luck in a very difficult juggling act, a career.

Isn't It Romantic allows Wasserstein to assay her own definition of what it means to be an independent woman—if not a feminist, a humanist, or even impressive. Ending her fight with Harriet because, at her new part-time *Sesame Street* job, she has to "get up early with the letter B" (145), Janie changes the locks to her own apartment so that her parents can't barge in and makes Tasha repeat "My daughter is a grown woman" before she lets her mother enter her home (147). Throughout the play, Tasha and Simon have intruded on Janie's space, bringing first coffee, then a coffee table, then a safari-themed bar, and other odd items with which to literally furnish Janie's life, as well as, more outrageously still, Vladimir, an immigrant Russian filmmaker/cabdriver who they think might be marriage material. (A sweet and clueless comic foil, Vladimir invites Janie to see *The Sorrow and the Pity* with him [115].) None of their offerings have anything to do with Janie's reality; instead they reflect the person her parents want her to be.

Their final gift of the play is a mink coat, which "is very small, a size 4. Janie hunches to pull it around herself" (148). This ultimate misrecognition of not just her values but the shape and scale of her body prompts Janie to insist that her parents see her for who she is. "I don't see how I can help you understand what I'm doing," she says. "Neither of you ever lived alone; you never thought maybe I won't have children and what will I do with my life if I don't" (149). Desperate for her parents to understand the array of new choices confronting their daughter, Janie quotes Tasha's advice, which she related to Harriet early in the play: "Always look nice when you throw out the garbage; you never know who you might meet. . . . Always walk with your head up and chest out. Think, 'I am'" (85). At the play's end, Janie tells Tasha that she can take care of herself and says, "Mother, don't worry. I'm Tasha's daughter. I know; 'I am'" (151). Mollified, Tasha leaves, wearing the mink coat that fits her perfectly (metaphorically signaling that the gift has been about Tasha all along).

Finally alone in her apartment, determined to unpack the long-ignored boxes of her things, as the answering machine plays yet another message from her whiny, floundering friend Cynthia Peterson, Janie begins to tap dance. As she finds her feet in the rhythm, she dons a hat and lifts an umbrella as a "spot[light] picks up Janie dancing beautifully, alone" (153). The bittersweet image rather brilliantly integrates Wasserstein's themes. Like Milty Schlimovitz, Janie fashions for herself a vaudeville routine reminiscent of Grossinger's entertainment in the Catskills. Like her mother, Tasha, Janie quickly picks up the dance style popularized by African Americans and poached by Jews. Alone in the spotlight, Janie plays for an unseen, unknowable audience, always aware that she's being watched and no doubt judged by forces to which she's somehow beholden. But nonetheless, she feels a happy freedom in her solitude and her physical freedom, finally unconcerned with her weight, her prospects, or her singularity.

Depending on how the moment is performed, Janie's last scene could be triumphant, ironic, or devastating. But I prefer to read it as hopeful. Janie might be dancing as fast as she can, but at least, in the end, she's made choices.[6] She's resisted what she earlier described as her father's sense of her "manifest destiny" (151) and made it this far on her own, even if her next journey is merely to go on location to Canada with the letter C for *Sesame Street* (147). Janie's life has indeed begun, answering one of the questions Wasserstein poses throughout this play and her subsequent work: If a woman refuses the conventional script of marriage and children, how does she know that her life has started?[7]

In both of her first two plays, Wasserstein uses disembodied voices at the beginning of each scene to inject a bit of pointed social humor. In *Isn't It Romantic* Janie's telephone answering machine provides this commentary, recording the voices of various would-be employers, of Tasha and Simon, and most frequently, of Janie's and Harriet's old friend Cynthia Peterson to gild each scene with a bit of satire. In the 1983 Playwrights Horizons production that followed the 1981 Phoenix Theatre premiere, the voices on the answering machine were recorded by already famous actors who'd passed through Wasserstein's stable of talents, including Kevin Kline, Swoosie Kurtz, Meryl Streep (who'd performed in *Uncommon Women*), Patti LuPone, and director Jerry Zaks. The rather inside joke of these actors lending their voices to these parts no doubt helped to enhance the humor for those who recognized them and helped secure what was fast becoming Wasserstein's New York cultural capital.

The episodic style connoted by those taped messages also became Wasserstein's hallmark, although *Isn't It Romantic* boasts a more well-made play structure than the earlier *Uncommon Women*. Scenes shift back and forth from Janie's and Harriet's apartments to Central Park South, where the women, their boyfriends, and their mothers meet for lunch and conversation. In one of her first scenes with dialogue between two older women, Wasserstein lends Tasha and Lillian common cause when they bump into one another in the park. The scene allows these women to empathize with one another, while it also amplifies the theme of ethnic differences that color scenes between Janie and Harriet. Tasha confides to Lillian, "Listen, I know you people don't like to get very intimate, but since our daughters are such good friends, I want to tell you I always admired you" (122). Tasha's presumptions about non-Jews are as egregious as Lillian's and Harriet's are about Jews. Tasha shares Simon's expression "Everything presses itself out" to describe her faith that their daughters will find their way. "I don't understand why they're fighting it so hard," she muses (120). Lillian echoes her later, saying reassuringly, "Sooner or later you can have everything pressed" (121), the imposition of WASP practices on Yiddishkeit presentiment.

The misinterpretation of the ethnically inflected saying is Wasserstein's charming depiction of the benign gulf in understanding between Christians and Jews. Even Harriet, who's supposed to have known Janie all her life, consults the *Oxford Companion to Jewish Life* to see how to mark the occasion of Janie's new apartment ("I'm not familiar with this companion," Janie retorts wryly [102]). Act 1, in fact, closes on a scene in which Harriet's misunderstandings provide the comedy as Janie's inability to fix Marty a chicken makes her frantic. After Janie hurriedly describes Hymie's Delicatessen and Marty's nephew, Schlomo, Harriet gets things gloriously confused and announces, "Janie, people named Homo and Schymie! I feel our move back to New York has been very successful. I've met a sadist vice president and you've become involved in a shtetl" (116).

Isn't It Romantic is less often produced than other Wasserstein plays, but in some ways the script is the most moving and astute about issues that preoccupied the playwright her entire life. As a play about mothers and daughters, it continues to be rare in the American canon (and at least Janie didn't kill herself, as the young protagonist did in Marsha Norman's Pulitzer Prize–winning play about a mother and daughter, 'night, Mother, in 1983). Her sharp humor allowed Wasserstein to stay unsentimental and clear-eyed about the mother-daughter relationship, as she captured the vexations of women attempting to meet their mothers' expectations when the country was exploding with new possibilities for white middle-class women's success. Wasserstein's play crystalized the enormity of the paradigm shift, even if she couched her inquiry in humor.

In between the original 1981 production and the 1983 revival, Wasserstein tweaked and streamlined Isn't It Romantic. Critics, however, traced the line between Janie and Harriet and Wasserstein's early characters from Uncommon Women and Others while adding a soupçon of ethnic references to their generally approving but dismissive reviews of the Playwrights Horizons production. Douglas Watt, in the Daily News, hardly a Wasserstein fan at this point, noted that the play "is primarily the story of a nice Jewish girl who finally rejects a nice Jewish boy . . . and life as a Brooklyn housewife in favor of going it alone."[8] Many of the reviews refer to the "nice Jewish girl" stereotype, which, when used by Jewish girls ironically (as Wasserstein does in Isn't It Romantic) points out the weight of the caricature for those trying to live rich, well-rounded lives. Critics from powerful mainstream newspapers used the cliché mostly to keep Wasserstein and her play in their places. Clive Barnes, writing condescendingly in the New York Post, described her characters as "spoiled brats" who are "out to find themselves and their place, and do so most amusingly, and with a great deal of chic and fancy charm."[9]

Other critics noted the ethnic comparisons the play foregrounds. Richard Corliss, in Time, suggested that Wasserstein "writes about Jews and WASPS without a tincture of sitcom condescension, finding poignant similarities in perpendicular lives, giving just about every character equal time and a fair number of laughs."[10] Elliot Sirkin, in the Nation, on the other hand, wrote, "What Isn't it Romantic really dramatizes is an old racial myth: Jews are warm and emotional, and WASPs, especially on Park Avenue or Wall Street, are cold fish."[11] He sees Janie as an "ethnic waif" who seems "less like a person than a tourist attraction," "at least partly because she so resembles Rhoda on the old Mary Tyler Moore Show."[12] Sirkin's sarcastic criticism also reminds me that the pointed, satirical way in which Wasserstein wrote about New York Jews was fairly rare in the popular culture of 1983. While lots of Jewish playwrights had become famous in the American theater—Arthur Miller, Kaufman and Hart, and Neil Simon among them—the kind of ethnic humor that Wasserstein plied so explicitly might rankle even some Jews who worried about one-dimensional, anti-Semitic caricatures. Mel Gussow, on the other hand, in the *New York Times*, writing of the original 1981 production, said, "The heroine . . . has a seemingly inexhaustible supply of one-liners and quick comebacks, many of them transliterated from the Yiddish. She is a card-carrying kvetch, a female version of Woody Allen's woeful stand-up persona."[13] Gussow's comparison put Wasserstein in the company of another Jewish cultural icon, implicitly elevating her stature.

Interestingly, five years after *Isn't It Romantic*'s revival at Playwrights Horizons, the play that would catapult Wasserstein into real success and fame wasn't very Jewish at all. But that play, *The Heidi Chronicles*, engaged directly with the feminist movement in ways never before seen in mainstream theater.

CHAPTER FOUR

The Heidi Chronicles

The Heidi Chronicles (1989) proved to be Wasserstein's first breakout success and remains the play most associated with her career and her concerns. The play could be seen as a companion piece to *Isn't It Romantic*, as it describes the travails of Heidi Holland, a Janie Blumberg–style feminist professor (a character type that recurs throughout Wasserstein's subsequent plays), as she tries to make sense of her career and her personal life against the backdrop of recent U.S. history. Told in flashbacks from the early 1960s to the then-present of the late 1980s, *Heidi* compares pre-feminist heterosexual women's ability to roll up their poodle skirts and roll down their bobby socks while they smoked and twisted on the dance floor to a poignant sense of what's been gained and lost by women who gradually thought more of themselves and their capabilities.

The play traces Heidi's rise from a confused might-be feminist tagalong to a well-established art historian who successfully documents women artists' lives and work but can't quite get her personal life in order. Wasserstein's take on what was quickly becoming the media-proclaimed demise of feminism in America struck a cultural chord. *Heidi* won the 1989 Pulitzer, Tony, Outer Critics Circle, Drama Desk, and Susan Smith Blackburn awards and had a healthy run on Broadway. The play remains a perennial favorite in the regional theater circuit and received frequent revivals shortly after the playwright's death in 2006. A 2015 Broadway revival garnered a great deal of media attention, even though it closed after eighty performances.

The play began Wasserstein's association with director Daniel Sullivan, who championed an early version of *Heidi* at Seattle Rep, the regional theater in Washington State he then headed. In the original Broadway production, Joan Allen starred as Heidi, Boyd Gaines as Peter, and Peter Friedman as Scoop. Heidi's character (and Allen's casting) began Wasserstein's move away from the ethnic stand-ins on whom her earlier plays centered. While Heidi has a certain diffidence and ambivalence in common with Holly Kaplan of *Uncommon Women and Others* and with Janie Blumberg of *Isn't It Romantic*, she's emphatically not Jewish. The play's ethnic humor is reserved for Scoop Rosenbaum, the arrogant, striving, upper-middle-class man who first flirts with Heidi at a mixer for Eugene McCarthy in 1968 and dates her through their young adulthoods before he marries Lisa Friedlander, a Jewish children's book illustrator from Memphis. Peter Patrone, whom Heidi meets at a high school dance in Chicago, where they both go to private schools, is Italian and eventually comes out as gay, while Susan, Heidi's lifelong, chameleon-like best friend, is unmarked as anything but white, upper-middle class, extremely ambitious, and sexually flexible. With Jewishness reserved for Scoop, who is perhaps the play's most unapologetically polarizing and unappealing character, though he boasts a certain slick charm, Wasserstein moved away from ethnic specificity to make a more mainstream statement about the status of gender in the United States, as America anticipated the end of the twentieth century. Perhaps as a result, she struck a chord that allowed her work to resonate in a large public arena for the first time.

The Heidi Chronicles polarized feminist spectators and critics when it was produced on Broadway in 1989. Some, myself included, felt that Wasserstein's play participated in what was by then a cultural dismantling of the gains feminism had made for American women since the movement began in the early seventies. By hopping and skipping quickly through the decades from 1965 to 1989, many critics felt that Wasserstein's episodic race through political history, accompanied by pop songs that marked each moment more specifically than some of the plot points, belittled feminist accomplishments by painting them with such a broad, pop culture brush. Wasserstein's trademark wit and humor also perturbed some spectators. No one suggested that feminists couldn't be funny—an unfortunately common (and persistent) stereotype—but many debated whether Wasserstein was laughing at or with the movement.

The play's insistently individualist perspective in fact angered many feminist critics. Wasserstein's heroine sits outside the circle of women at the Ann Arbor consciousness-raising group to which Susan drags her in 1970, and even if she does finally make common cause with the odd group assembled to empower themselves, the scene is one of the most parodic in the play. And although Heidi goes on to become a famous art historian committed to women and art, she never finds her way back to the collective feminist analysis that consciousness-raising begat. The play leaves her stranded (as Heidi complains bitterly to an alumni group from Miss Crain's School to which she delivers a speech, she feels stranded by her life, too) without the important community of women that feminism has always insisted is politically necessary. Wasserstein's play was derided as liberal sour grapes, in which a woman playwright used the popular Broadway forum to gesture to a history she intimated was finished and a politic she suggested was spent. Many feminists saw *The Heidi Chronicles* as a sellout, a sop to dominant culture just when the social movement needed a powerful public champion.

I agreed with and even promoted this feminist critique of the play. But read in the context of Wasserstein's previous and subsequent plays, and the context of the ongoing history of the status of women in the United States, I'm now persuaded that *The Heidi Chronicles* does a certain kind of important cultural work. All of Wasserstein's by now well-established themes echo through the play: men speaking for women, foretelling their futures, as Scoop does (so presciently) when he first meets Heidi; women striving to "have it all," to find husbands, bear children, and exceed these traditional achievements with the even more ambitious careers to which women of a certain class, by 1989, could at least presume to aspire; and ambivalent relationships with men who are too confining for a heroine who wants more independence, wants more from herself, and sees herself with more to contribute to the world than just another cozy nuclear family. Wasserstein extends these themes by lifting them out of the confines of a small Seven Sisters school or a relationship between Jewish and non-Jewish friends in New York and placing them in the realm of American history, writing her picaresque heroine's story against the backdrop of a turbulent, unpredictable moment in politics and culture. Wasserstein's bid to speak more broadly heralded both her achievement and her new level of vulnerability to artistic critique.

I feel more charitable toward *The Heidi Chronicles* now, perhaps because my own politics have become less radical and more liberal since 1989 or perhaps because an additional twenty-five-odd years of American history have accumulated through which to see the play's strengths and weaknesses. When *Heidi* premiered on Broadway, the feminist movement was still vibrant and visible in American culture, although it had already begun to suffer the backlash that journalist Susan Faludi would go on to document in her 1991 book about the "undeclared war against American women."[1] Feminism already felt precarious in 1989, especially to those critics, scholars, and activists who remained committed to its potential as a movement for human rights advanced through the lens of gender.

I recall speaking at a conference on a panel with several other theater scholars when *The Heidi Chronicles* debuted. We all approached the production from different critical perspectives (semiotic, psychoanalytic, scenic, etc.). As the lone feminist speaker, I excoriated the play for what I found to be its retrograde politics and was cheered on by the large crowd of women who attended the panel so that they, too, could share the forum for their mostly outraged viewpoints.[2] But such a response has to be put in the context of the moment. In 1989, feminist theater and performance scholars were still finding their footing and fighting to be taken seriously by an academic field that was recalcitrant about acknowledging the gendered nature of power and knowledge. The theater industry, too, blithely disregarded feminists who advocated for women playwrights to be produced in numbers equal to men in the most visible, powerful venues. Given the complexities of the era, that *The Heidi Chronicles* was produced on Broadway and received all of 1989's top theater accolades seemed offensive, given what many feminist critics read as its flippant ambivalence about the movement (most egregiously advanced in the consciousness-raising scene and in Heidi's lecture at her alma mater).

More than twenty-five years later, I remain an avowed feminist theater scholar. But American culture and the academy have both changed. Feminist theory and ideas now underpin the most important theater and performance studies scholarship, which has more recently considered transgender lives and performance, as well as disability and other, more intersectional aspects of identity and subjectivity. In some ways, in fact, the status of "women" qua women is less important and debated now than it was then. A lot of work remains to be done on women playwrights and directors, especially, as well as on gender writ large in American and global theater and performance. But the academic field's politics have moved decisively to the left since 1989.

Of course, such a shift might make current feminist scholars even more suspicious of *The Heidi Chronicles*, and some might feel even less generous toward the play. I find myself taking a longer view. If university and college students perform the play, the script offers them a chance to engage critically with the history it narrates (a history with which many students remain unfamiliar). Heidi can be a terrific role to play—witness Elisabeth Moss's excellent performance in the 2015 Broadway revival. And most importantly, many years after its premiere, because the fortunes of feminism have devolved rather than improved, the play is situated differently within a historical conversation about women and equal rights.

Astonishingly, the play remains one of the few by a woman to win both the Pulitzer Prize for Drama and the Tony Award for Best Play, and one of the very few to boast a major Broadway revival (a production I'll discuss below).[3] Only one woman playwright since Wasserstein—Theresa Rebeck—has been regularly produced on Broadway, especially without the debilitating workshop process that often distorts plays before they're even seen by large audiences. Given this still-appalling track record for women in the most powerful theater forums, Wasserstein's success in the 1980s and 1990s demands respect and attention. Likewise, because feminism is even less visible in mainstream culture since she wrote her play, the fact that anyone took the movement seriously enough to write about it for Broadway audiences now seems remarkable.

The Heidi Chronicles begins with a trademark Wasserstein framing device. But rather than the "man's voice" that moves the ironic commentary of *Uncommon Women* or the telephone answering machine voices that provide the satiric counterpoint to Janie's ongoing life dramas, *The Heidi Chronicles* actually embodies its heroine at the top of the play. Heidi Holland (played first by Joan Allen and then by Christine Lahti in the award-winning original Broadway production) stands in front of a screen in a lecture hall, teaching a class about the history of women artists.[4] As she moves through a survey of work from Sofonisba Anguissola in 1559 to Lilly Martin Spencer in 1869, Heidi's opening gambit sets up Wasserstein's themes. Heidi's knowledge of women's history is vast, and her contribution to the academic feminist project to recover formerly invisible women is clear. She lectures that despite Sofonisba Anguissola's renown as a painter in her day, art history textbooks fail to mention her. "Of course," Heidi says as an aside, "in my day this same standard text mentioned no women 'from the dawn of history to the present.'"[5] Heidi's revisionist project aligns with Wasserstein's. In her own history, the playwright, too, plans to rectify the persistent invisibility of women.

And yet the monologue also establishes one of the problems with both Heidi's and Wasserstein's tone. As the art historical images flash onto the screen, Heidi looks up at one of the paintings and says, "Hello, girls" (160). The comment is casual, if a bit coy, the ploy of a teacher who wants to be liked. But it also undercuts the artists' and Heidi's authority in a rather typical Wasserstein way. The jokes mask the analysis; while the audience laughs, they might not hear the more potent critique and feminist contribution in the lines that follow. As she analyzes the final slide of Spencer's *We Both Must Fade*, Heidi points out that the "vanitas" painting reminds the viewer of "mortality and time passing, while the precious jewelry spilling out is an allusion to the transience of earthly possessions. This portrait can be perceived as a meditation on the brevity of youth, beauty, and life. But what can't?" (161). Heidi's analysis anticipates the course of Wasserstein's play, which in many ways is itself a mediation on the brevity of youth, beauty, and life. But the shrugging "But what can't?" helps persuade Heidi's students and perhaps Wasserstein's audience not to take very seriously the stature of these artists or of the professor/playwright herself. Heidi waves us into the past to chronicle a certain slice of American feminism—white, upper-middle-class, college-educated, as usual—through which Wasserstein provides a whirlwind tour. But she's already undercut the project by making it just a tiny bit twee and prosaic.

Heidi's meditations usher the audience into the play's first scene. As the professor muses on the painting and helps her students remember salient details for the upcoming test, she remarks that *We Both Must Fade* "reminds me of me at one of those horrible high-school dances. And you sort of want to dance, and you sort of want to go home, and you sort of don't know what you want. So you hang around, a fading rose in an exquisitely detailed dress, waiting to see what might happen" (161). This musing prologue to the play's action positions Heidi/Wasserstein as the passive observer to the course of her own life and to the American history she recalls and also suggests that art appreciation requires personal identification. That the painting reminds Heidi of herself suggests to her art students—and to the theater spectators—that the way to understand art is to identify with it personally, to connect it to a life experience with which you can relate.[6] This individual, personal mode of interpreting art characterizes Heidi and Wasserstein. They ignore a more collective, socially acute analysis of art history and theater and, in the process, let their spectators and many of their interlocutors off the hook. Nonetheless, the comment and strategy provide a useful dramatic device. And as Wasserstein's play flashes back to a high school dance in 1965, using the same reflective structure with which *Uncommon Women* began, Heidi's thoughtful prologue at least resonates. Wasserstein encourages spectators to see each episodic scene from the perspective of 1989's present, to be at least a bit critical of how we got from "there" to "here." And the scenes do reverberate, as each hopscotching moment rings with foresight or a poignant observation about what will or does happen to the women of Heidi's generation and upbringing.

At the 1965 high school dance that opens the play's history lesson, returning to a moment twenty-four years earlier than the play's prologue, Heidi and her best friend Susan sing "The Shoop Shoop Song" together as they look out onto the floor for appropriate men. The flirtatious, already ambitious Susan demonstrates more affinity for the project than the rather aloof, ambivalent Heidi. Susan schools Heidi in the proper way to attract a man: "The worst thing you can do is cluster. 'Cause then it looks like you just wanna hang around with your girlfriend. But don't look desperate. Men don't dance with desperate women" (163). Susan serves as Heidi's teacher throughout *The Heidi Chronicles*, ventriloquizing social mores that shift with trends and fashion over the decades. As she rolls up her skirt to show off her legs, Susan tells Heidi, "You know, as your best friend, I must tell you frankly that you're going to get really messed up unless you learn to take men seriously" (164). Susan goes off to dance with a boy whose signature style is twisting and smoking at the same time, but happily, as Heidi settles in by herself to read a book (*Death Be Not Proud*, of all things), she's approached by Peter Patrone, the caustically funny, soon-to-come-out-as-gay young man who will become another lifelong friend. With inflections that anticipate his campy style, Peter observes of Heidi, "You look so bored you must be very bright" (165).[7] As he and Heidi connect instantly, Peter concocts a dramatic scenario that allows both of them to pretend they're somewhere else:

> PETER: Don't apologize for being the most attractive woman on the cruise.
> HEIDI: Cruise?
> PETER: She docks tonight in Portsmouth. And then farewell to the *Queen Mary*. . . . Our tragic paths were meant to cross. I leave tomorrow for the sanatorium in Zurich. *Coughs.*
> HEIDI: How odd! I'm going to the sanatorium in Milan. *Coughs. He offers her his handkerchief. She refuses.* (166)

That Heidi can play along with Peter marks them both as outsiders to the heterosexual occasion at hand, comrades in a subtle but present critique. As they dance with parodic flair to the night's final song, Peter asks Heidi if she will marry him:

> HEIDI: I covet my independence.
> PETER: Perhaps when you leave the sanatorium, you'll think otherwise. I want to know you all my life. If we can't marry, let's be great friends. (167)

Peter's remark is of course prophetic, in the way of all Wasserstein's male characters. Because he's gay, Heidi and Peter will never marry, but they will indeed be lifelong friends, charting shifts in the zeitgeist from their own identity perspectives. In fact, the next time the audience sees Peter is in a scene Wasserstein sets in 1974 outside the Art Institute of Chicago, where Heidi and a humorless female colleague, dressed all in black, protest the exclusion of women artists from the *Age of Napoleon* exhibition. The protest, however, fizzles when no one stops to listen. When Peter shows up unexpectedly, he chants, "No more master penises! No more master penises!" implicitly both belittling and getting to the heart of the protest's political claims (185). Heidi scolds Peter: "Peter, this is *serious*!" (185, italics in original). But now in even better command of his light and witty gay wordplay, Peter brushes aside Heidi's claims on the political moment, reminding her that Nixon's impeachment is happening at the very same time. Feminist demands for more recognition for women artists compete with a political crisis that, by contrast, is more important to the course of history.

But rather than arguing that women artists should be equally vital to cultural progress, Wasserstein subtly allows Peter to shift the focus, first to Nixon and then to his own identity claims as a "liberal-homosexual-pediatrician" (188). At first Heidi thinks he's joking as usual, finding ever new ways to ridicule her own ideological attachments. But Peter insists,

> Heidi, I'm gay. Okay? . . . And *my* liberation, *my* pursuit of happiness, and the pursuit of happiness of other men like me is just as politically and socially valid as hanging a couple of goddamn paintings because they were signed by someone named Nancy, Gladys, or Gilda. And that is why I came to see you today. I am demanding your equal time and consideration. (189)

Sadly, for the feminism that Wasserstein puts on the Broadway stage for one of the first times in history, before act 1 ends, the women's movement is already competing with gay liberation for social attention and legitimacy.

Although addressing both movements might have allowed the playwright to knit them together into parallel and equally important civil rights struggles, Wasserstein writes Peter with such charm and charisma (and such good, funny lines, for which Heidi serves as his "straight man") that he overshadows Heidi and her nascent political analysis. Heidi's colleague Debbie, the protest organizer, takes an instant dislike to Peter. She tells him, "I find your ironic tone both paternal and caustic. I'm sorry. I can't permit you to join us. This is a women's march" (189). Debbie's gender separatism sets off Heidi's alarm bells: "But I thought our point was that this is *our* cultural institution. 'Our' meaning everybody's. Men and women. Him included," she says (190, italics in the original). In the middle of a scene about demanding equality for women in art, Wasserstein already moves Heidi toward the humanism that overshadows her feminism throughout the play. To rub salt into that wound, Peter quips that Debbie should have let him march because he knows the curator, another gay man. His access to power and influence will always exceed Heidi's.

When he becomes the best pediatrician in New York under forty later in the play, and when HIV/AIDS descends on his community, Peter's political status again trumps Heidi's. In the play's penultimate scene, set in 1987, Heidi arrives near midnight to donate books and records to the New York children's hospital ward Peter runs, as she intends to leave the next morning to take a teaching position in Minnesota. Heidi's life has foundered and she feels sad, despite her relative fame as an art critic and professor, so she's accepted an offer to teach and finish her new book in the Midwest. But Peter is angry at her and at the world, burdened with the AIDS pandemic and its effect on the children for whom he cares and on his own community. Pressed to be honest, he says,

> Okay. Heidi, I'd say about once a month now I gather in some church, meeting house, or concert hall with handsome men all my own age, and in the front row is usually a couple my parents' age. . . . And we listen for half an hour to testimonials, memories, amusing anecdotes about a son, a friend, a lover, also handsome, also usually my own age, whom none of us will see again. After the first, the fifth, or the fifteenth of these gatherings, a sadness like yours seems a luxury. (237)

Peter's critique is harsh. Wasserstein implicitly allows the play to establish a hierarchy of suffering in which gay men, devastated by HIV/AIDS, inevitably trump what Wasserstein and Heidi describe as the discomforts and sadness of a feminist political movement that hasn't quite paid off as expected.

But the comparison is unfair. American feminist and lesbian activism in the 1980s and 1990s in fact embraced HIV/AIDS as an activist cause, lending political energy and support to gay men, many of whom were radicalized by the virus's ravages. Years later, commentators would point out that feminists and lesbians sometimes sacrificed their own issues to work with ACT-UP and other gay activist movements and that gay men never repaid the solidarity by advocating, for instance, for breast cancer research. Most troubling in how Wasserstein tells this story is that Peter's suffering so clearly dwarfs Heidi's. Peter speaks for a community and Heidi appears to speak only for herself. Women's activist struggles are reduced to the individual and seen as trite compared to the life-or-death terror confronting gay men and HIV/AIDS.

Peter persuades Heidi not to leave for Minnesota by reminding her that "in our lives, our friends are our families," a truism that Wasserstein models throughout the play and in her entire opus (238).[8] Unlike *Isn't It Romantic*, in which Simon and Tasha Blumberg and Lillian Cornwall figure so centrally as parents against whom Janie and Harriet compare the choices available to shape their own lives, Susan, Peter, and Heidi's on-again, off-again boyfriend, Scoop Rosenbaum, compose Heidi's family. On the one hand, Wasserstein suggests that this is a liberal kind of progress. Untethered to traditional notions of kinship, people like Heidi and her friends are free to make new ties and commitments.[9] But at the same time, because their milestones are differently marked, it's difficult to know when they've arrived at adulthood.[10]

This persistent quandary in Wasserstein's plays threads through *The Heidi Chronicles*, too. Scoop, who dropped out of Princeton to found the magazine *Liberated Earth News* and later accrues power and influence as the editor of *Boomer*, a magazine for the baby boom generation, tends to assign grades to everything, from potato chips at the McCarthy mixer where he and Heidi first meet to his own fiancée, Lisa, whom he rates when Peter asks if he loves his soon-to-be wife. Scoop remarks to Heidi, "Do I love her, as your nice friend asked me? She's the best that I can do. Is she an A+ like you? No. But I don't want to come home to an A+. A–, maybe, but not A+." Heidi responds, "Scoop, we're out of school. We're in life. You don't have to grade everything" (201). This reminder might be specious, but in Wasserstein's universe, the question of when people really become adults remains open, as the measurements for success and arrival become ever more elastic.

What it means to be "in life" shifts, in fact, as Wasserstein chronicles the fickle history of American popular and political culture for these two and a half decades. Scoop represents the white male (though Jewish) trajectory of American success, moving as he does from Princeton to *Liberated Earth News* to *Boomer* to, by the play's end, the possibility of running for Congress. Along the way, although he's married to the benign Lisa, his affairs with other women are legion and well-known among his friends, as Wasserstein paints Scoop as a typical man of privilege and power who's more than a bit of a cad. He, like Peter, has been the play's prognosticator, predicting Heidi's future in ways she's unable to do for herself. At their first meeting, in 1968, Scoop criticizes Heidi for her diffidence ("You don't have to look at the floor. . . . Why are you so afraid to speak up?" [172]) and then predicts, "You're the one this is all going to affect. You're the one whose life this will all change significantly. Has to. You're a very serious person. In fact, you're the unfortunate contradiction in terms—a serious good person. And I envy you that. . . . You'll be one of those true believers who didn't understand it was all just a phase" (173).

Heidi is irritated by Scoop's self-assurance. In one of the rare instances of women in Wasserstein's plays talking back to the men who control their lives, Heidi tells Scoop, "I was wondering what mothers teach their sons that they never bothered to tell their daughters. . . . I mean, why the fuck are you so confident?" (171). But despite her frustration with Scoop's blow-hard bossiness, he still gets the last word, and his predictions to a certain extent come true. At the play's end, when Heidi tells Scoop about her fantasy that her adopted daughter, Judy, will achieve the feminist gains for which Heidi has continued to fight, Scoop comments, "So I was right all along. You were a true believer" (247). And although he is indeed right, his smug self-satisfaction detracts a bit from what might otherwise be the achievement of Heidi's lasting commitment to her ideals.

Perhaps more perniciously, Wasserstein uses the character of Susan as a foil for Heidi's steadfast feminist-humanism. If Susan instructs Heidi about the importance of men at their high school dance in 1965, by 1970, in a scene set in Ann Arbor, Michigan, Susan is the incipient feminist who has dragged Heidi to her first consciousness-raising meeting.[11] Heidi is just visiting, literally and metaphorically, but her appearance on the scene allows Wasserstein to parody the excesses of an early moment in a certain strand of American feminist history, when women tried hard to empower one another, offering affirmations that had too long been withheld. Set in a church basement, the scene gathers an array of types, including the middle-class housewife, Jill, who's trying unsuccessfully to put herself first in the context of a demanding family life; Fran, the Army fatigues–wearing, lesbian "fuzzy physicist" who swears like a soldier; and Becky, the teenager abandoned by hippie parents to an abusive boyfriend, who is looking for a community to save her from herself. When Susan and Heidi join the scene, the women's assertions of love for one another ring superficial and facile, as though they're practicing a feeling they

haven't quite yet achieved. In fact, much of early consciousness raising was about letting feeling follow form, about willing community
into existence and then filling it with substance. But Wasserstein's
parody is so adept, the humor becomes unwittingly mean-spirited.

This scene offered one of the first representations of a
consciousness-raising group ever seen on the Broadway stage.
Whether Wasserstein meant her parody affectionately or not, the
scene allowed audiences to affirm their stereotype of this crucial
feminist practice as, frankly, silly.[12] Feminism is also already compromised in the play. Susan, the play's bellwether for shifting political and social trends, tells her friends, "I was seriously considering
beginning a law journal devoted solely to women's legal issues. But
after some pretty heavy deliberation, I've decided to work within the
male-establishment power base to change the system" by accepting
a position on her school's law review (178). Although in actuality,
1970 was a little early for self-avowed feminists to be making these
compromises, the debate over how to be a radical and effective
change agent was very real in feminism. Susan's choices reflect po-
larities in the feminist movement, debates over how to make social
change happen.

But as Susan decides to work within the system, Wasserstein also
sets her trajectory toward unfortunate accommodations. After law
school, where Susan and Scoop wind up clerking for the same judge,
Susan joins the Montana Women's Health and Legal Collective (194).
At Scoop's wedding to Lisa in 1977, Scoop remarks that Susan "could
have been brilliant" but "brilliance is irrelevant in Montana" (195).
By Lisa's baby shower in a scene set in 1980, Susan has what Wasserstein calls "a new look, with pants, heels, and a silk blouse" (206).
She's just graduated from business school, in which she enrolled to
help make her Montana women's collective more financially self-
sufficient. But now, Susan has decided to take a position in L.A. as
"an executive VP for a new production company. They wanted someone with a feminist and business background. Targeting films for the
twenty-five-to-twenty-nine-year-old female audience" (209). Of
course, as Susan herself might have said ten years earlier, using feminism and business in the same sentence was once oxymoronic, but
Susan moves fluidly into the Hollywood power set and happily
adopts its market-based mentality.

By 1984, in a scene in which Heidi and Susan meet for a New

York power lunch, Susan is wildly successful and determined to co-opt Heidi's experience with women and art for a television sitcom she wants to develop. Heidi thinks they're meeting for a soulful conversation and asks her friend, "Susie, do you ever think that what makes you a person is also what keeps you from being a person?" Susan brushes her off, saying, "I'm sorry, honey, but you're too deep for me. By now I've been so many people, I don't know who I am. And I don't care" (224). Susan morphs from one identity to the next, as Wasserstein uses her to chart how feminism, in the playwright's estimation, has accommodated itself to capitalism and become a fashion trend that, in the right hands, can pay off handsomely. Susan plans a television series about three young women about to turn thirty, "three gals on the town in an apartment. Curators, painters, sculptors, what have you," character types with which she presumes Heidi can help. Denise, Lisa's younger sister, who enrolled in women's studies courses at Brown and is now Susan's assistant, says of the show's women, "They're ambitious, they're professional, and they're on their way to being successful":

> SUSAN: And they don't want to make the same mistakes we did.
> HEIDI: I don't want to make the same mistakes we did. What exactly were they?
> DENISE: Well, like a lot of women your age are very unhappy. Unfulfilled, frightened of growing old alone.
> HEIDI: It's a good thing we're not doing a sitcom about them. (226)

Offended at this version of her generation's history, Heidi declines to participate, "because I don't think we made such big mistakes. And I don't want to see three gals on the town who do" (227). But Susan protests, "In L.A., everyone creates their own history," as she air-kisses Heidi good-bye and runs out of the restaurant to catch up with Diane Keaton (227).

As in so many of the play's other scenes, Wasserstein critiques the very social styles she uses humor to parody. She delivers part of her analysis through Heidi's responses, in this case to Susan's glib prosecution of feminist values for pecuniary ends. But Heidi has been a reactive, passive character, embodying the observant wallflower she predicted in her art history lecture at the very top of the play. Wasserstein disarms her ability to provide a real alternative to Susan's bastardization of the feminist cause and to Peter's co-optation of equality as more important for gay men than for women. Wasserstein places Heidi's climactic monologue directly following her lunch scene with Susan, in the guise of a lecture Heidi delivers at the Plaza Hotel for the Miss Crain's School East Coast Alumnae Association. The theme of the lunch is "Women, Where Are We Going," to which Heidi responds with an impromptu complaint about how stranded she feels by the women she expected to be her comrades in the struggle to improve gender inequality. Instead of feeling supported, Heidi reports comparing herself unfavorably to women at her gym who wear all the cool exercise shoes and clothing and eat all the latest faddish foods and who, Heidi presumes, have affairs behind their husbands' backs or "trendy" lesbian liaisons, but from whom she feels utterly separate, inadequate by comparison yet certainly superior, as well as sad and alone.

She confesses to her alumnae audience,

> I'm sorry I don't want [the locker room] women to find out I'm worthless. And superior. . . . I'm envying women I don't even know. I'm envying women I don't even like. . . . And suddenly I stop competing with all of them. I'm just not happy. I'm afraid I haven't been happy for some time. . . . I don't blame the ladies in the locker room for how I feel. I don't blame any of us. We're all concerned, intelligent, good women. *Pauses.* It's just that I feel stranded. And I thought the whole point was that we wouldn't feel stranded. I thought the point was that we were all in this together. (231–32)

Wasserstein's by now notorious diagnosis of how feminism has let women down by not providing the formula for "having it all" sounds, in Heidi's monologue, like whining about personal unhappiness, instead of fury that society hasn't changed to account for women's aspirations and needs. Heidi bemoans a lack of community, but Wasserstein has depicted her as a character who always removed herself from the political coalition feminism made an option. Heidi sits outside the consciousness-raising circle; she throws her lot in with Peter at the demonstration for women in art; she can't get behind Susan's and Denise's desire to cash in by creating a popular version of her feminist generation for mainstream television. Wasserstein construes scenes in which Heidi clearly suffers from misogyny, as though the problem stems from Peter's and Scoop's individual blindness and insensitivity rather than social inequity. This choice is exemplified in the painful albeit hilarious scene Wasserstein writes for the three friends in which they appear together on a breezy talk show called *Hello, New York*, on which the two men boast and gab with April, the fawning show host, and never let Heidi get a word in edgewise.

Given the play's humor and realism, it takes some work to extrapolate Heidi's condition to that of women in general. Instead, the character appears to be a talented, smart, relatively privileged woman who's chosen the wrong friends. Fran, the fuzzy lesbian physicist in Ann Arbor whom the play implicitly ridicules, promotes the most potent analysis of Heidi's flaws. She asks Heidi if her dissertation about images of women in art is feminist, to which Heidi demurs, "Humanist" (180). In response, Fran repeats her motto, "You either shave your legs or you don't," suggesting that feminism can't be managed with halfhearted, accommodationist, humanist politics (178). Heidi's expressed commitment to humanism over feminism ("All people deserve to fulfill their potential," she asserts [173]) in fact leaves her with one leg shaved and one hairy, which hardly equips her to blame her disappointments on feminism as she later does in her Miss Crain's speech.

The play's 1989 success left feminist theater critics feeling ambivalent. On one hand, it was hard not to applaud Wasserstein for starting a conversation about feminism on Broadway in a full-length, multicharacter, multiactor play at a moment when most feminist politics represented in theater were performed in solo shows or at small venues in downtown New York or around the country. At the same time, it was amply clear why some feminist commentators bemoaned the fact that this dialogue was launched for the first time around a heroine with such a vexed relationship to the movement, distancing herself from its goals while expecting to reap its rewards. In one of the most cogent feminist reviews published in the trade presses, Alisa Solomon, writing for the *Village Voice*, said, "Like *Uncommon Women and Others* and *Isn't It Romantic*, *The Heidi Chronicles* looks wittily at intelligent, educated women, and assures us that they are funny for the same, traditional reasons women have always been funny: they hate their bodies, can't find a man, and don't believe in themselves."[13] Solomon says, "If Wasserstein's play offered a serious critique of bourgeois feminism amid its polished one-liners . . . I'd feel a sisterly sympathy for Heidi's disillusionment. . . . But *The Heidi Chronicles'* own vision of feminism, like its dramaturgy, is itself entirely bourgeois."[14] "And while Heidi's understanding of feminism is about as superficial as you can get (she refuses the f-word and insists on being called a 'humanist') Wasserstein punishes her for it, as if it's feminism's fault that she didn't have both a career and a family."[15] In my own negative reading of the play at the time, I wrote, "*The Heidi Chronicles* is a 'postfeminist' mainstream play that distorts the political history of U.S. feminism from the mid-1960s to the late 1980s. The play trivializes radical feminist gains, suppresses feminist rage, and acquiesces to the dominant culture's reading of the end of feminism. The play's traditional realist form helps to promote its essentially conservative ideology."[16]

The Heidi Chronicles remains a vexing play, in part because even in 2017, it is still one of the few to even attempt to tell the history of contemporary American feminism.[17] Sullivan's original production played up Wasserstein's sharp and frequent jokes and wound up belittling the very feminist movement the playwright was trying to parse while telling the story of Heidi's life. Director Pam MacKinnon paced her star-studded 2015 revival more deliberately and emphasized its drama alongside its comedy. Elisabeth Moss's starring turn as Heidi offered a thoughtful and smart, richly nuanced rendering of the character that made her warm and deeply present, where Allen had played her in a way that many reviewers described as "steely."

The revival offers ample opportunity to reconsider what the play might mean to new generations of spectators. MacKinnon, invited by *Playbill* to reflect on her production's relevance, said,

> I don't think it's a dated play in any way, shape or form. . . . I wish it were dated more than it is, but it does feel like the issues of today and fulfilling your potential and having it all—there's this complicated psychology of being a woman as well as the sociology of making your way in your own career and thoughts of family—are still very, very current in our country.[18]

Although the revival was generally well reviewed, some critics disagreed with MacKinnon's generous assessment. Alisa Solomon, writing this time for the *Nation*, remarked that "the passage of time reveals *The Heidi Chronicles* to have been catching the rise of the neoliberal feminism that prevails in elite precincts today: that every-woman-for-herself kind of leaning in that makes no demands on the workplace or the state and builds no solidarity with others."[19] Solomon protests that the play doesn't even pass the notorious Bechdel test, which requires two women in the same scene in a film, especially, to speak directly to one another about something other than a man.

More mainstream critics tended to see the revival as successful and timely. The *New York Times'* Charles Isherwood argued in his review that the play's questions did still "resonate today as strongly, and at times as painfully" as in 1989; he admitted that he had "some anxiety on the question of the play's durability," but he believed that "fortunately . . . the play's humor retains its buoyancy" all these years later and attested to "how germane the play's questions remain."[20] For a *New York Times* reviewer who can be stingy with praise for women playwrights, this is a real rave. Likewise, the *Chicago Tribune* reviewer, Chris Jones, who produced a thoughtful obituary about Wasserstein when she died, wrote, "This remains one of the most honest, accessible, and involving plays of the 1980s, and Heidi is a (time-capsuled) heroine with whom to be reckoned now and forever."[21] *Deadline*'s Jeremy Gerard praised this "still remarkable" play and wrote, "I'm sure some will criticize *The Heidi Chronicles* as dated, but that strikes me as criticizing *Selma* [Ava DuVernay's 2014 movie about Martin Luther King] on the same grounds, as if those once-crucial issues have faded or been resolved. What nonsense."[22] Although the *Selma* comparison seems a bit specious, Gerard described *The Heidi Chronicles* as something of a fictionalized history play, one that narrates a moment in time that will never outlive its importance to public or national memory. The *Huffington Post* critic, David Finkle, concurred, writing, "It occurs to me that because it's now 2015, some theatergoers will think Wasserstein's vision of a particular past quarter-century is now dated. If so, they're confusing the concept of 'dated' with the concept of indelibly recreating a specific date, time and place. The late and very much missed Wasserstein has impeccably done the latter."[23]

The *Jewish Daily Forward* critic, Jesse Oxfeld, said that "two and a half decades later, it's still fantastic," and added,

> The writing in *Heidi* . . . is so sharp—so funny, so insightful (and, perhaps conveniently, so much of it set even further in the past)— that it doesn't feel dated today. In an era past aerobics classes, alligator-skin planners and high-end Zeus sneakers, the particulars of

our arguments may be different. But, for better or worse, the arguments about women's lives are the same. And even more deeply, even with the gender-role politics stripped from the show, *Heidi* is about something universal to the aspirational, overeducated classes in middle age: What if I don't achieve what I was supposed to? What if everyone else does better?[24]

When the play was first produced, few people looked for the universal in *The Heidi Chronicles*, as Oxfeld did here. While Marsha Norman's 1983 play *'night, Mother* was regularly sifted for indications that its mother-daughter themes might resonate, like *Death of a Salesman*, in a wider American landscape, *The Heidi Chronicles* was seen very specifically as a chronicle of twenty-five years of American feminism and as very particular in its address.[25] That Oxfeld saw the play in 2015 as raising broader questions for the "aspirational, overeducated classes in middle age" perhaps does speak to the continued or even growing relevance of Wasserstein's worldview; that is, if, as Oxfeld proposed, you strip it of its gender politics. And then what would be left?

Entertainment Weekly's Melissa Maerz wrote ambivalently about what the revival demonstrated had or had not changed for Wasserstein's strata of American women. Maerz wrote,

> The good news about the Broadway revival of *The Heidi Chronicles*? The famous monologue about the failures of feminism still holds up. The bad news? It still holds up. . . . Feminism has changed a lot since Wasserstein wrote that scene. Today, *The Heidi Chronicles* might seem like the product of second-wave issues that aren't relevant anymore. But after nearly 30 years, that monologue is still just as powerful, and, sadly, for many women, it's probably just as easy to relate.[26]

She acknowledged that "that time-capsule vibe might be hard to overcome, especially when Heidi lectures about feminist debates that went out of style decades ago. (Is there something *'uniquely female'* about women's painting? Ugh.)" But, she noted, "If *The Heidi Chronicles* doesn't always translate for the 21st century, maybe we should be happy, too. Isn't that a sign that some things have gotten better?"[27] In one swoop, Maerz criticizes the play's second-wave values (looking for something essential about women's difference), suggests that our distance from them indicates that history has moved profitably on, and then cautions that feminism is in fact still leaving women stranded. The play's confusions continued, in 2015, to touch something similar in some of the critics who wrote about the revival.

In 2015 the history of the United States from the midsixties to the late eighties that Wasserstein narrates feels that much more remote from current political concerns. Contemporary radical feminist activists now tend to think intersectionally about race, ethnicity, and sexuality and about multiple, rather than binary, gender positions. But as feminist historian Joan Scott insisted in her 2015 Meredith Miller Memorial Lecture at Princeton University, American feminist activism of the 1960s, 1970s, and 1980s cannot be dismissed, given how it galvanized and inspired however partial a swath of women at the time and after.[28] Written just as the backlash against that activism was filling the mass media, Wasserstein's 1989 play appeared to lend credence to mainstream dismissals of feminist politics. The Ann Arbor consciousness-raising scene in the play's first act was particularly painful for feminists to witness in 1989. The antiessentialist academic feminist theorizing of that period had roundly dismissed consciousness-raising groups, alongside the media's disdain for feminism in general. Those dual critiques made consciousness-raising easy to lampoon, since even feminist revisionist histories portrayed the groups as white women kvetching together, rather than acknowledging their work as motivating, theory-inspiring occasions for political awakening.

But many feminist spectators cried foul in outrage when, in *The Heidi Chronicles*, the consciousness-raising group's members seem belittled in a scene that felt too cruelly satirical. In Sullivan's production, Heidi literally sat outside the circle. Although the others warn her not to judge them, Joan Allen played the scene with chilly antipathy for the proceedings. Her example urged the audience, too, to see themselves as superior to these silly, striving women. MacKinnon's production, and especially in Elisabeth Moss's wonderful performance (for which she received a 2015 Tony nomination for Best Leading Actress in a Play), conceived of Heidi as essentially warm, strong, and thoughtful. Rather than blending into the scenery, apologizing for herself, or blandly refusing to participate, Moss's Heidi worked every moment she was onstage to figure out what she thinks and where she stands (and there's not a scene in the play that doesn't include her). When the character decides to make common cause with the consciousness-raising group women, for example, Moss's Heidi deliberately committed wholeheartedly, joining the women proudly in their collective rendition of Aretha Franklin's song "Respect." Even though the women might say "I love you" a bit too freely to everyone and anyone, MacKinnon and Moss and the other actors played the scene with affection and intelligence that honored, instead of demeaning, the history of consciousness-raising.

Throughout the play, MacKinnon's revival invited spectators to witness Heidi's awakening to her own agency and her gradual understanding that women of her generation were encouraged to let men make decisions and speak for them. When Peter (Bryce Pinkham) hijacks the women in art demonstration, Heidi has to explain feminist activism to him (and to the audience). When he comes out to her as a gay man in that scene, Moss registered Heidi's disappointment and her acceptance that their relationship will never be sexual. In all of her scenes with her occasional and always inappropriate boyfriend, Scoop (Jason Biggs), Moss let spectators see Heidi's realization that being with him works against her own interests as an independent person.

Given Moss's precision, intelligence, and likability, the moments when the play lets Heidi down were more glaring in the 2015 Broadway revival. The climactic monologue in the second act, when Heidi delivers her Miss Crain's School speech, remained strident and maudlin and overly personal because that's how it's written. Moss worked through the speech beat by beat to find its essential humanity and tried to make it land for a community rather than just for the character. That she did not succeed, and that the monologue still sounded like an indictment of feminism, wasn't Moss's or MacKinnon's fault. Wasserstein, speaking with Mervyn Rothstein in the *New York Times* in 1988, explained that she intended the play to "track change, social change, and how all these movements affected people's lives." She in fact told him that it was the *Good Housekeeping* advertisements and articles of the reactionary late 1980s that prompted her thinking:

> Sometimes I see these Good Housekeeping ads for a return to traditional values, and . . . I just think, 'What's happened? How has all this happened?' I read all the stuff about a gentler, kinder life, and all of that, and I find it very upsetting. Are they saying that the women who decided to fulfill their potential have made a mistake? That's com-

pletely unfair. It makes you feel stranded. It makes you feel part of a tidal wave.[29]

In this quote Wasserstein seems to blame the backlash *against* feminism for prompting women to feel stranded. But the monologue she wrote for Heidi has always been received as an indictment of feminism and of women's inability to "have it all," which feminism purportedly promised.

But even in Heidi's perhaps most difficult, selfish moment, Moss made compelling Heidi's struggle to figure out her life in relation to the people around her. That she's surrounded by privileged women more concerned about where to buy the latest athletic apparel, a particular breed of New Yorkers who make her feel "worthless and superior" at the same time, constrains what Heidi (and Wasserstein) can say about the feminist movement. The speech appears to indict feminism, but if you hear it as accusing only Heidi, for comparing herself to exactly the wrong role models, it sounds differently. The moment is about *the character*, but the problem is that it's always read as about *the movement*.

Perhaps Wasserstein's most cynical gesture in the play was to use the character of Susan to represent options for feminism. Susan shifts lightning fast from being a radical feminist "shepherdess" on a feminist "dude" ranch in Montana to editor of the law review at Yale to an MBA-powered television producer trying to exploit stories about quirky and powerful women. Playing Susan in the revival, Ali Ahn nailed Susan's shifts in tone, style, and costume, in a performance that was broad without succumbing to parody. Casting an Asian American woman as Susan might also address the charge that feminism in this period was only for white women. But Susan is written as shallow and self-serving from the start, making Heidi's expectations for their friendship peculiarly misplaced. It's really *Susan* who leaves Heidi stranded without an empathetic female friend to give her the reality check she so desires. Not feminism.

With Susan reduced to offering Heidi air-kisses before she chases after celebrities in a restaurant, Heidi turns to the men in her life for support. In the revival, Bryce Pinkham beautifully played the stalwart, sarcastic gay pediatrician, Peter, with humor and knowingness. Jason Biggs, well cast and on target, played Scoop. Her encounters with these two very different men—Scoop indicted but admired for his patriarchal ambitions and adulterous predilections, and Peter ennobled by working with infants with HIV/AIDS—become determining for Heidi. She's attracted to Scoop even though she knows he's a cad, and she adores Peter even though he demands she accept that his life is more important and tragic than hers. Neither can really see her, but Heidi has nowhere else to turn in Wasserstein's world.

The play's other women characters, even in the revival, are caricatures. Lisa (Leighton Bryan), Scoop's southern belle wife, is a gifted children's book illustrator but is used narratively only as the butt of Scoop's infidelity. Denise (Elise Kibler), Lisa's sister, learns about feminism in her women's studies courses at Brown and has carefully planned her life so that she can have it all. April (Tracee Chimo), the superficial, power-mongering television host, facilitates the conversation on her vapid morning show between Scoop, Heidi, and Peter in which the men speak over Heidi and publicly silence her. Fran, of the Ann Arbor consciousness-raising group, was fleshed out in the revival by the brilliant (double cast) Tracee Chimo's loving portrayal but remained famous for her declaration that "either you shave your legs or you don't," a rather reductive mantra for feminism, even in the early 1970s. Given these choices, to whom might Heidi turn for empathy, experience, and insight?

Moss is a strong, emotionally acute actor who brought humor and strength to Heidi's plight. The character *laughed with* instead of *at* the others, and what the script offers as self-deprecating, apologetic humor, Moss reinterpreted as smart, if kooky, lightheartedness. Her Heidi was in control of herself and her emotions and could laugh at herself even as she felt her way through the rough patches. Spectators could see her struggling to find her place among each of the groups in which Wasserstein places her. She was angry at the end of the *Hello, New York* taping, ecstatic when she embraced the Ann Arbor consciousness-raising group, and indignant on Lisa's behalf when she told the women at Lisa's baby shower that she saw Scoop in Central Park with his mistress at the rally mourning John Lennon's assassination. Moss gave Heidi spine, intelligence, and emotional depth, which made her a much more captivating guide through the history Wasserstein sketches.

John Lee Beatty's set used a stage revolve and blank white walls on which to project snippets of history as it passes through the play. Critics over the years, David Savran chief among them, have commented on how Wasserstein superficially telegraphs history through her choice of song lyrics, played under the top of each scene to mark the narrative's march through time. In MacKinnon's production, however, projections of newspaper headlines from significant moments, as well as television set-shaped photos of American presidents, advertisements, and other evocative cultural images, played against the walls more schematically than literally and better helped the music situate the story in history. The revival's design respected the story and did justice to history more than the 1989 original.

The great theater historian Oscar Brockett always encouraged us to ask "Why this play now?" as the central dramaturgical question for any production. The answer to why *The Heidi Chronicles* should have been revived on Broadway in spring 2015 remains vague. The much-touted, critically acclaimed production closed after only eighty performances. Yet as playwright Lisa Kron insisted in a *New York Times* article about the production's imminent closing, people tend not to ask whether David Mamet's plays remain relevant when they close quickly on Broadway.[30] The revival of *Heidi*, for whatever reason, didn't take. The high ticket prices, the play's pat solutions and privileged women's plight, or the fact that in 2015 young feminists might not have known the play or the playwright, or have cared about its issues, as Chloe Angyal of the feminist website feministing. com suggested in the same *Times* article, might have all contributed to the revival's short run.

Or perhaps the marketing campaign didn't help. The publicity featured its star cast, posed against an empty white background, with Moss wearing a sexy red dress in front of Pinkham and Biggs. Marketers might have presumed that star casting would be enough to entice people to see the play. The advertisements and posters didn't offer any insight into the play's content or style. It was impossible to know it was a comedy, let alone about thirty years of American history, including feminism. Even the large political-style buttons handed out in the theater's lobby during the run were cryptic. Against a bright pink background (of all things), the buttons proclaimed, "I am 'Heidi'" #HeidiOnBroadway. This in itself demonstrates the limited way in which the producers saw the potential audience: as only white, upper-middle-class women who would identify not just *with* but *as* Heidi? How unimaginative.

In the revival, a beautiful moment capped the end of the hospital scene, the penultimate in the play, when Heidi decides she'll postpone the year of teaching she'd planned to accept in the Midwest and stay with Peter in New York. He's confessed his grief over losing his friends to AIDS and relayed his anger that Heidi would abandon him when he needs her. Although her choice to stay could be seen as still another of Heidi's self-sacrifices, Moss played the decision as born of her love for her oldest friend. She and Peter embraced at the scene's end, and Heidi cupped his face in her hands to peer gently into his eyes with a gaze full of fondness. As the stage lights dimmed and the scene transition started, I could see Moss repeat the gesture in the dark, as an actor expressing affection for her scene partner. I don't know if the moment was planned or spontaneous, but it struck me that this is what made the difference in this production. Moss appeared to love Heidi, as well as the other characters and the actors who played them. Her bighearted, affectionate, and intelligent performance suffused the play with welcomed new meanings.

When a play like *The Heidi Chronicles* was and remains the only one on Broadway telling even a partial, personal history of American feminism, the character and the playwright bear the burden of representation. Before she died, Wasserstein urged people not to saddle her with such responsibility and argued forcefully and rightly that there should be more plays about women and feminism, so that she could tell her story without the impossible necessity that it represent *all* women's stories. Would that her wish had come true.

CHAPTER FIVE

The Sisters Rosensweig

The Sisters Rosensweig, too, became a popular choice for regional theaters after it was produced on Broadway in 1993. The play demonstrates Wasserstein's affinity for the theater of Chekhov, Kaufman and Hart, and Noel Coward, as it mingles the angst and immobility of the Russian dramatist's characters with the farcical family maneuverings of the American duo and the drawing-room comedy of the British stylist. But *Sisters Rosensweig* is also perhaps Wasserstein's most autobiographical play. The central characters are loosely based on Wasserstein and her sisters, Sandra and Georgette, and although it is set in London, its themes and conflicts represent those of upper-middle-class, New York–bred Jewish women trying to fashion their lives in the best way they can. Wasserstein uses the play to address the tug of artistic aspirations and socially progressive activism against the constraints of conventional professional ambition and the requisites of an emotional and romantic life. In this, as in her earlier plays, she continues her preoccupation with the balance between work and love and considers how those marginalized by gender or ethnicity manage to navigate a dominant culture that includes them by class but excludes them otherwise. *Sisters Rosensweig* also shows Wasserstein delving into an ambivalence about Jewish ethnicity that was then new in her work.

In fact, by the early nineties, when the play was first produced, Wasserstein had swung back and forth between portraying her heroines as Christians or as Jews. The *Uncommon Women* were mostly WASPs, except for Holly Kaplan; *Isn't It Romantic* split the difference with its two main characters and made ethnicity part of its debate; and *The Heidi Chronicles* presented Heidi Holland as a non-

Jewish protofeminist at a time when many of the most visible women in the American movement happened to be Jewish. Wasserstein actually said she didn't think it was an accident that she won her highest acclaim for a heroine named Heidi Holland, instead of Holly Kaplan. But in *Sisters Rosensweig*, Wasserstein took the risk of immersing her characters in her own ethnicity, a strategy that didn't seem to affect the play's success on Broadway or in regional theater circulation. Still, Wasserstein perhaps hedged her ethnic bets by setting the play in London, where the three sisters play out old family struggles against the backdrop of global capitalism and international struggles for human rights. Questions of assimilation and self-interest pull against their desire to change the world. Although the sisters' struggles with men, with one another, with themselves, and with their rightful place in the world offer Wasserstein a variety of spokes to trace, the hub of family dynamics turns the play's wheel along the axel of domestic comic melodrama.

Sara Goode is the oldest of the Rosensweig sisters, a stately, accomplished corporate executive who moved to London to launch her fabulously successful career. Her daughter, Tess, provides her counterpart, the next generation of "Goode" women who is still forming herself against and alongside her mother's choices. While Sara is conservative in her tastes and catholic in her affections, Tess is attracted to "bad" boys and radical social issues. Tess's boyfriend, Tom Valiunus, is a working-class Brit with whom she plans to travel to Lithuania to participate in its social revolution. (The play is set in 1991.) Tess's choices contrast with Sara's more measured, safe decisions, and the affectionate tension between them establishes one of the play's motivating conflicts.

Sisters Rosensweig also sits alongside *Isn't It Romantic* as a play at least partly about mothers and daughters. No patriarch looms here in the family drawing room, although male-dominated culture remains a stricture against which these women are forced to define themselves. Because the Rosensweig matriarch recently died, Sara becomes her sisters' de facto mother, anchoring the perambulations of Gorgeous Teitelbaum, the middle sister, who is a housewife and talk-show-radio host in Newton, Massachusetts, and Pfeni (née Penny) Rosensweig, the youngest sister, who is a peripatetic journalist with a penchant for romantic attachments with gay and bisexual men. Her would-be boyfriend, Geoffrey Duncan, is a theater director whom she met sitting beside him in the audience at a performance of *Giselle*. Although Geoffrey fantasizes about a life with Pfeni, by the play's end, he admits that he misses men and leaves her for a long-time, on-again off-again boyfriend. Pfeni is Wasserstein's stand-in in *Sisters Rosensweig*; as Julie Salamon details in her biography of the playwright, Wasserstein's most intense romantic involvements were with gay men taking a temporary hiatus from relationships with their own sex.

But in *Sisters Rosensweig*, Sara, too, chooses inappropriate mates. Her current partner, the ultra-British Nicholas Pym, whom Tess calls a fascist and Gorgeous more pointedly calls a Nazi, serves to establish Sara's would-be WASP credentials more than he provides real companionship and caring. When Mervyn Kant (née Kantlowitz) appears at her door to provide costume pieces for Geoffrey's current theater production, he instantly sees beyond Sara's gentile affectations and calls her back to the Jewish ethnicity she forsook to enhance her career. Although each of the three sisters grows through the play, Sara moves the furthest, from a withdrawn, rather uptight, buttoned-down captain of industry who refuses to sing for her daughter to a warm, ethnically identified mother who ends the play crooning a duet to "Harvest Moon" with Tess.

Sisters Rosensweig is perhaps most notable for what Wasserstein declares as her intent. She writes in the introduction to the published script that her characters are "grownups whom we don't get to see on stage often enough."[1] In fact, Sara is a woman in her midfifties, and her romantic relationship forms the play's trajectory. Hers is a mature version of the story Janie and Harriet tell in *Isn't It Romantic*, after professional choices have been made and relationship issues supposedly put to rest. Sara appears to have given up her roots for her career, preferring to erase what she sees as the hobbling particularities of Jewishness and gender. For instance, Tess has been assigned one of her aunt Pfeni's books for the "women's segment" of her college English class, but Sara dryly remarks that although her sister's books are brilliant, "having a separate category for women's writing is counterrevolutionary" (6). According to Tess, however, as Sara approaches her fifty-fifth birthday, she is in "desperate need of hope and rebirth" (7). The play charts Sara's progress toward personal renaissance through her re-embrace of her female and Jewish specificity.

London, where Sara has made her home and career, becomes a

placeholder for a kind of "no place," a city where someone like Sara can disappear into a nondescript sameness. By stark contrast, the middle sister, Gorgeous, lives in a suburb of Boston that's a notable Jewish enclave. To underline her ethnic commitments, Gorgeous has come to London with a group of women from her synagogue's sisterhood. Her personal and spiritual advisor is Rabbi Pearlstein, and she insists that Sara observe the Sabbath while she's visiting. Gorgeous's overt and insistent ethnicity makes Sara that much more "white"—or nonethnic—by comparison. In the play's Broadway production, Jane Alexander played Sara and Madeline Kahn played Gorgeous. Alexander's patrician bearing and nonethnic features and voice must have erased all traces of Sara's Jewish birthright, while Kahn's low-comedy, ethnically inflected reputation and performance style no doubt brought a bit of the Borscht Belt along with Gorgeous to Sara Goode's London flat.

Between them, Frances McDormand's Pfeni probably served as a happy fulcrum in the original production at Lincoln Center Theater. (Christine Estabrook replaced McDormand as Pfeni when the play transferred to Broadway.) McDormand is now known as more of a character actor, someone who can play everything from the chief of police in the Coen brothers' film *Fargo* (1996), where she employed a hilarious, now-infamous broad midwestern accent, to the Boston working-class single mother in David Lindsay-Abaire's *Good People* on Broadway in 2011, or the salty, emotionally reticent wife and mother on the television miniseries *Olive Kitteridge* in 2014. Casting her as the middle sister who changed her name from Penny to Pfeni, with her chameleon style, makes the character the pivot point between her sisters' two extremes. Pfeni is a successful journalist, author of several books, and a world traveler, giving her a kind of rootless appeal. If anything, Pfeni is a wandering Jew (103), who needs her experiences with global difference to give her life the sharp edge of meaning. She says, "Somewhere I need the hardship of the Afghan women and the Kurdish suffering to fill up my life for me. And if I'm that empty, then I might as well continue to wander to the best hotels, restaurants, and poori stands" (77). Wasserstein stops short of damning her character for her restlessness, but she does portray her as a successful woman who can't quite settle her emotional life.

As in all of her plays, Wasserstein's preoccupations here redound to what it means to have a focused and purposeful life. The three sisters provide a continuum of choices, none of which Wasserstein considers definitive. That their mother has recently died and that Sara has recently recovered from "female troubles" that turn out to be ovarian cancer and is about to celebrate a significant birthday means that the sisters palpably face their mortality, peering into the last part of their lives with fear (if not loathing) and wonder. Gorgeous holds the most conventional views of what it means to be settled and very much wants to see her more socially accomplished sisters adopt lives that might better echo her own. But although Gorgeous is married and lives in an upper-middle-class Boston suburb, even she is not quite what she seems. Her Chanel suit is a knockoff, and as she walks the streets of London with the Temple Beth-El sisterhood, she longs for a pair of real, good shoes (Manolo Blahniks come in for some good-natured lusting after and laughter). Gorgeous's lawyer husband, Henry (never seen here), hasn't worked in two years; his partnership was dissolved because of the recession and he now writes mystery novels in the family basement, playing at being Raymond Chandler (93).

Gorgeous's sisters find it easy to belittle her "lay analyst" (93) talk show and her traditional Jewish spiritual values, tinged as they are with a familiar, "Jewish American princess" materialism. But Wasserstein lends Gorgeous a great deal of verve and grit. When the sisterhood women send her a gift for leading their tour of London, it turns out to be a real Chanel suit with all the requisite accessories. Gorgeous is nearly orgasmic with glee but instantly knows she'll return every piece of the gift. She says, "Somebody's got to pay for tuition this fall, and better Chanel than Henry or me" (103). She does try the suit on before she takes it back, then insists Pfeni go return it with her: "Pfeni, we'd better hurry or I'll lose my will power. It's very hard for me to postpone gratification. If I have something in my hand for more than two minutes, I want to keep it or at least eat it" (103). Underneath Gorgeous's name-brand airs lies a sober, pragmatic woman well aware of her role in keeping her household afloat.

By contrast, for all her pretenses otherwise, Sara's control of her life is much less secure. She's involved with a man who epitomizes British pretension, dates other women, and isn't a serious life mate. Nick Pym is tall and aristocratic and frequently peppers his remarks with the adjective *marvelous* ("This is marvelous cheese, darling" [40]). Tess accuses him of British perversion, imagining that he "takes sixteen-year-old models to dinner at Annabel's and then goes home alone and puts panty hose over his head and dances to *Parsifal*" (51). Since Wasserstein creates him as a foil for the Merv Kant character, she makes Pym ignorant about matters of cultural difference and allows him to unwittingly exemplify the subtle anti-Semitism that Merv addresses at Sara's birthday dinner. When Merv appears for dinner dressed in a flamboyant shirt he borrowed from Geoffrey's apartment below, Geoffrey applauds his choice, saying, "And see his amazing Technicolor shirt of many colors!" (44). Nick Pym adds, "So many Jewish American men I know, professional mostly, wear those shirts. Why is that, Merv?"

> MERV: It's a money-lending uniform.
> NICK PYM: Beg your pardon.
> MERV: They're so well designed, you'd never know it costs a pound of flesh to get them. (45)

Wasserstein's stage direction indicates that Sara "looks at Pym as the room laughs with Merv" (45), illustrating Sara's understanding that her would-be paramour is oblivious to his own offensive presumptions and to how her company subtly pokes fun at him with Jewish references (to the stereotype of Jews as bankers and Shylocks) that go over his head.

In fact, as the play progresses, Merv, the Jewish furrier from New York, begins to win Sara's affections. Merv is unabashedly ethnic. In his first scene, he uses Yiddish expressions, joking with Geoffrey, who makes his entrance from a service door: "Geoffrey, mazel tov, you've finally come out of the closet" (21). Merv is traveling in Europe with the American Jewish Congress, first to Budapest and soon to Ireland to "have brunch with the Rabbi of Dublin" (22). Although Merv has arrived to drop off some costumes for Geoffrey's play, he's intrigued with Sara's apartment and soon with Sara herself, rather shrewdly understanding that she's remade herself in the U.K.

> MERV: So you and your sister are from New York?
> SARA: My sister is a traveler, and I live right here in Queen Anne's Gate. . . .
> MERV: Well, you're the first Jewish woman I've met to run a Hong Kong bank.

By coming out himself as a Jew whose name was Anglicized, Merv subtly indicates that he shares Sara's assimilated past. But Merv is also frank and open with his Jewish identifications, quick to out himself while Sara prefers to erase her own ethnicity. Later, when Merv is introduced to Tom, he announces, "And you must be . . . Tom, the Lithuanian nationalist. You know, before the Holocaust, Vilnius was home to about 65,000 Jews. . . . Tessie, I suspect your mother is one of those hostesses who prefers that a guest not come into a room and immediately bring the conversation around to the Holocaust" (41). Of course, Merv is right, but he can't keep himself from using his own Jewish commitments to call Sara back to her derelict ethnic roots. Alone together in the scene that ends the first act, Merv begins to call Sara "Sadie," the less biblical, more colloquial nickname for a Jewish lady (recall Barbra Streisand as Fanny Brice singing "Sadie, Sadie, Married Lady" in the musical *Funny Girl*). The nickname reminds Sara of her childhood, since her grandfather once called her by the same term of endearment.

Even as Merv chips away at her self-enforced Puritanism, Sara resists his charms, insisting, "Merv, we're too old for this" (54). He retorts, "When did you figure out that you had all the answers?"

> SARA: High school. I knew what the teacher was going to ask before she asked it. I knew what was going to become of every girl in my class, and I knew, for some reason, I was different from them.
> MERV: You weren't a nice Jewish girl.
> SARA: Why do you always come back to that? (54)

Irritated that Merv sees everything through a persistently Jewish perspective, Sara insists on her own difference. And yet soon after, they realize that Merv was the first guy to have sex with Sonia Kirschenblatt, who was the valedictorian at Sara's high school. In a fast game of Jewish geography, they establish not just an emotional connection but a past shared with a young woman who sports an obviously Jewish name.

Ever resistant, Sara warns Merv that he doesn't know her as well as he might think:

Look, Merv, if you're thinking, 'I know who this woman is sitting next to me. I grew up with her, with women like her, only sometime in her life she decided to run away. She moved to England, she dyed her hair, she named her daughter Tess and sent her to Westminster. She assimilated beyond her wildest dreams, and now she's lonely and wants to come home,' you're being too obvious. Yes, I'm lonely, but I don't want to come home. (57)

Sara might not want to come home to New York, but as the second act proceeds, it is clear she does want to come home to Merv, to the Jewishness he represents, and to a familiar ethnic identification that reminds Sara of comfort, ease, and family.

The second act returns all the characters to some essential understanding of who and what they are and might become. Pfeni and Geoffrey begin to plan their common future. Pfeni is (not) working on her book on gender and class (she says it's writing itself in a Crock-Pot somewhere in Tajikistan [68]) and Geoffrey is waxing poetical about how fleeting is time. In a speech reminiscent of Peter's hospital scene in *The Heidi Chronicles*, in which he mourns the loss of so many friends to HIV/AIDS, Geoffrey declares,

I've changed address books three times this year because I couldn't bear to cross out any more names. I've lost too many friends. I've seen too many lights that never had their chance to glow burn out overnight. I've tried for years now to make sense of all this, and all I know is life is random and there is no case to be made for a just or loving god. So how then do we proceed? In directing terms, what is the objective? Of course, we must cherish those that we love. That's a given. But just as important, people like you and me have to work even harder to create the best art, the best theatre, the best bloody book about gender and class in Tajikistan that we possibly can. And the rest, the children, the country kitchen, the domestic bliss, we leave to others who will have different regrets. Pfeni, you and I can't idle time. (69)

If some of Peter's anger and cynicism about the HIV/AIDS crisis is gone from Geoffrey's version of the plaint, Wasserstein replaces it with urgency about honoring the lost by making the best possible art. One can imagine Wasserstein's friends and intimates making just such a speech, surrounded as they were in the early 1990s with gay men dying of a virus that quickly reached pandemic proportions.

At the same time, Geoffrey has less gravitas than Peter and becomes a plot device through which Pfeni makes a commitment to herself. While Geoffrey is out giving a talk to Gorgeous's sisterhood buddies, Gorgeous tells Pfeni that she's become too eccentric for her own good: "Wandering around the world alone at forty, Pfeni, you're wandering yourself right out of the marketplace. And don't tell me you have Geoffrey. I know you can't judge a book by its cover, but sweetsie, you're at the wrong library altogether. Pfeni, don't you want what any normal woman wants?" (72). Gorgeous might be played as a bit of a wise fool, but even to her, Geoffrey's sexual preferences are clear. When he returns from having his "consciousness raised by the full assemblage of the Temple Beth-El sisterhood" (85), Geoffrey has also had a change of heart about his future with Pfeni and decides that he misses men. He tells Pfeni,

> You really don't understand what it is to have absolutely no idea who you are. . . . For all your wandering, you're always basically the same—you have your sisters, your point of view, and even in some casual drop-in way, your God. Pfeni, the only time I have a real sense of who I am and where I'm going is when I'm in a darkened theatre and we're making it all up. Starting from scratch. But now I want a real life outside the theatre, too. So maybe I will regret this choice. I know I'll miss you. But I'm an instinctive person, my luv, and speaking to those ladies, it all just clicked. Today this is who I am. I have no other choice. I miss men. (88)

Pfeni's only comeuppance is her retort: "It's all right, Geoffrey, I do, too" (88). Geoffrey, though, is ennobled by embracing his essential gay self. His wavering sexuality is explained by his involvement in the wily chimeras of the theater. Pfeni, whose trade is to chronicle real-life conditions in the world's hot spots, has to accept her status as a wanderer and returns to writing her book. As with other Wasserstein women, her self-acceptance is wistful and tinged with loss. She admits to Gorgeous, if "you make sure to fall in love with men who can never really love you back, one morning you wake up at forty in your big sister's house, and where you should be seems sort of clear" (101). Pfeni exits with Gorgeous, who is off to return her real Chanel suit.

As each of the sisters settles into her life, emerging from the dust cloud that Sara's birthday and their brief reunion has kicked up, they approach themselves with a bit more clarity. Sara leaves open a future with Merv; even as he leaves to visit the rabbi of Dublin, their affection for one another is clear. Sara and Tess sit together and Tess asks her mother some questions to complete the paper Tess is writing about Sara for her oral history assignment. Early in the play, Sara has announced to Pfeni that the thesis of Tess's project is "to prove that my early years have no bearing on my present life. Frankly," she sniffs, "I can hardly remember my early years" (13). But as Tess turns on her tape recorder at the play's end and asks Sara to state her name for the record, Sara responds proudly, "My name is Sara Rosensweig. I am the daughter of Rita and Maury Rosensweig. I was born in Brooklyn, New York . . . I first sang at the Hanukah Festival at East Midwood Jewish Center. I played a candle" (107). Sara indeed remembers her early years and has finally come to recall her origins fondly. When Tess asks her to sing, of course, Sara complies, and the mother and daughter end the play on a refrain of "Harvest Moon": "So shine on, shine on, harvest moon. For me and my gal" (109), evoking the Tin Pan Alley tradition that also resonates with Jewish culture.

Her acceptance and proud announcement of her Jewish roots indicate that Sara has come to embrace the identity she kept at a distance, and her willingness, at the end, to sing with her daughter also demonstrates her return to a past she had held at bay. The ending is one of Wasserstein's more optimistic, and one of the few in which mothers and daughters in her plays actually reconcile. In *Uncommon Women*, mothers aren't at all in evidence, their in loco parentis authority represented by the arch Mrs. Plumm. In *Isn't It Romantic*, Janie's and Harriet's mothers seem to have more in common with one another than with their daughters, who make their choices nearly in opposition to the models their parents establish and desire for them. And in *The Heidi Chronicles*, Heidi's motherhood might be her crowning achievement, but Wasserstein defers its real challenges and accomplishments to the future.

But in *Sisters Rosensweig*, although Tess and Sara appear to have a typical Wasserstein relationship of comic tension, they arrive somewhere quite different by the play's end. By planning a trip to Lithuania with Tom, Tess appears to reject her mother's conservative corporate values for a more progressive politics of liberation. But shortly before their planned departure, Tess realizes that the Lithuanian freedom struggle isn't hers. She admits to Pfeni, "I went with Tom to the rally last night, and everyone was holding hands and singing Lithuanian folk songs. But the more they smiled at me and held my hand, the more apart from it all I became. Aunt Pfeni, are we people who will always be watching and never belong?" (100).

As she moves into adulthood, Tess, like her mother and aunts, confronts her own ambivalences about who she is and whom to throw in her lot with. Sara at first accuses Tess of being like Pfeni. Tess tells her aunt, "My mother says she worries about me because I'm so much like you. She says you compulsively travel because you have a fear of commitment, and when you do stay in one place, you become emotional and defensive just like me" (7). Though Pfeni responds wryly, "Tess, honey, I'm so sorry, I didn't know it was contagious" (7), Tess does seem caught among a variety of options for how to be in the world, none of which suit her perfectly. Neither her mother nor her two aunts provide the perfect role model. When she informs her mother she's not going to Lithuania, Sara thanks her for changing her mind:

> TESS: I didn't make this decision for you. I made it for me. You have
> to have your own life.
> SARA: Really, I can't have yours?
> TESS: You wouldn't want mine. I don't even know what mine is.
> Mother, if I've never really been Jewish, and I'm not actually
> American anymore, and I'm not English or European, then who
> am I? (106)

Tess poses the existential question that most of Wasserstein's ambivalent heroines share, drawn and quartered as they are across ethnic and here national identifications. But rather than tussle with her mother as other Wasserstein characters do, Tess, like Sara, is self-aware about the intricacies and codependencies of their relationship, and the two end the play in a warm alliance.

Like *The Heidi Chronicles* before it, *The Sisters Rosensweig* is set at a moment of profound social change. If *Heidi* narrates the history of second-wave American feminism in its episodic, time- and place-hopping settings, *Sisters Rosensweig* observes the conventional dramatic unities of time, place, and action, using one set and one day to observe the characters' arc. Their moment in time, however, is at the beginning of the end of the Soviet Union, when states like Lithuania are fighting for independence. Tess comments, "It's just like my mother to have a dinner party on the night the Soviet Union is falling apart" (39). As a result, the evening is peppered with references to world events past and future that make the central scenes in *Sisters Rosensweig* rather Shavian in their attention to politics, even though Wasserstein's obvious model for the play was Chekhov and his *The Three Sisters*. But unlike Shaw, whose characters seriously ponder political, moral, and ethical quandaries, politics seem to be more of a plot device for Wasserstein, who leavens her characters' seriousness with jokes.

Wasserstein could be critiqued for supporting her characters' shallow sense of history. The play equivocates about taking a stand on world affairs. In response to Tess and Tom's compassion for the Lithuanian people's struggle, both Pfeni and Nick Pym associate Vilnius, the country's capital, with a "decent old restaurant" (39). Pfeni tells Tess that "Vilnius was once the Jerusalem of Lithuania. . . . There's also a good restaurant, the famous and traditional Old Cellar. Also, for plays, check out the Central Theatre of Vilnius" (10). While Tess and Tom fantasize about going to Lithuania as freedom fighters, Nick Pym and Pfeni think of it as a site for capitalist and cultural consumption. Even Pfeni, the world-traveling journalist, who needs the pain of third world women to give shape and meaning to her life, wavers between political reporting and restaurant reviewing.

Wasserstein creates an equivalence between nations—especially those that aren't Western, American, or British—and cites them as exotic places of difference. So while her characters struggle with their own place in the world as lapsed American Jews, the rest of the world reassures them by being different from them and strangely equal to each other. When Nick Pym leaves Sara's dinner party, he breezily says good-bye to Tess, wishing her and Tom good luck in Latvia (51). Latvia and Lithuania are all the same to him. His parting line is, "You know the shocking thing about all of this business with the Soviets is one questions what in God's name the entire twentieth century was for" (51).

As global politics play out on the world stage, however, the Rosensweig sisters and their men and daughters focus their dramas internally, on how they reconcile an ethnic family heritage with their individual futures. As the Soviet bloc dissolves into separate nations, the Rosensweigs move in reverse, reasserting their belonging with and to one another as family. Pfeni and Gorgeous admire Sara as their new matriarch, snuggling with her on her sofa toward the play's end:

GORGEOUS: You know what I wish with all my heart?
SARA: What?
PFENI: What?
GORGEOUS: I wish that on one of our birthdays, when all the children and men have gone upstairs to sleep . . .
SARA: What men?
GORGEOUS: And we finally sit together, just us three sisters . . .
PFENI: Around the samovar.
GORGEOUS: And we talk about life!
PFENI: And art.
SARA: Pfeni!
GORGEOUS . . . That each of us can say at some point that we had a moment of pure, unadulterated happiness! (97)

Sara and Pfeni contemplate Gorgeous's wish and agree with her, then Sara breaks the mood with mock solemnity, telling Gorgeous, "There's something I've been meaning to share with you. . . . Your neck is very dry" (98). In a few short scenes and bits of dialogue, Wasserstein moves her characters from the stage of world politics, to a simpler wish for individual happiness, to a still more prosaic preoccupation with dry skin. This very cycle, she suggests, is the stuff of women's lives. We spend our days on the stage of global history and art (that the sisters quote lines from Chekhov's play to describe their own lives is part of Wasserstein's knowing comedy), but at the end of the day, we worry about how to rejuvenate our skin.

Comedy has always traded in the low, in references to bodily functions sometimes not suited for more polite company. In many ways, despite its pedigree of influence by Kaufman and Hart, Coward, and Chekhov, *Sisters Rosensweig* draws its humor from the collision of gendered ethnic bodies, as Wasserstein's characters try to determine what goes where and who goes with whom. Geoffrey says that he is "the only theatre director who can ignite the stage with true female sexuality," insisting, "gender is merely spare parts" (50).

Sara is persuaded to go to bed with Merv after she hears his story about "shtupping" Sonia Kirschenblatt when they were teenagers. Wasserstein's characters long to connect and belong, but the comedy keeps them rooted to their bodies as a way to heal their souls. At the same time, because this Jewish family is displaced to London—which becomes in Wasserstein's hands the "origin" country for America but clearly not for the Jews—the characters evince a rootlessness that requires their ethnic identifications (and its comedy) to cement their relationships. Ironically, Lithuania is a much more likely place for a pilgrimage for people of their stock, but Tess's desire to go there to celebrate the nation's liberation is mocked throughout the play. Wasserstein's comedy here relies on peculiar rules of equivalence. Ruminating on her life choices, Pfeni admits that she uses other women's struggles to fill up her life, rendering her politics only personal, as global struggles serve to self-actualize a white, middle-class woman. And yet Merv's authenticity as a Jew is secured by his own references to the Holocaust, evidence, once again, of the slipperiness of Wasserstein's use of politics and history to anchor her characters' identities.

Critical response to *The Sisters Rosensweig* was mixed, with the most prominent writers writing along party lines. Kevin Kelly, in the *Boston Globe*, continued to disparage Wasserstein's writing (he had earlier suggested that *The Heidi Chronicles* won the Pulitzer Prize for Drama in 1989 because the play had no competition). Kelly wrote, "Sitcom is probably where Wasserstein's true talent lies, and in 'Sisters Rosensweig' it works better than it has before."[2] He compared her to Neil Simon without really complimenting her facility for comedy and explicitly dismissed her work: "Wasserstein has determined to be commercially viable at the expense of saying anything that might prove either (unduly) provocative or (passingly) profound. Everything is turned toward the joke (yes, Simon-like). When the current threatens to run serious, the flow is impeded with pebbles and boulders, titters and howlers."[3] Mel Gussow, on the other hand, who was the second-string critic at the *New York Times* through Wasserstein's early career, felt more affinity for her work. He called *The Sisters Rosensweig* a "captivating look at three uncommon women and their quest for love, self-definition, and fulfillment" and noted, "In dealing with social and cultural paradoxes, Ms. Wasserstein is, as always, the most astute of commentators."[4] He read this play in the context of the ongoing stories Wasserstein's work told, writing, "As the characters in Ms. Wasserstein's plays have become older, moving on from college to New York careers to the international setting of the current work, the author has remained keenly aware of the changes in her society and of the new roles that women play. In her writing, she continues to be reflexively in touch with her times."[5]

CHAPTER SIX

An American Daughter

Wasserstein's play *An American Daughter*, which premiered on Broadway in 1997, is probably her most effective in terms of addressing national issues and melding them with personal questions about identity. Its politics and theatrical form fit comfortably into the liberal feminist canon in which most of her plays reside, as the play describes women trying to make their way through and even to succeed and prevail in established systems of power dominated by men. Although the play maintains the wry, comic tone and socially acute, witty observations for which Wasserstein is known, the more sober aspect of *An American Daughter* concerns women's ability to achieve social status and political power according to rules that seem written to exclude them.

All of Wasserstein's preoccupations reappear in this play, from the liberal feminist notion that women can "have it all," to the conflict between a professional life and a family life, to the basic inequity in how women's lives differ from men's, even in the most privileged echelons of American society. *An American Daughter*, even more than *The Heidi Chronicles*, is perhaps Wasserstein's most topical play, as its plot mirrors an actual political debacle around a President Bill Clinton–era political nominee. The story continues to resonate in how Wasserstein depicts a rabid, corrupt media and the self-serving interests of those who purport to be the country's intellectual and political leaders.

An American Daughter's heroine, Lyssa Dent Hughes, is a direct descendent of Ulysses S. Grant. She is a wealthy, highly educated professional woman vying to be nominated by the president as his surgeon general. Lyssa's father, Alan, is a famous U.S. senator from

Indiana, and her husband, Walter Abrahmson, is a much-published, often-quoted sociology professor. Although Lyssa's own achievements are equally impressive, she is sandwiched between the patriarch and the husband, both of whom accrue power and status without working nearly as hard as Lyssa. Wasserstein uses this gender triangle in many of her plays, most famously in *The Heidi Chronicles' Hello New York* scene, in which Heidi sits between her friends Scoop and Peter on a talk show host's couch and watches silently while they send their verbal volleys over her head, preempting her remarks every time she begins to speak. In *Heidi*, both Scoop and Peter love and even respect Heidi, but when it comes to public preening, Wasserstein shrewdly demonstrates how they revert to the old entitlements of male privilege that blind them to how they're erasing her.

Lyssa, likewise, is subtly overshadowed by her father and essentially undone by her husband. Although Lyssa is clearly the best candidate for surgeon general, Walter inadvertently sabotages his wife. He tells a reporter who is profiling her in anticipation of her nomination an anecdote about a jury summons Lyssa misplaced and then ignored. When the unctuous reporter feels ethically bound to report her indiscretion, the predatory media contrive to make the honest oversight seem a careless exercise of class presumption and a criminal neglect of her civic duty. In the news cycle that follows, Walter and various younger, strategic hangers-on and erstwhile spin doctors encourage Lyssa to bend to public opinion, to be contrite, and to compromise her ideals in order to return to favor, an assault on her integrity that Lyssa refuses to withstand. Finally, even though Lyssa's credentials are impeccable and she is a passionate advocate, especially for women's health, the perception that her class status helped her avoid a civic responsibility makes her nomination too distasteful to go forward and she withdraws her name from consideration. Lyssa is left at home, in the domestic space in which the story takes place, entering online chat rooms to talk about health care while her two young twin sons babble to her from offstage.

Wasserstein finds *An American Daughter*'s inspiration in the gendered betrayals of Bill Clinton administration–era political duplicity. Lyssa's dilemma mirrors the Zoë Baird and Kimba Wood "Nannygate" cases, in which these two early Clinton nominees for attorney general were both disgraced by the press when background checks revealed they'd employed undocumented immigrant domestic workers. Wasserstein's heroine finds her own potential similarly compromised when a rather quotidian oversight becomes a national outrage. As in the real historical examples, the fictional president who nominated Lyssa declines to support her candidacy, despite their warm private friendship. Wasserstein's plot also recalls the Lani Guinier affair, in which Bill Clinton nominated an old Yale classmate with whom he'd long been friendly to head the Civil Rights Commission, only to back away from her politically when the media dubbed her the "quota queen" and smeared her public image.

By modeling the plot of *An American Daughter* so closely on these real and then-recent political examples, Wasserstein clearly intended to offer an alternative reading of what happened to these women. Her play looks resolutely at the events from Lyssa's perspective and tracks the private devastation wrought by her public ruin. Zoë Baird and Kimba Wood were never afforded such a platform for their perspectives, and Lani Guinier spoke out about her treatment at the hands of dominant power only much later, excoriating Clinton for betraying their friendship and his political ideals. Wasserstein gives these women their day in the court of public opinion by relating a similar story and demonstrating how they were demonized symbolically in ways that had more to do with gender than with their actual employment practices.

The play also echoes the media spectacle over Hillary Clinton's early 1990s "why should I stay home baking cookies" remark and the media frenzy it inspired, and the ways in which Bill Clinton's first presidential campaign manipulated his wife's image to control the damage after her retort caused such consternation among "women of America" who were defensive about their own choices to stay at home baking. In *An American Daughter*, a similarly faceless, patently constructed gang of "women of America" rally against Lyssa's descriptions of her mother in Indiana making icebox cakes and cheese puffs stuffed with pimento. Reporters twist her affectionate remarks into disparagements instead of faithful observations about her mother's domestic habits. Lyssa gets a one-two punch; she is accused of being too privileged and busy to answer her jury summons and too professional and important to cook for her family.

That Lyssa's misdemeanors echo real events gives Wasserstein a structure on which to hang a discussion about women and power, the corruption of the media, and the callowness of the American federal government. But Wasserstein sorts through its many layers in a way the mainstream media failed to do when the Baird-Wood-Guinier nominations pressured Clinton's administration. Wasserstein interrogates the other side, setting *An American Daughter* in the domestic/private space where Lyssa suffers her ignominious public defeat. In this case, while she might lose her shot at political power, her situation at least helps shift some of the privilege away from her father and husband. Although Lyssa is the daughter of a conservative Republican senator, she is quite liberal in her views on women's health, including abortion and reproductive issues. Her own ambitions challenge those of the family patriarch, and even though she loses the nomination, she puts up a fight that besmirches a bit of her father's reputation, too. Her husband, Walter, is ultimately a weak man who is willing to compromise his wife's integrity to get her elected, a choice she finally decides not to make. He urges her to listen to the advice of her father's political consultants, who suggest she wear a headband (more shades of Hillary) for her interview of contrition (echoes here of Bill and Hillary's televised confession about Bill's affair with Gennifer Flowers) and otherwise pander to the masses to save her nomination. Lyssa tries but finds herself unable to impersonate someone she is not.

Wasserstein surrounds Lyssa with people who represent a range of social and public opinions more than they serve as full-fledged characters with complex interior lives of their own. Lyssa and Walter's friend Morrow is a young, gay Republican who fills the role gay men often play in Wasserstein's work: he is comic relief, a witty commentator, and a fount of pop-cultural references. But he ultimately helps destroy Lyssa, because he refers to her unanswered jury summons in front of Timber Tucker, the television reporter conducting Lyssa's first public interview on his show, *Time Zone*. Morrow also boasts other traits of the typical Wasserstein gay male character: he is knowing, a bit cold, narcissistic, and colorful, but ultimately unsupportive of the female heroine's dilemmas.

Many of the character names in *An American Daughter* are slightly absurd and wryly reflexive, signaled by their alliterative appellations. The slick, ambitious Timber Tucker cuts Lyssa down by announcing her ignored jury summons and causing a media firestorm. Quincy Quince, a female former student of Walter's, is the author of *The Prisoner of Gender*, a bestselling book about the post-feminist generation. Although her name sounds *Mayflower* blue-blooded (or as Lyssa's friend, Judith, piquantly notes, like "there's a president lurking in [her] bloodline"), her Greek father actually changed their last name to Quince from Quintopolous "when he noticed the jelly at a breakfast function."[1] A next-generation version of the assimilated immigrant, Quincy has styled herself as a feminist pundit who uses the occasion of Lyssa's troubles to self-promote her way into a regular spot on *Time Zone*, the television show on which Lyssa's fate is sealed.

Quincy's name is purposefully gender-free, marked by whiteness, and ultimately conformist, a cookie-cutter name for an unoriginal woman with public pretensions. Wasserstein positions her as the voice of third-wave feminism, the movement that retains a critique of gender but refashions it as a commodity in the marketplace of ideas. Quincy's genealogy aligns her with Denise, Lisa's younger sister in *The Heidi Chronicles*, who majored in women's studies at Brown but adapts feminism to neoliberal, individual goals of striving for success. In response to a suggestion that she should run for public office, Quincy demurs, "No, sir. I have two more books to write and I want to start my family before I focus on my public life. My generation wants to do it all, but we want to have some fun, too" (35). In contrast, the play's older women, Lyssa and Judith, espouse their beliefs with passion and commitment and understand in a more material, experiential way how feminist ideology affects real women's lives. Lyssa is a figurehead to Quincy and little more—Lyssa is Quincy's ticket to a seat of authority at the table of public opinion created and manipulated by the media.

Critics noticed that these three characters, in particular, seemed "stock" rather than conceived with experiences, psychologies, and backstories. Gail Ciociola, in her book on Wasserstein, writes, "As devices . . . Morrow and Quincy . . . function less . . . as flesh-and-blood characters, and instead perform conceptual work in what Wasserstein herself declares as a 'play of ideas.'"[2] David Sheward, in *Backstage*, writes that the show "comes across as a panel discussion on contemporary topics rather than as a portrayal of real people in a plausible situation. . . . Wasserstein didn't go deeply enough beyond her issues and into character."[3] In this case, Wasserstein needed these characters to mark out the poles of a political debate and settled for stock types to draw her argument.

Like several of Wasserstein's heroines, Lyssa is not Jewish. Instead, Lyssa's best friend, Dr. Judith Kaufman, bears the weight of ethnic and racial difference. Judith is an oncologist who, like her friend, also specializes in women's health. She has known Lyssa since their days at a boarding school called Miss Porter's, which Lyssa must disguise in her nomination interview as something more public and generic than the privileged private school the name represents. Judith, an African American Jew, attended the school on a scholarship. She married a man who turned out to be gay and has been trying for many years to have a child through fertility treatments and artificial insemination, all strategies she laments as unsuccessful.[4] Judith is also religiously observant and spends much of the play practicing the rituals of the Jewish New Year, Rosh Hashanah. She participates in the Taschlich ceremony, in which Jews visit a moving body of water in which to symbolically throw away and expunge the year's sins. This so-called Festival of Regrets serves metaphorically to frame the play, as Judith and Lyssa reflect on the choices they have made, the paths they have not taken, and as in all of Wasserstein's plays, their chances for real happiness.

Judith's African American Jewishness carries and sometimes becomes the butt of Wasserstein's comedy in *An American Daughter*.[5] Judith always enters Lyssa's house through the garden, chiding Lyssa and Walter for leaving their gate open and inviting trouble from the "*schvartzes*"—the Yiddish word for "dark" that's a colloquialism for African Americans—and other supposed ruffians.[6] But Lyssa's nomination is not in fact sabotaged by intruders at her gate. Instead, it is destroyed from within, by Walter and Morrow. Trouble is always already there, in the family and its company, circulating in dominant ideology and just waiting for its chance to land on someone who wants to promote real social change.

Despite her sharp and incisive commentary, Judith, as a woman, an African American, and a Jew, can't protect Lyssa from her public demise. Judith regrets that although she's a doctor, she "can't make life or stop death," underlining the limits of anyone's power (although she can't "make life" only because she has been unable to bear children, a deficit in Wasserstein's worldview that persuades the character impulsively to try to commit suicide). Lyssa accuses Judith of being arrogant to think that she can make life or stop death, but Judith burns with care and compassion; she really wants to make a difference in the world. The play's bitter medicine is that in the end, both women are forced to try to change the health-care system while they remain off the nation's most public stages.

While Lyssa unsuccessfully prepares to assume her rightful place in the panoply of white Anglo-Saxon power, as a Jewish African American Judith is the character in *An American Daughter* who does not quite belong. Judith is Heidi's inheritor from *The Heidi Chronicles,* and her interloper's perspective is more aligned with Pfeni's in *The Sisters Rosensweig.* She delivers the knowing outsider's perspective—her long monologue at the end of *An American Daughter*'s first act is reminiscent of Heidi's story in *The Heidi Chronicles* about going to the gym and feeling so lost and alone. Wasserstein writes Judith's speech in an almost identically contrite, part-resentful, part-resigned tone. When Judith arrives dripping wet in Lyssa's living room, she tells her friend that she joined a Taschlich service by the banks of the Potomac, where she observed old religious men and younger lawyers discharging their religious obligations:

> I stood there feeling my familiar distance and disdain. And then, almost involuntarily, I began shredding my low-fat cranberry-orange muffin. I wanted this God, this Yaveh, to know me. . . . "Oh, Lord, my God, I distrust most people I know, I feel no comfort in their happiness, no sympathy for their sorrow." A tiny cranberry sits still upon the water. "Oh, Lord, our God . . . I regret the men I've been with, I regret the marriage I made, I regret never having children, I regret never having learned to be a woman." I pull off the entire top and a wad of muffin sails like a frigate towards the Washington Monument. "Oh, Lord, my God, Mighty of Mighty, Holy of Holy, I can't make life and I can't stop death. Oh, Lord, my God, the Lord is one, I've wasted my life," and I jump in. (55–56)

Just like Heidi's speech to her audience at Miss Crain's School for Girls, Judith's monologue is full of the little, specific details (the cranberry-orange low-fat muffin, for example) that brand it with Wasserstein's trademark wry social commentary. And the upshot of the story, although it is about a suicide attempt, arrives leavened by humor. Lyssa asks Judith what happened after she jumped in the

Potomac, and her friend responds, "It seems I'm still a very good swimmer."

> I was great. I was bobbing up and down in my pearls and Liz Claiborne suit, when I noticed a box of Dunkin' Donut holes floating along. And suddenly I remembered the slogan from my mother's favorite donut shop, "As you ramble on through life, whatever be your goal, keep your eye upon the donut and not upon the hole." And I began laughing and laughing. Now I had a purpose. Now I had a goal. I must rescue the donut holes and bring them here to you on N Street. Lyssa, these are the donut holes of my discontent. (56)

As in much of Wasserstein's work, what could be a truly tragic or psychologically fraught and traumatic moment is undercut by ironic, self-deprecating comedy.

Like so many other Wasserstein heroines, Judith is a single woman who wants to have a child, although by the play's end, she has given up on infertility treatments and resigned herself to what Wasserstein regards a bit too heavy-handedly as her barrenness. The fact that Judith, too, is a highly accomplished professional woman seems diminished by her overwhelming desire to bear children, but Wasserstein tries, again, to build a character who can "have it all" and still maintain her politics, her passion, and her integrity. Regrettably, Judith is unable to succeed (although strangely, adoption, which was a happy alternative for Heidi, does not seem a choice here).

The High Holidays, on which the play opens and to which Judith frequently refers, are a time of reflection and renewal in Judaism, during which people atone for past mistakes and indiscretions and prepare for the rejuvenation of the coming year. But despite Judith's personal and spiritual attempts at rebirth and regeneration, Wasserstein suggests that the Potomac's waters are muddied by the dirt of politicians and reporters determined to cloud the idealism of those who might really have progressive effect in Washington. The play ends on a much more bittersweet note than many in Wasserstein's canon. Lyssa stays with her husband, despite his infidelity and his betrayal of her political ideals; she withdraws her nomination for surgeon general; and at the finale, she types on her computer, entering social debates from her home as a way of participating in public life.

When the play opened on Broadway, the clutch of powerful New York reviewers mostly dismissed Wasserstein's play of ideas, demonstrating, as usual, their ambivalent opinions about the playwright's aspirations and her audiences. Ben Brantley, in the *New York Times*, spent his lede describing spectators' anticipation with barely concealed contempt: "The members of the audience practically purr, like cats anticipating a favorite meal in a warm kitchen, when the curtain goes up at the Cort Theatre. There before them is a tasteful but comfortable environment that evokes affluence, education and reassuringly human disarray."[7] In other words, Brantley positioned Wasserstein's play and her audience within the disdainful realm of the middlebrow, the cultural sphere in which consumers are given what they want, not asked to aspire higher or to think too hard, and formulas are repeated for profit rather than provocation. Brantley admired Wasserstein; he called her "one of the few American playwrights since S.N. Behrman to create commercial comedies of manners with moral and social heft."[8] But he chided her for packing too many ideas into the play ("Ms. Wasserstein often seems to be operating from a Filofax overstuffed with lists of things to accomplish: issues to address, emotional buttons to push, jokes to sell, plot points to chart") and said that "at its best, 'American Daughter' is a bit like watching C-Span with a shrewd, wisecracking friend . . . working principally in bite-size slices of sound, sentiment, and humor."[9]

Brantley has never been particularly generous as a reviewer, and especially not to women, so his denigration of Wasserstein and her play is not surprising. But his take on *An American Daughter* also illustrates how difficult it was for Wasserstein to be taken seriously as a woman with ideas and a political viewpoint, given that her most comfortable theatrical idiom was comedy. In her preface to the published version of the play, Wasserstein responds to Brantley and other critics on just this point:

> It's a great mistake to view comedic writing as a comforter cloaking an excruciating bed of nails. And, in my opinion, it is an even greater mistake to dismiss witty repartee as just a series of one-liners. My intention with *An American Daughter* was not to overhaul but to widen the range of my work: to create a fractured fairy tale depicting both a social and a political dilemma for contemporary professional women. In other words, if Chekhov was the icon of *The Sisters*

Rosensweig, then Ibsen would be the postfeminist muse of *An American Daughter*. The topicality of the play would be merely a container for a deeper problem. (viii–ix)

Would that critics could have seen the play through her eyes. Clive Barnes, in the *New York Post*, sided with Brantley, saying, "The writing suffers from a certain smartassed cuteness—at its lamest in such asides as 'organized religion always gives me migraines,' at its best in sharp, unexpected topical thrusts of wit such as describing Lyssa's best friend, a black and Jewish woman doctor, as 'a walking Crown Heights.'"[10] Howard Kissel, in the *New York Daily News*, agreed with his colleagues, saying the play is full of "glib opinionizing" and "wishing [it] had more moments where it rose above its own fray to put things in a larger perspective."[11] He continued,

> The play too seldom gets beyond its constant verbalizing. Characters are rarely developed; too often, they seem mere mouthpieces or plot devices. . . . Wasserstein said she wanted to do something topical. Maybe she should run symposiums on Beatty's set. For topicality, you can buy newspapers or cultivate friends who give stimulating dinner parties. You don't need to go to the theatre.[12]

I can't help but sense a gendered reaction from these powerful white male New York critics. By 1997 very few women, still, had won the Pulitzer Prize for Drama, and just that year, Garry Hynes and Julie Taymor became the first women ever to win Tonys for direction (Hynes for Martin McDonagh's play *The Beauty Queen of Leenane* and Taymor for *The Lion King* musical). The reviews of Wasserstein's play sniff about her style and preoccupations, but one wonders if, for instance, Neil Simon had written the play, the critics' responses might have been different.

While *An American Daughter* perhaps is not the strongest of Wasserstein's plays, I admire her choice to address recent events with such spot-on precision, from an insider's perspective that had been very much repressed in the mainstream media. That is, once Zoë Baird and Kimba Wood withdrew their nominations for attorney general in the first one hundred days of Bill Clinton's first administration, they were barely heard from again. Lani Guinier, who suffered similar slights from her one-time-friend-in-high-places when Clinton threw her, too, under the bus of the nomination process for assistant attorney general for civil rights in the Justice Department in 1993, took to the airwaves shortly after to advance her own analysis of what it meant to be dismissed as "the quota queen." Even Hillary Clinton, the candidate's wife, was silenced after her infamous remark on her husband's campaign trail about refusing to stay at home to bake cookies. Friends' and supporters' efforts to remake Lyssa Dent after her quip about her mother's icebox cakes is similarly misunderstood in *An American Daughter*, mirroring Hillary Clinton's public shaming and disciplining. Wasserstein's play tried to see these betrayals from the women's point of view.

Perception is, in fact, everything in the American media. In *An American Daughter*, Wasserstein uses comedy to atomize the costs of stifling public scrutiny for accomplished women who want to contribute to political life. Wasserstein gives Lyssa and Walter twin sons who are heard but never seen, making them the first married couple with children to assume leading roles in one of her plays. The twins, however, are kept offstage, where they serve as a kind of Greek chorus, reporting to Lyssa, for instance, on the media's response to her jury summons oversight. The boys' voices, too, ground Lyssa in domesticity, reminding us of her role as a mother even while she fights for her opportunity to be an influential public figure. In the end, Lyssa accepts that she does the most good in her own smaller sphere of influence. But Wasserstein asks us to regret that she is kept out of a wider, more consequential arena for reasons that have nothing to do with her qualifications and everything to do with skewed public perception that slips out of her control.

In most reviews of Wasserstein's work, male critics refer back to her "uncommon women," the shortcut they take for grounding Wasserstein's viewpoint in her first notable protofeminist play and for tracking her progress and the trajectory of white, upper-middle-class, heterosexual American women through contemporary history. Although the critics' references always sound a bit condescending, Wasserstein's work does build on her own ideas and her well-established formula. *An American Daughter* includes all the archetypes of her catalog, from little choices to the more central. Walter calls his powerful wife, Lyssa, "Lizard," echoing the animal nicknames and diminutives many of her male characters adopt to subtly diminish their female counterparts. As in *The Heidi Chronicles*, especially, Wasserstein uses music to mark the historical moment, as well as to convey information about her characters (Lyssa and Judith listen to an oldies station that markets itself as "now" music for grown-ups, and Walter is nostalgically fond of the Beach Boys). As in all of her plays except *The Sisters Rosensweig*, voiceovers at the top of scenes situate us in history, provide social commentary, and forward plot points. In *An American Daughter*, television newscasters overheard broadcasting their stories fill this function.

Like most of Wasserstein's heroines, Lyssa has Judith to serve as her best friend, a female foil who also has unfulfilled desires or choices she makes differently. Although the fact that she is African American and Jewish makes her exceptional in Wasserstein's plays— and gives the character quite a heavy burden of representation— Judith provides a variation on the theme of Susan in *The Heidi Chronicles* and Harriet in *Isn't It Romantic* and prefigures Nancy, Laurie's best friend in Wasserstein's last play, *Third*.

Quincy Quince fleshes out the position of Tess, Sara's daughter in *The Sisters Rosensweig*, and Denise in *The Heidi Chronicles*, the Brown graduate who took classes in women's studies, all of whom contemplate feminism from an academic perspective while they presumptuously reap the rewards of the social movement in their personal and professional lives. At Lisa's shower scene, which opens *The Heidi Chronicles*' second act, Denise says, "Once my career's in place, I definitely want to have my children before I'm thirty. I mean, isn't that what you guys fought for? So we could 'have it all'?"[13] Quincy Quince follows Denise's genealogy, exploiting her pseudo-feminist insights for the payback of public thought leadership while never once considering how gender might in fact imprison Lyssa. Older feminists—Lyssa here, Heidi earlier, and Laurie in *Third*—no longer retain pride of place as pioneering thinkers or activists. The next generation consigns them to the dust heap of history and proceeds to reap the financial, professional, and personal rewards their elders' leadership made possible.

Other characters in *An American Daughter* echo Wasserstein's stable of types and preoccupations. Morrow is cut from the mold of Peter in *The Heidi Chronicles* and Geoffrey in *The Sisters Rosensweig*, white gay men who use their cutting wit for social observation and self-aggrandizement and ultimately prove that their solidarity lies elsewhere. Although Walter first shares the anecdote of Lyssa's misplaced jury summons, Morrow feeds it to Timber Tucker, precipitating his friend Lyssa's downfall. When Judith asks him why he betrayed Walter and Lyssa, Morrow says, "I was just making a point. Like writing a column. I forgot they were people I know and like" (78). Relationships in this political enclave are transactional and tenuous. Morrow here also borrows some of Scoop Rosenbaum's prescient preening.

Interestingly, heterosexual men are rather neutralized in *An American Daughter*. Lyssa's father, of course, is a senator, but Alan Hughes is more an old-school patriarch in ways that confine his power, and Lyssa's husband, Walter, is hapless, thoughtless, and inept. In the play's penultimate scene, Wasserstein sandwiches Lyssa between Walter and her father for Timber Tucker's second television interview, for which various consultants have encouraged her to wear a headband, look feminine, and try to curry favor with the populations she has supposedly alienated. The scene mirrors Heidi's miserable moment taping the television segment on *Hello, New York*, the puerile talk show on which Scoop and Peter, flanking Heidi, speak over her and don't let her join the conversation as they promote their own agendas. But in *An American Daughter*, Wasserstein's character refuses to be erased or handled by political operatives. Walter and her father try to compliment Lyssa's work as a mother and shore up her history as a dutiful daughter. But Lyssa chafes under the men's control of the dialogue:

> TIMBER: Do you think your wife's embattled nomination is indicative of the conflict inherent in liberalism and your "greening of America" generation?
> WALTER: Let's not get academic here, Timber. Lyssa and I are just two real people who happen to be in a little trouble.
> LYSSA: I made a mistake. I should have answered the notice. It was an oversight. And I apologize. It was simply bad juggling by a working mother. (87)

This is the first time she speaks during the interview, interrupting Walter, Timber, and her father volleying back and forth about and above her. Lyssa tries to put the controversy to rest with simple, pointed truths. But Timber will not relent. He probes Lyssa's reputation, suggesting that her ten-year run on the *Ladies' Home Journal*'s list of "American Women Role Models" perhaps makes other women "envious." "Are you too perfect?" Timber asks smugly (90). He dwells on Lyssa's mother and her relationship with her father, proposing that her mother's resentment toward her powerful husband mirrors American women's feelings about Lyssa. He forces an irritated Lyssa to propose, "Timber, I don't believe we can really judge who will make the best surgeon general based on their mother's marital happiness" (91). But he continues to push, until Lyssa explodes, enumerating all the real political issues women in America should care more about than her own mother or her jury summons, including their reproductive rights, the underfunding of research for women-specific cancers, and teenage drug addiction and pregnancy rates. Finally, she says,

> There's nothing quite so satisfying as erasing the professional competency of a woman, is there? Especially when there's such an attractive personal little hook to hang it on. Oh, we all understand it now! She must have hated her mother! That's why she's such a good doctor. She must be a bad cold person. That's why she achieved so much. And anyway it would be all right if she were a man and cold. That man would be tough. No one would give a damn what he felt about his mother! But a woman? A woman from good schools and a good family? That kind of woman should be perfect! And if she manages to be perfect, then there is something distorted and condescending about her. (92)

Critics might find this "opinionizing," but the speech marks one of the first times in Wasserstein's work that she allows one of her characters to actually speak the social critique that is always just under the surface of her comedy. Delivered by Kate Nelligan, who played Lyssa in the Broadway production (to very good reviews), the monologue diagnoses the condition of accomplished women caught in conflicting gender presumptions. These are the fruits of "having it all"—class resentments and social judgments that come from deep-seated conservatism about the proper ceiling on women's aspirations in the first place. Ending her humiliating interview with Timber Tucker and withdrawing her doomed nomination, Lyssa tells her husband remorsefully, "I really wanted that job, Walter. I would have been good" (96). Lyssa, unlike Heidi or Janie Blumberg, at least can articulate what she has lost as she is kept from fulfilling her professional promise on a national scale.

A 2016 production of *An American Daughter* at the Williamstown Theatre Festival in Massachusetts, during the height of that year's presidential election season, demonstrated that even topical drama can have staying power, especially when it addresses gender and power as accurately as Wasserstein's play does. Directed with empathy and insight by Evan Cabnet, the production found new layers and resonances in a play that was by then twenty years past its Broadway premiere. The production also reminded me that Wasserstein was a fabulous craftsman; she knew how to write a tightly constructed scene with sharp, pointed dialogue, and she excelled at leaving audiences laughing. The play's unified narrative addresses just one moment in time and unfolds on one set. But in a political climate in which the media derogated still another woman politician—this time Hillary Clinton, during her historic run for president—Wasserstein's play felt poignant, its humor more mordant than flippant.

Although Wasserstein set the play in 1996, around when the actual events regarding Bill Clinton's cabinet nominations took place, I found it difficult to see the Williamstown production as historical. How do a director and a design team evoke the 1990s for an audience in the 2010s? No one in the play speaks into or writes text messages on a cell phone, which these characters certainly would do today. Instead of surfing the web, the characters watch a lot of television and listen to a lot of radio, hungry for the information—which would now most likely come by email or the Internet—that ultimately determines their fates. In perhaps the most obvious mark of the historical moment, Walter enjoys playing music albums, shuffling them on and off the turntable to make a point or to establish a mood (just as Wasserstein selects music to play under scenes for similar reasons). The characters' clothes in the Williamstown production appeared just a little out of style, to evoke the 1990s.

But it might have been interesting for Cabnet and his designers to set the play in the present; although for those who remember, it refers to past media debacles, *An American Daughter* resonated urgently with gender politics on the most visible political stages of the moment. In the second act, in which Wasserstein pulls the net entrapping her heroine ever tighter, Lyssa's revelation of frustration and refusal during the *Time Zone* taping was very moving, partly because she embodies a type we still see in the media today: a woman who has to "soften" herself and wear the metaphorical equivalent of a headband to win people's trust in a climate in which commentators remain more eager to talk about women's families and relationships than about their work. Hillary Clinton's failed candidacy was blamed in part on her personal coldness and explained by persistent cultural misogyny, both issues that Wasserstein diagnosed as pitfalls for political women twenty years earlier.

Cabnet's excellent direction punctuated the Williamstown production with unexpected pauses, moments of penetrating sorrow when the performers did not rush to the next punch line but just sat with the irony and sadness of what they had said (for instance, after the humiliations of Lyssa's interview with Timber Tucker, and after Walter admits that he did indeed sleep with Quincy Quince). Cabnet trusted the play, and the smart, sharp edge of Wasserstein's humor, which gave the production real dignity and depth.

An American Daughter's critique of the media also hit home in Cabnet's production since, if anything, the way Internet journalists and conservative pundits ridicule progressive causes has only grown worse in the last twenty years. The slick Timber Tucker, who invades Lyssa and Walter's home to destroy their reputations, is an even more familiar type, although now a woman in Lyssa's position would recognize his danger and would never dismiss him on the air without truly causing an uproar. Scenic designer Derek McLane's subtly moneyed living/dining/foyer space clarified how trapped Lyssa is in the domestic. When the large television crew arrives to thread cable everywhere and disrupts the furniture in her living room, Cabnet used the scene to stage a perfect analogy for the invasive destruction they cause in Lyssa's life.

While in the Broadway production, Timber, Walter, and Morrow seemed righteous in their betrayals of Lyssa, at Williamstown Stephen Kunken, as Walter, Roe Hartrampf, as Morrow, and Jason Danieley, as Timber, played these men with narcissistic self-absorption and arrogance. Morrow still seemed clueless about his disloyalty to his friends, perhaps even more so because gay men *do* have families now and are less often portrayed as outside the kinships structures in which Morrow is presumed to take solace in Wasserstein's play. Because gay characters are ubiquitous onstage in 2016 and tend to be fuller, richer, and more complex, Morrow's camping in the Williamstown production seemed tired. But Hartrampf's gym-buff body (though more 2010s than 1990s) signaled his shallowness (in a way that perhaps Quincy Quince's anorexia—as embodied by Kerry Bishé—did hers, too).

Kunken played Walter as egotistical and whiny. Lyssa insists that this debacle concerns her, not him, and his complaint that he's "disappearing" registered as a jealous bid for attention from a man concerned that his days as a bold-faced, quotable name have passed. Kunken's Walter mopes, can't resist his former student's flirtations, and doesn't provide his wife with the emotionally or politically astute advice she needs. In fact, Judith and Lyssa were the play's true couple in this production. Judith's monologue about jumping into the Potomac wearing her Liz Claiborne suit before her epiphany with the box of Dunkin' Donuts solicited more audience sympathy than Walter's admission that he hasn't written anything worthwhile in five years. The shift of empathy to the women characters deepened Cabnet's feminist reading of Wasserstein's play.

The women characters in this production did seem to find new common cause. Deborah Rush, playing Senator Hughes's fourth wife, nicknamed "Chubby" (because of her desperate thinness) played what could be a minor character with a steely knowingness that belied her reputation as empty arm candy. Rush clarified that Chubby knew exactly the score and the necessary trade-offs for power in public life. Although her one-liners still sang, Rush brought élan and intelligence to what might have been a caricature. Even Quincy Quince did not register as quite as striving in Cabnet's production. Bishé played her as lithesome and smart, and although she is trying to advance her career, suggested she is also really trying to advance an analysis. Lyssa could only see her as a sexual and intellectual adversary, but in this production, though Quincy remained blithely unaware of her sometimes cutting presumptions, she seemed truly eager to trumpet Lyssa's feminist cause.

The Judith character, in 2016, continued to carry the play's ethnic humor. Wasserstein burdens the character with racial and religious difference, as well as comedy, but Judith is written in such a way that a good actor can give her self-esteem and depth. The late Lynne Thigpen played Judith with fatigued empathy in the Broadway premiere, for which she won a Tony Award (Thigpen died of a cerebral hemorrhage five years later, in 2003). Saidah Arrika Ekulona (who received critical acclaim as the lead in Lynn Nottage's play *Ruined* at Manhattan Theatre Club in 2009) played Judith in the Williamstown production with a great deal of charm and strength and in many ways became the play's conscience. Ekulona balanced the character's personal sadness with her keen attention to the state of the world and presented her as a knowing, acutely observant interpreter of her friend Lyssa's media firestorm. Ekulona communicated Judith's intelligence through Wasserstein's dialogue, but also as a silent and forceful presence. Cabnet frequently placed the actor downstage left, so that the audience could watch Judith observing the action. Ekulona's excellent comic timing and pointed reactions grounded Wasserstein's critique.

Ekulona and Diane Davis, who played Lyssa at Williamstown, captured the palpable chemistry and affection of two lifelong friends. Watching them perform—often sitting together on Lyssa's couch, casually holding hands or massaging one another's feet—I was reminded of how well Wasserstein portrays female friendships and their physical, emotional, and intellectual intimacy. In fact, a moment that seems a throwaway in the script and in the Broadway production worked in Cabnet's vision to bring the play's ending a whole new tone. In her first scene, Judith realizes she's forgotten to bring an article she wants Lyssa to read about research in their common field of women's health. At the end, Judith hands her friend the essay, in a gesture that underlines the importance of their work. Judith has decided to end her fruitless fertility treatments and Lyssa has withdrawn her nomination as surgeon general, but the simple act of sharing an article indicates that they will continue to assert their professional commitments to activism for women's health. When Judith leaves, rather than appearing cowed or defeated and retreating upstairs to join her sons on those Internet chat rooms, Lyssa picks up the article, puts on her reading glasses, settles into an armchair, and gets to work.

Cabnet and his actors, as a result of these choices, draw the audience's attention away from the media's condemnation of Lyssa Hughes Dent and toward her determination to keep working and fighting for her ideals. Knowing how the 2016 Republican presidential nominee Donald Trump pilloried his opponent, the ending of this production of *An American Daughter* (which ran during the summer prior to the November election) offered hope that a candidate like Hillary Clinton will be smart and resilient and will overcome whatever setbacks the media and Trump construct to force her to stumble. The production's final image offered a timely, resonant reading not just of the events of 1996 but of the presidential politics of 2016. That Clinton didn't garner enough electoral votes to win the election, and that the contempt she was shown by her competitor helped usher him into the Oval Office all seem foreshadowed in Wasserstein's play.[14]

In fact, given the contemporary significance of the Williamstown production, I can only wonder how Wasserstein would have rendered this presidential election season. How might she have narrated, as years passed, Trump's public comments about Hillary's bathroom break during the primary debates, or the way he constantly baited her about being a woman? Surely Wasserstein would have been outraged and inspired to turn politics into art, as she did with *An American Daughter*.

CHAPTER SEVEN

Third

Wasserstein's last play, *Third* (2005), in many ways repeats the themes of *The Heidi Chronicles*, revisiting a feminist professor (now of literature) safely tenured at a small, elite college in New England of the sort that the playwright once attended. But this time, a male student, called Third, has his say, launching a liberal critique of Professor Laurie Jameson's idiosyncratic feminist analysis of *King Lear*. In their debate over free speech and in Laurie's open contempt for Third's discourse of "tolerance," Wasserstein offers a rather pernicious portrait of a feminist academic stuck in what the playwright portrays as shopworn suspicion of dominant male power. But the play also stages a conversation about the limits of entrenched belief and the potential transformations in middle-aged, intellectual women's lives in a way rarely seen in commercial theater.[1]

Third premiered at the Lincoln Center Theater in New York in September 2005, directed by Broadway regular Daniel Sullivan, Wasserstein's frequent collaborator. The Lincoln Center production starred Dianne Wiest as Laurie Jameson, Jason Ritter (John's son) as Woodson Bull III (otherwise known as "Third"), and Amy Aquino (a longtime favorite Wasserstein actor) as Laurie's friend Nancy. *Third* offers all of Wasserstein's staples: at the top of each scene, voiceovers from various television commentators, heard while Laurie watches them obsessively, place the narrative in history (the start of the war in Iraq in 2002). Laurie's long, punctuating monologues let the audience glimpse her inner life, as a respite from the bright, witty, rapid-fire dialogue that otherwise moves the play. The playwright's concern with mortality—tragically revealed when Wasserstein's own terminal illness became clear after the play opened—is represented here in Laurie's father's Alzheimer's disease and her faculty friend Nancy's recurrent breast cancer.[2] The ineffectual academic husband character also recurs, as he did in *An American Daughter*, though this time he's never seen (only heard, as the weights he lifts fall against the floor upstairs from the action onstage and startle the other characters).

As the play opens, Laurie speaks to her students (for whom the audience substitutes). She is fifty-four years old, dresses in a funky retro style, and, according to Wasserstein's stage direction, "takes very good care of her skin."[3] This parenthetical remark reveals as much about Wasserstein's observations as it does about the character. As in Sara's reference to Gorgeous's dry skin in *The Sisters Rosensweig* and the obsessive ablutions of the coeds in *Uncommon Women*, Wasserstein always grounds her comedy in the particularities of women's bodies. Laurie prepares the students to whom she speaks for her own idiosyncratic interpretation of *King Lear*, in which she urges them to sympathize with Goneril and Regan and to see Cordelia as weak and wimpy. Enrolled in the class is Third, a self-declared straight white male student who is on the school wrestling team. He quickly realizes he has an assignment-scheduling problem that requires special dispensation, which Laurie refuses. When he does turn in his work, Laurie believes he has plagiarized his paper, since she can't imagine that an athlete like Third—whom she also assumes is rich and probably a legacy student, because his real name is Woodson Bull III—could also be smart. The play pits the two against each other, staging their disputation to question how a veteran feminist teacher can become trapped by her own dogma. Wasserstein also uses the play to think through what it means to age—physically, politically, and intellectually—and to consider the challenges of trying to paint widespread social change from the limited palette of an academic institution.

As in all her plays, Wasserstein also probes the mother–daughter relationship and female friendships. *Third* sets Laurie against her postfeminist daughter, Emily (played by Gaby Hoffman, now of *Girls* and *Transparent* fame, in the Lincoln Center premiere), who lobs criticisms and complaints about her mother's single-minded and blinkered political correctness. In some ways, Emily's position nods to third-wave feminism, which Wasserstein might have also been alluding to in her title. Unlike second-wave feminists who, with their more radical politics, launched a structural critique of social power and demanded transformation, third-wave feminists often seem complacent with the status quo, while they advance more individualist demands for women's equality.[4] This friction between feminist as well as family generations plays out in Laurie's relationship with Emily. Likewise, although Laurie and Nancy exemplify the female friendships portrayed across Wasserstein's plays, their relationship is difficult, less pliant and secure than those between her usual women pairs. Nancy, for instance, votes against Laurie during Third's disciplinary hearing, and Laurie's charge that Third plagiarized his paper is dropped. Wasserstein implies that Nancy has realized there's more to life than scholarship, or feminism, for that matter.

Third focuses on Laurie, but other characters propel her eventual transformation by commenting on her choices and judging her motives. Third and Jack (Charles Durning at Lincoln Center), Laurie's elderly father, are the play's only male characters. Jack serves as a Lear-like figure and suffers from advanced Alzheimer's. Laurie's husband is a political science professor, whose adequacy as a scholar and a man she regularly doubts; in fact, he remains an invisible presence whose choices counterpoint Laurie's. He's converted Emily's bedroom into a home gym and eventually buys a motorcycle to ride around on with other middle-aged bikers. Laurie can't take him seriously because until her climactic epiphany she continues to strive for the academic success and approbation that he's given up.

Like most of Wasserstein's plays, Third rejects subtext and psychology. In Wasserstein's Shavian style, Laurie shares three thoughtful monologues—similar to the two that Heidi Holland performs in The Heidi Chronicles and the one that Judith delivers in An American Daughter—that locate her commitments and her excesses and forward the play's action. Wasserstein uses these speeches to extend Laurie's personality beyond the fourth wall, addressing the audience either as though they are students in Laurie's class or as the play's actual spectators. In her monologue at the beginning of the play, Laurie speaks to her students, announcing her goal for her class: "Our job here is to renew our scholarship by eliminating any heterosexist, racist or classist barriers. Rest assured, this classroom is a hegemonic-free zone" (5). In her next monologue, during Third's hearing before the college ethics committee near the end of the first act, Laurie sweats profusely, either because of the situation, or hormones, or both. Removing her soaking shirt, she launches into a fantasy—Third and Nancy freeze and the stage lights dim during her monologue—in which she confesses directly to the audience her desire to hold Woodson Bull III accountable in a way that she can't hold responsible the country's president or vice president for their dishonesty and corruption. She implicitly admits that she's displacing her fury at world politics onto a student whose personal politics she presumes align with the gender, race, and class privilege of the president. By her third and final monologue, Laurie's lecture to her class detours into a tangent about her relationship with her husband. When she realizes how far the personal has intruded into the professional, she apologizes sheepishly and ends the class early.

These speeches let Wasserstein reveal to the audience what Laurie thinks and feels. They represent the "telling" that Wasserstein used throughout her career to make a pact with spectators, to invite them in, to preach to a presumptively converted, liberal crowd who would ridicule radical feminist excess while feeling good about its own commitment to empowering women. While they take the place of other dramatic techniques Wasserstein might have used to reveal character, these pedagogical monologues teach the audience things— about women, in particular. The speeches extract Laurie from the play to reveal her intellect, her seething rage, and her thwarted desires in a deeply gender-marked style. In fact, Frank Scheck, reviewing *Third* for the *New York Post*, said, "And having the prof fanning herself while in the throes of hot flashes would have seemed awfully sexist if it had come from a male playwright."[5] Maybe so. But Wasserstein's insistence on putting the side effects of diminishing female hormones on view in the theater recalls her equally radical choice to have a character fill a diaphragm with Ortho-Crème onstage in *Uncommon Women* earlier in her career. Although Laurie remains rather remote and even unlikeable to the other characters in *Third*, Wasserstein allows her to bid for the spectators' allegiances by making her fully, intimately human. If we identify with Laurie, Wasserstein suggests, perhaps we'll understand and forgive her ideological extremes.

Aside from Laurie's rather confessional monologues, no secrets and little deep psychology add nuance or complexity to *Third*. Only the question of whether or not Third plagiarized his paper on *Lear* propels the action. As the debate about Laurie's charge simmers and flares, Third presents evidence against Laurie and her accusations and, at least tacitly, against feminism writ large. Third accuses Laurie of reverse discrimination, insisting, "You have a problem with me because I'm happy. . . . I'm straight. I'm white. I'm male. . . . Why are you wasting time on someone as insignificant as me? If you're angry, pick on someone powerful" (23). Although he belittles her for attacking an insignificant college student such as himself, Third also implies that power is not suffused across identity positions, that his social identity means nothing. Wasserstein suggests that Laurie over-reads and Third under-reads the complexities and influence of identity vectors, perhaps representing some pivot point on which feminism balanced in 2002–3, the academic year in which the play is set.

Contemporary feminism in many ways opened doors for students like Third. He enrolls in classes like Laurie's—and his gay and lesbian literature class, and the course in "Third World" culture he also takes—with the entitlement of someone for whom identity politics are detached from personal experience and for whom the lives of the aboriginal lesbians he studies, and even the lives of middle-class, aging, white feminist women, for example, are fair game for any student to consider. (Wasserstein makes "Pinky," the aboriginal lesbian whose memoir Third reads in his gay and lesbian literature class, the unfortunate butt of too many jokes. The references to Pinky devolve until the figure becomes an offensively tidy symbol at whom the white, straight characters—and the audience—all scoff.) But without a foundation in emotional or political identification, these courses become as academic for Third as his Shakespeare class. Third's ecumenical magnanimity makes him seem liberal, but part of Laurie's accusation is that he can't possibly understand what it means to read *Lear* from a feminist perspective the way she can, given that she is living her own version, playing Cordelia to her father's mad king. For Third, his paper successfully engages original ideas, but Laurie views his work as inauthentic because, in many ways, it *is* academic, only an idea, not a passion or a politic. This conflict encapsulates the flaw in Laurie's thinking. She's mired in the essentialisms of an earlier kind of contemporary feminism, one that presumes women really do see and experience the world differently. Third, on the other hand, sincerely believes he can proceed from intellectual curiosity into the study of lives that aren't his own.

Third investigates these conflicting values and principles but also meditates on larger questions of belief. Faith stands as an open, pressing question in the play. Although Nancy accuses Laurie of being a "religious cynic," she admits that Laurie is "the one who always had faith in the future and the work we had to do" (40). She tells Third that "Laurie Jameson is still holding the torch. . . . To Professor Jameson, it all still really matters" (24). Her remarks resonate with Scoop's, who told Heidi in her *Chronicles* that she and other "true-believing girls" would have a long, hard way to go because of their confidence in the possibility of feminist transformation.[6] Wasserstein tries to distinguish faith from dogma, wondering how to give up entrenched truths that no longer illuminate people's lives as history moves forward.

But faith hovers over the play as an urgent necessity, not as religion; in fact, *Third*'s characters lack ethnic flavor. Laurie Jameson, like Heidi Holland, is a non-Jewish and nonspecifically Christian character. Nancy begins dating a male rabbi she meets during her chemotherapy infusions to treat a recurrence of her breast cancer, but otherwise, the characters are not religiously or ethnically inflected. Perhaps Wasserstein wanted to reach for a more unmarked sense of identity, one more widely available for spectators' identifications in ways that the Borscht Belt inflections of characters like those in *Isn't It Romantic* or *The Sisters Rosensweig* would disallow.[7] Faith, after all, is a more general pursuit than the particularities of religion, especially one as culturally and socially marked—with its accents and gestures, its shtetl-hewn tribalism and attachments to subaltern history—as Judaism.

Third's humor and Wasserstein's familiar ability to couch current events in personal, domestic situations makes its ideas easily digestible.[8] The play is frequently performed by regional theaters across the country. I saw the 2007 Geffen Playhouse production in Los Angeles, starring Christine Lahti and directed by Maria Mileaf, which suffered from a sitcom effect that made the play seem flip and superior about the feminist lives it describes.[9] Lahti played Laurie as a self-deprecating smart woman; the role reads differently from Heidi (which Lahti also performed on Broadway, after Joan Allen originated the part), in that Laurie is not the shrinking spectator of her own life.[10] But Lahti's physical elegance (and skeletal thinness), decorated in the Geffen production with stylish, contemporary clothes, and her habit of laughing off Laurie's seriousness of purpose by undercutting her lines with raised eyebrows and dry laughter, meant that Lahti embraced too heartily the irony that Laurie eschews at the play's end.

At the Geffen, Wasserstein's play became the vehicle for a critique of feminism, because it positioned Laurie as prey to the criticisms of her third-wave or postfeminist daughter and Third. Lahti's Laurie didn't transform—she capitulated, giving in to a harsh appraisal of her own values as rigid, dogmatic, and old-fashioned. As Third, Matt Czuchry (who went on to star as the character Cary Agos in the television series *The Good Wife*) offered a charming but vague performance that made him an unworthy adversary, and Jayne Brook, as Nancy, didn't provide much of a foil for Laurie's ambivalence. Even Laurie's daughter, Emily (Sarah Drew), sounded shrill rather than thoughtful as she rejected her mother's life choices.

In the 2008 Philadelphia Theatre Company (PTC) production of *Third*, Lizbeth MacKay played Laurie with a completely different investment in the character's commitments. From her first monologue, in which Laurie shares her feminist critique of *King Lear*, MacKay's choices proposed Laurie's argument as idealistic rather than strident. Mackay's Laurie started the play in an ankle-length jean skirt, wearing a loose-fitting top adorned with the chunky turquoise jewelry favored by progressive women of a certain age. Her graying hair was pulled back from her face but cascaded down her back in the long, loose style of 1970s feminists. She looked like someone who had been on the battle lines of the women's movement, and her world-weariness showed on her face. When Laurie reassured her class—and MacKay her audience—that the course would be a "hegemony-free" zone, she meant it, making spectators much less inclined to laugh at the notion that such an ideologically safe space is possible. At the Geffen, Lahti-as-Laurie snickered knowingly at the idea of a "hegemony-free" zone, bringing the audience into the joke she made of the line, and held the performer blameless for her character's ideology. The PTC production addressed the play's concerns with more sincerity.

Will Fowler played Third at PTC as truly wounded by Laurie's plagiarism accusation, offended that his earnest intellectual talents could be suspected. When at the play's end Third confesses that Laurie's attentions, though negative, made him more interesting than he will probably ever be again, the actor delivered his lines sheepishly, as if to acknowledge how bankrupt unmarked male, white, middle-class, heterosexual power is in a world that is so culturally and politically diverse. Third's losses in the PTC production could not be cut by the Pyrrhic victory of his exoneration by the college ethics committee. He returns reluctantly to the fold of normativity that even he knows is too barren to embrace. He plans to break up with a girlfriend who has already written their life scenario with the predictable plot of heterosexual middle-class white propriety secured. Even Third cannot go along with the ruse that there is no "outside" to that story—even Third, in the PTC production, wants more from his life. Making the characters less one-dimensional opponents helped the play feel more thoughtful.

Nancy was played by Melanye Finister, an African American actor, in the Philadelphia production, a casting choice that also gave it more nuance and relevance (although the night I attended, the PTC audience was overwhelmingly white, with only a handful of obviously African American spectators). Perhaps because of their racial differences, the skirmishes Nancy and Laurie withstand appeared more fraught, and the expense of being on opposite sides of important issues much higher. When they return to an uneasy though hopeful solidarity by the play's end, agreeing to forgive one another for their disagreements and betrayals, the two characters illustrate the fragility of relationships not just between women, but between women who are different in as many ways as they are similar. The compromise was harder won, its import more fundamental.[11] The casting also mirrored the character relationships in *An American Daughter*, in which the white protagonist's best friend is an African American woman.

The mother-daughter relationship in the PTC production also underlined the complexities of reconciling different feminist generations. Because Laurie was played less as a successful, corporate working woman (as Lahti styled the character) than as an academic, intellectual, CNN junkie, and because the daughter, Emily (Jennifer Blood), was performed with complex vulnerability more than flip disregard for her mother's choices, the two actors managed to illuminate their conflict in a way that also heightened its larger political importance. When Emily rejects Laurie's values, insisting she doesn't want to embrace her mother's rigid dogmatism or her exacting, narrow definitions of political efficacy, the younger woman is left wondering how she will fill the hole her choice will leave in her life. Emily more incisively critiques her mother's pretensions in this production—Laurie's name-dropping, her supercilious, unthinking class snobbery, and her thwarted academic ambitions—but the daughter cannot yet fathom what new values she will replace them with.[12] As she walks away from her Swarthmore education to live with an older man who is a bank teller, Emily's rebellion offers her less security than her critique of her mother's feminist values might assume. What she leaves behind is clear, but what she moves toward seems uncertain.

Although the relationship between Laurie and Emily remained tense, the actors' choices illustrated how Laurie and Third grudgingly learn from each other. While they do not reconcile in the end, they reluctantly admit that they have forced one another out of their respective comfort zones, with transformative results. Laurie's plan to take an extended leave of absence signals her new willingness to escape the narrow confines of her worldview. Third decides to enroll at Ohio State University on a wrestling scholarship, but he has learned that he cannot escape the cultural power of his gender privilege, however little it actually suits him.

The PTC production cast several young actors as stray students, using them to move furniture between scenes and to perform small gestures that represented campus life during transitions. They tossed Frisbees and footballs, teased and flirted, and otherwise drew in broad strokes the interactions of young people on a quad between classes. The choice situated the play nicely in the tumult of its campus environment, if not exactly in a more specifically drawn historical moment. But Laurie Jameson was still left alone, the isolated elder stateswoman rushing purposefully along ivy-lined paths to and from her classes. Laurie examines her choices in the isolation of her monologues and suffers her daughter's rejection and her student's wrath without a best friend, let alone a larger community, to which to turn, since her overbearing obsessiveness turns Nancy away from her, too.

Perhaps because it was Wasserstein's last play, regional and community theaters around the country regularly mount productions of *Third*, most with varying degrees of success or social relevance. Critics' reviews of these productions tend to find fault with the play and what they see as its contrivances. But their repudiations reveal a gendered response typical of how reviewers wrote about Wasserstein's work throughout her life. Most of the critics sniff at Laurie Jameson as an "unlikable," arrogant character, though one, reviewing the Hangar Theatre production in Ithaca, New York, in 2016, suggested, "What makes Wasserstein's last work so unusual is that her mouthpiece is not always right, and her dramatic arc rises with her comeuppance."[13] Reviewers generally see Third, the wrestler student, as genial and likable, while Laurie's brains and ego make her distasteful ("he's as engaging as she is off putting," said a Seattle critic, continuing, "She's not an understanding mother or a merciful friend, and her husband is smart to keep out of her way").[14] Another reviewer, writing about a 2008 production in San Antonio, Texas, called Laurie's investigation into Third's potential plagiarism a "witch hunt."[15] Reviewing the Philadelphia Theatre Company's production, critic Steve Cohen said, "[Third] is intelligent, sensitive and open-minded but he seems to be from blue-blood Republican stock, and consequently Laurie immediately dislikes him. I like him a lot."[16] In the Hangar Theatre's production, the daughter, Emily, was performed by an African American woman, repeating some of Wasserstein's tropes about race and the similarities and differences among women from An American Daughter. But embodying Emily's third-wave feminism as African American, in distinction to her mother's second-wave feminist stance, also hints at an often-launched critique of white feminism that could render Laurie even more unsympathetic. Critics line up against this intellectual, powerful female character partly because her sense of control and entitlement chafes. Even when, over the course of the play, Laurie comes to better understand her hubris, most critics can neither empathize with nor see Laurie as representative of anything more than a haughty woman.

Other productions of Third over the ten years since it premiered in New York pull other threads from the tapestry of Wasserstein's life and work. Uncommon Women or The Heidi Chronicles haunt most critical engagements with her work. For example, Tim Dunleavy, reviewing the Philadelphia Theatre Company production, said, "Wasserstein's final play, Third, offers an interesting take on the playwright's long-running chronicle of the modern American woman and her place in society."[17] We get it—Wasserstein's work, like her character Heidi's life, is a chronicle. But Dunleavy's assignment of Wasserstein to a narrow slice of the American story separates and constrains her. Would these critics suggest that Arthur Miller or even Neil Simon specifically chronicled modern American men and their place in society? I think not.

In addition, although the trope of "having it all" doesn't appear explicitly in *Third*, many reviewers insist on seeing Laurie Jameson as a descendant of her predecessor, Heidi Holland, another woman professor who worried about this particular cultural condition. (The reviewer of a 2011 production in Germantown, Pennsylvania, said, "Laurie is essentially Heidi about 20 years later.")[18] Although *Third* has little to do with Heidi's struggle to make sense of the complexities of her life, critic Michael Sommers, reviewing a 2014 production at the Two River Theater in Red Bank, New Jersey, for *The New York Times*, called Laurie Jameson "a middle-aged woman who indeed has it all."[19] He also called the play Wasserstein's "study of an 'uncommon' woman at a midlife crossroads," a reference to *Uncommon Women and Others* that practically becomes a tic in reviewers' references to Wasserstein's plays.

Reviewing a 2011 production of *Third* in Durango, Colorado, Judith Reynolds said, "Wasserstein took contemporary women who 'wanted it all,' frustrated them mightily, and then found a way for them to confront reality, adjust and maybe even change."[20] Not exactly high praise for a feminist playwright, to suggest that adapting her characters to social constraints is a neat and positive trick of the trade. And for critics to suggest that Laurie's feminism boils down to the acquisitiveness of liberal feminism, when the professor herself preaches ideas much closer to cultural feminism in how she essentializes gender, misreads Laurie's objectives and simplifies the history of contemporary feminism. To look at Wasserstein's oeuvre as solely about women who want "it all" and cannot get it flattens the complexity of her characters and their ideas. And to consider Laurie as "a menopausal sister of Heidi from 'The Heidi Chronicles,'" as Charles McNulty did in his review of the Geffen production for the *Los Angeles Times*, reduces Wasserstein's thinking about women's fortunes and social engagement to a reflection on the physical cruelties of aging.[21] Laurie Jameson suffers from hot flashes in *Third*, but Wasserstein invites the audience to laugh *with* her at her own discomfort, rather than belittle her for her female body's betrayals.

Bob Verini, in a *Variety* review of the 2007 Geffen Playhouse production, said more generously than most,

> "Third" is by no means a perfect play, thin in places and sometimes too explicit thematically. Laurie doesn't get to defend her views as cogently as she could; Third himself is a bit too good to be true; and the "King Lear" parallels seem forced. . . . But Wasserstein's goal was to bring Laurie Jameson from blind rage to enlightenment, and stacking the deck a bit was a price she didn't mind paying. In sending Laurie out to rethink the last third of her life, Wasserstein must have been cognizant of her own borrowed time, but one likes to think she was even more mindful of the country that, as her body of work proves, she loved deeply. Not uncritically, but in the way of the clear-eyed idealist . . . who hasn't given up on America, already one-third of the way through its third century.[22]

To Verini's credit, he sees Wasserstein on a plane with other (unmarked, male) playwrights and gives her the benefit of enough doubt to see her as a deeply American writer whose love of country propels her feminist critique of idealism and values.

Toward the end of her life, Wasserstein confessed that her plays were becoming less autobiographical and more concerned with the history of her own ideas.[23] *Third* addresses gender as both a site of identification and a scene of struggle over affiliations in the social imagination, positioning Wasserstein as a playwright engaged in public conversations about political and personal issues. The play opens ways of thinking about social concerns that other popular media in the mid-2000s considered differently and less incisively. Wasserstein once told an interviewer, "The theatre is not television. Not as many people will ever see my plays in one night. But what you can do with theatre because it's not a big business initially—even when it is big business it's not big like the other things—you can begin to say things that then sort of filter into the culture. I think that's a good thing."[24]

What feminist critics like myself once saw as Wasserstein's rejection of feminism now seems to me a rather true portrait of the tension between realizing and valuing women's social differences and wanting to be part of something intimately, rightfully, largely human. I admit—with some chagrin—that I identify with Laurie Jameson. After all, I'm a middle-aged, white, female, feminist college professor. I bristle when Wasserstein positions Laurie as an antiexample, as a feminist trapped by her own blind spots who needs to be taught a lesson or two about compassion and political generosity. I resent that spectators are encouraged to deride Laurie's extremes and to applaud her choice to let go of what the play considers her harshest feminist assumptions. But I, too, find myself a "true believer" and very much want to practice my faith and belief in the power of ideas to change social relationships. After many years working to achieve these goals, I appreciate a play that even attempts to study what this kind of political faith might mean and to tally the costs for those of us who continue to believe.

That *Third* was Wendy Wasserstein's last play makes its missteps bittersweet. Reviewing the original Lincoln Center Theater production, Scheck, in the *Post*, said, "While 'Third' lacks the strength of narrative and characterizations that marked 'The Heidi Chronicles' and 'The Sisters Rosensweig,' it again displays Wasserstein's gift for dissecting the emotional and social states of a certain breed of upscale, highly educated women."[25] But he believed "there's a forced quality about the play that undercuts its effectiveness."[26] Likewise, Michael Feingold, writing briefly about the play in *The Village Voice*, said,

> Compassionate by nature and passionate in her desire to speak up for female equality, Wasserstein is nonetheless a satirist by instinct, an artist whose desire to be part of the ruling elite is only equaled by her impulse to ridicule it, and whose most deeply felt social avowals are counterbalanced by an apparently irresistible desire to puncture all deeply felt social avowals with the pearl-headed pin of comedy. At times, Wasserstein has been able to balance her warring impulses; her new play, *Third*, shows that they can also pull her work apart.[27]

John Lahr, in *The New Yorker*, said, "The absence of event is what scuppers Wendy Wasserstein's genial but aimless new play. . . . Wasserstein provides no real drama . . . [her] characters live onstage as illustrations, not as people."[28] If the lack of real dramatic incident in the play meant that it "rolls along like a car in neutral, arriving at its destination without ever picking up momentum," perhaps *Third* captured a more meditative mood.[29] By the end of the writing and staging process, Wasserstein surely knew she was dying, although, as

Salamon details in her biography, the playwright told no one of her critical illness until her health had completely deteriorated. Laurie Jameson signals that the sabbatical she intends to take at the end of the play might be an extended one, and that in fact she might not come back to her now less than fulfilling academic life. Perhaps Wasserstein, too, was saying goodbye to all that and letting Laurie's ruminations on good choices and bad serve as her own farewell.

Conclusion

What remains remarkable about Wendy Wasserstein's career and the enduring popularity of her work is how few playwrights before or since her death attempted a discussion of contemporary feminism—or more generally, the status of women in American society—in the public forum of popular theater. Lily Tomlin chronicled second-wave feminism in *Search for Signs of Intelligent Life in the Universe* (1985), in which Geraldine Ferraro's nomination as the first female vice presidential candidate came as a sound cue to which Tomlin's character listened—and showed the audience how to listen—with fervent, quivering joy. I recall my own goose bumps as a spectator of the production at that moment, in 1985, when history was being made and the theater was used to mark it and to celebrate.[1] That moment was the first in which I can remember an extended discussion of American feminism launched on a Broadway stage.

The Heidi Chronicles, premiering on Broadway in 1989, gained significance from the still-new discussion it, too, proposed about feminism. Other women playwrights who had achieved the Broadway forum eschewed this particular topic, although Beth Henley, in *Crimes of the Heart*, in 1981, and Marsha Norman, in 1983's *'night, Mother*, at least wrote about women. In the years shortly after *Heidi*'s success, Wasserstein's subsequent plays—*The Sisters Rosensweig* and *An American Daughter*—were the only ones written by a woman about women to find a Broadway audience. Theresa Rebeck has subsequently garnered her share of Broadway success, but her work—especially the play *Seminar* (2012), in which a female writing student uses her sexuality to promote her career with her misogynist male professor—sits uneasily in the feminist canon. Gina Gionfriddo's play *Rapture, Blister, Burn* (2013) considers a famous feminist professor who worries about her life choices and arranges generations of women within conversations about the wages of the social movement and the critique it launched. The play was a finalist for the 2013 Pulitzer Prize in Drama. Although it has been produced off Broadway and in regional theaters to positive reviews, it has not received a Broadway production.[2] Danai Gurira's play *Eclipsed*, which addresses the status of African women during a war in Liberia, ran on Broadway for four months beginning in February 2016, starring Lupita Nyong'o and seven other women of color. The production, directed by Liesl Tommy, moved from the Public Theater downtown.[3] In spring 2017, Pulitzer Prize–winning playwright Paula Vogel's play, *Indecent*, will be produced on Broadway, after its successful run at the Vineyard Theatre in downtown New York.[4] For Vogel, whose plays have been produced successfully off Broadway and at regional theaters around the country for thirty years, this Broadway debut is long overdue. But these examples simply underline that Wasserstein's visibility and popularity on Broadway during and after her lifetime continue to make her work singular among women playwrights.

I still find *The Heidi Chronicles* a flawed play, one whose disavowal of feminism when it was first produced damaged perceptions of what was then still a thriving social movement. But Wasserstein's writing changed over time. What many once viewed as her insufferable upper-class white privilege evolved into sharply drawn satire of that stratum's excessive wealth and social acquisitiveness.[5] As critic Christopher Bigsby suggests,

> Beneath the humor, the failed ideologies and even the legitimate crusades, what lies at the heart of her work is the dilemma of the individual, alone even in the company of others, struggling to make sense of a personal life, conscious of passing time, negotiating with the competing demands of those around her and finally making the only commitment which matters, namely to the need to shape her life into a form in which she can take pride.[6]

This fierce individualism is exactly what makes Wasserstein's work so frustrating for critics who would prefer to see feminism as a movement in which women find camaraderie not just in gender identifications or from empathizing through their differences but through rigorous analysis of the structural social foundations of gender and race that result in unequal power and wealth. But at least Wasserstein scrutinizes her characters' choices to ask: How does one do the right thing in the world? How does one make progressive social change happen from within existing political systems? In what sphere can women operate most effectively to influence public opinion? How can women conduct their lives ethically and honorably without being blinkered and hobbled by values that calcify, as *Third* suggests? In her *New Yorker* profile of the playwright on the occasion of *An American Daughter*'s premiere, Nancy Franklin wrote,

> Wasserstein's characters have a lot of questions about identity and self-determinations, questions that women used to ask silently, if at all: What should my life be like? What if I do this? If I do this, can I still have that? What do I want? And do I really want it, or am I just supposed to want it? And if I don't want it, what do I do then?[7]

Wasserstein's plays are commercial, popular theater, but they do advance conversations that matter about women's status and desires, their work and dreams. Her plays might be liberal, but surely they're feminist, too.

Wasserstein's plays are also quite Jewish. While at one point in American theater history it might have been possible to characterize Broadway as a welcoming home for Jewish playwrights, its ethnic identifications have changed over time. These changing demographics also increase the ongoing importance of Wasserstein's work, as her plays are replete with a kind of ethnic humor that now seems more at home on television than it necessarily does on Broadway stages. For example, Jill Soloway's *Transparent*, the series that debuted in 2014 on Amazon Prime and addresses her father's gender transition into womanhood, is rooted in the particularities (and comedy) of being Jewish in Los Angeles. Likewise, the third season of Jenji Kohan's *Orange Is the New Black*, a Netflix series that began streaming in 2013, gets quite a lot of mileage from one African American character's attempts to broker her way into Jewish ethnicity so that she can bump up the quality of her food by requesting kosher meals.[8] The Jewish humor, often spoken by African American characters, peppered throughout the episodes as a result is notably funny. And the character's eventually sincere embrace of Jewish faith was quite moving. But I can't think of a contemporary (woman) playwright who has inherited Wasserstein's mantle as a chronicler of Jewishness or feminism in theater.[9]

Jewishness works in Wasserstein's plays as a kind of in joke. Knowing Yiddish (even a few scattered words, but certainly its inflections) gives a spectator and reader an advantage in parsing her work. And that peculiar brand of New York Jewishness marks her plays even more specifically. The landmarks her characters mention, the fashion trends they observe, the meals they detail, and the restaurants they describe all ring with the deep local knowledge of a life-long Manhattanite. This, too, requires spectators who appreciate the argot of the city and perhaps explains why Wasserstein was a Broadway darling.[10] Always eager to pay it forward, Wasserstein also worked with the Theatre Development Fund to establish a program called Open Doors, which brought disadvantaged New York City public high school students to the theater and matched them with artist-mentors to discuss what they'd seen onstage.

Yet Wasserstein's Jewishness also marked her as an inside-outsider in the socially elite world she and many of her characters inhabit. Her insights into the community of which she both was and wasn't a part were crowned by her novel, *Elements of Style* (2006), a vicious parody of a group of self-serving, social-climbing, Upper East Side, white New Yorkers and their vacuous, sometimes violent, ambitions. The novel, in fact, tonally resembles Wasserstein's plays. Her heroine/alter ego here, Frankie Weissman, is a well-known pediatrician who moves her practice from the center of the elite Upper East Side neighborhood to 102nd Street and Fifth Avenue, smack in the middle of Spanish Harlem, so that she can better serve the poor kids she sees as patients pro bono. The Upper East Side mothers who frequent her practice with their children fret about the move. In one priceless scene, Judy Tremont, the worst of the self-absorbed bunch, storms into Frankie's office demanding that her children be seen before they get cholera from the children of color sitting in the waiting room. To Weissman's (and Wasserstein's) credit, she throws Tremont out on her ear, and Wasserstein makes sure Tremont gets her full comeuppance later when she is accidentally killed on a ski slope by the very socially superior woman she's worked hard through the whole novel to befriend.

As in her plays, in *Elements of Style* Wasserstein revels in her deep knowledge of the foibles of the rich and the restless in New

York. The novel is peppered with fashion and product brand names that only the cognoscenti would know, and she uses the names to signal the shallowness of characters who are defined solely by what they buy and consume. The women in the novel are the worst offenders; their husbands open their checkbooks, but Wasserstein ruthlessly satirizes female social and amorous ambitions, as what passes for friendship among Judy Tremont's crowd is mostly counting social points for proximity to the famous and the powerful. Written in the early 2000s, after 9/11 rocked Manhattan and the world, Wasserstein's novel was one of the first to attempt a comedy of manners that engaged that cataclysmic event. She describes how the monied classes use the tragedy as an excuse for their indulgence, and the descriptions illustrate how their wealth sequesters them from real feelings, whether of fear, guilt, or melancholy. With their private planes at hand, they can easily get off the island, as many of them do when, in Wasserstein's fictionalized narrative, New York's first suicide bombing happens at a Starbucks across from Lincoln Center.

That Wasserstein would place this imaginary terrorist act in the neighborhood of the high-culture emporium that brought her so much visibility and success illustrates her self-critical abilities. The suicide bombing kills a character named Jil Taillou, the in crowd's favorite Sotheby auctioneer, who has told his admirers and hangers-on that he's a Hungarian refugee. Taillou's death reveals him as a closeted gay man with a perfectly normal, if secret, relationship with a successful young male architect. Wasserstein also unmasks the powerful auctioneer as Julius Tattenbaum of Brooklyn, New York. Jil was scamming his league of women followers as deftly as they cheat one another, but he managed to preserve a modicum of a decent life for himself beyond the clutches of the women's aggressive acquisitiveness.

With Heidi's scene with Peter in *The Heidi Chronicles* reverberating, Frankie visits her hospital's neonatal intensive care unit on Christmas day and has a pleasant exchange with a male nurse, just as Heidi visits Peter to donate her effects to his children's HIV/AIDS ward, intending to leave New York for the Midwest. Wasserstein always placed her characters close to medicine, whether she fashioned them as doctors, like Peter in *Heidi* or Lyssa Hughes Dent and her friend Judith in *An American Daughter*; as patients (Judith again, Sara in *The Sisters Rosensweig*, and Laurie Jameson's friend Nancy in

Third); or as women whose ambitions were meant to be linked to a physician's, as a wife or as a doctor herself (Janie Blumberg in *Isn't It Romantic*). Cancer, in fact, and more broadly, mortality, thread through much of Wasserstein's work, a harbinger of her own eventual death from lymphoma.

Although Wasserstein was criticized for writing only from the perspective of whiteness and wealth, *Elements of Style*, like many of her plays, demonstrates her acuity about racial difference. The novel includes a sharply satirical scene at a benefit for an independent film, held in Bedford-Stuyvesant (then a predominantly African American neighborhood in Brooklyn), to which all the white people come dressed in "ghetto." Judy Tremont and her husband attend as Ike and Tina Turner. Wasserstein reports, "The African American movie stars, on the other hand, were mostly in understated strappy gowns and fitted Armani suits" (146). Frankie's erstwhile boyfriend, Charlie, leaves the party on foot and congratulates himself for getting on the subway and making it all the way home without getting mugged. When he gets off the train in his own neighborhood, however, a white man wearing a "hooded Harvard crew sweatshirt" robs him (156).[11] Point made.

Elements of Style's tone switches abruptly from satire to earnestness at the novel's end, a shift that makes it difficult for a reader to know exactly what she's supposed to think. But the tonal ambivalence reminds me of Wasserstein's plays, too, with their moments of melancholy in the midst of their comedy and Wasserstein's persistence in posing hard questions while romping through funny plot points and witty repartee. The knife's edge between lightness and dark always rent Wasserstein's work, and while her fans preferred to call her funny, and the playwright herself hid her sober side behind a calculated façade of wit, self-deprecation, and good cheer, the poignancy of emotional terror always lurked around the corners of her plays.

A look back from what was perhaps her last writing in *Elements of Style* to her very first play ends my consideration of Wasserstein's career. Her first play, *Any Woman Can't*, which Wasserstein used for her application to Yale School of Drama, was never published. But the one-act has all the earmarks of what would become Wasserstein's comic style and presages most of her thematic concerns.[12] The comedy is dark and more absurdist than what became her trademark realism. The play's unsettling cynicism, its sober social critique, and its vaguely expressionist/absurdist trappings echo those of Israel Horovitz, the playwright with whom Wasserstein studied for her MA at City College. Horovitz won an Obie for his 1968 play *The Indian Wants the Bronx*, which explored a violent interaction of strangers over ethnic difference. Horovitz's style was influenced by Beckett, whom he knew personally. Wasserstein's first play clearly derived from this pedigree.

The play's narrative, however, sits squarely within the gendered commentary with which Wasserstein made her mark on theater and American culture. In the play, a young woman named Christina (called Chris, but not yet "Christ," as Janie Blumberg's mother calls her gentile sister-in-law in *Isn't It Romantic*) has recently graduated from Smith and has moved to New York City hoping to make her way in the world. In the opening scene, a group of anonymous men and boys infiltrate the theater from the aisles and the wings, catcalling to the women in the audience with obscene sexual suggestions. When Chris enters, they encircle her, bombarding her with their solicitations and unwanted attention. She barely escapes, segueing into a scene that seems a non sequitur but that ramps up the character's anxiety and inability to navigate an overwhelming world.

Chris attempts to be an instructor for a free, Arthur Murray–style dance class, although she knows very little about how to teach or move. (She nervously reads the students their instructions from a sheet of paper.) In this scene, too, gender complications prevail. Irv, one of her students, can't keep his hands to himself and shows her his moves in ways that have little to do with the social dance steps she's supposed to teach. The two couples (and one older woman) who compose her class are dismal specimens of heterosexual relationships. George and Hilda are married, but they detest one another and have appeared for the class only because each has been separately paid off by Hilda's mother. Irv's class partner, Natalie, desperately courts Irv's attention, until Hilda recognizes him as a man who frequents all the local dance classes and flirts with all the women. Natalie, it seems, thought she was special. Even in Wasserstein's very early theatrical universe, no woman is special enough.

In fact, Wasserstein's sharpest argument in *Any Woman Can't* seems to be that in a world where men prevail, women are extraordinary only if they distinguish themselves by their looks and their ability to service their men's needs. Chris's obnoxious, Princeton-graduate boyfriend, Charles (a version of which would morph into Charlie in *Elements of Style*), debates repeatedly whether he should get a business degree at Harvard or a law degree at Columbia or, he muses, perhaps both. The narcissistic man is completely oblivious to Chris's increasing panic over her own situation. Every time she goes out on the city's streets, Chris is accosted by anonymous men and boys, who catcall and whistle at her and reduce her to her body, calling her "Pink Pussy" and "cold cunt" and taunting her with their requests for explicit sexual favors.

Even Chris's brother, Markey (an overweight, controlling, but professionally successful bastard of a man), abuses his wife, whom he calls "Princess" while he yells at her and orders her around. Likewise, Charles flatters Chris and thinks telling her she is beautiful will mollify her; he can't understand her desire to be or do more. For a moment, Chris seems strong enough to try to leave Charles and live on her own, but the symbolically predatory men on the street finally terrify her into submission. The play ends with Chris baby-talking to Charles, asking for his protection as he absentmindedly uses her for sex and continues to contemplate his own professional choices.

The short play moves quickly from scene to scene, propelled by Chris's frantic desire to find a place for herself in an inhospitable world. Despite her intelligence, her gender forecloses Chris's options and reduces her to her body and her appearance. The characters in *Any Woman Can't* are mouthpieces for a worldview that is very much feminist in its analysis of gendered constraints and that sets out what would become Wasserstein's signature themes. Charles calls Chris "Teeny," a diminutive of the sort that most of Wasserstein's future male boyfriend or husband characters will use to subtly demean their smart, accomplished female partners (for example, Scoop in *Heidi*, Marty and Paul in *Isn't It Romantic*, and Walter in *An American Daughter*). Markey seems a thinly veiled, viciously satirical representation of Wasserstein's brother, Bruce, as the playwright began to mine the autobiographical vein she taps throughout her plays. (Chris's father invented velveteen, always a mark of Wasserstein's autobiographical beginnings.)

Chris's plaint about how to manage her life echoes Rita's in *Uncommon Women*, Janie Blumberg's in *Isn't It Romantic*, and Heidi's in the *Chronicles*. Chris says, "I'm busy biding time until something happens to me . . . and nothing happens" (20). She tells her unsympathetic brother, "But there must be something else I can do than be a lawyer or get married. I really did think I would be different" (27). And Charles impatiently tells her to buckle down and accept her constrained destiny: "Come on, Teeny, be a good girl. Ok, you're an uncommon woman. You're very talented. I just don't understand how everyone else works it out but you" (31). Indeed, Wasserstein fleshed out Chris's uncommon womanhood in the play that would become her Yale thesis project five years later.

As much as *Any Woman Can't* reveals the seeds of Wasserstein's discontent, the early play is less funny and much angrier and pointedly critical than anything she would go on to write. Chris's antiheroes here are Nancy and Pat, two women pushing baby carriages in parallel in a local park where she goes to meet Charles. They also represent some of Wasserstein's future stock characters, as women who capitulate to convention, see the world through jaded, sharply calculating eyes, and represent the antithesis of who Chris imagines she'll become. The two women banter in brand names, recognizing one another's handbags, for example, as Louis Vuitton. They compare orgasms and agree that clitoral is better, gesturing to the nascent 1970s feminism that infused the air around Wasserstein then, even while the characters seem to have compromised their sexual and other desires. Nancy and Pat recognize Charles, when he appears, as a Princeton man; they know the type. And none of the characters in the park scene realize that a man lying on a bench under a newspaper is actually dead. When his body is revealed, not one of these self-absorbed elite types cares much, either. The choice is perhaps heavy-handed, but because the play generally observes the rules of absurdism, the moment underlines these characters' lack of compassion.

Just as Heidi would in Wasserstein's play nearly twenty years later, Chris feels both lacking and superior at once. In a voice tape her brother, Mark, gives her to try to bolster her confidence, he says,

> Christina, this is your brother Markey and I want you to know how beautiful and intelligent you are. You are lovely, Christina, lovely, lovely, lovely. Don't be afraid. There are not so many strangers and people if you only concentrate on how important you are. You are my sister. Don't be afraid, I am always here with you and I know how very lovely and intelligent you are. And now, Christina, I want you to

breathe a sigh of relief as if all your anxietys [sic] and fears are gone. You can function happily, and beautifully, since inside you know that you are better than those around you and I am always here to help you. You are lovely, love, love . . . (46)

Like Chris, and so many of her struggling female characters, Wasserstein received similar mixed messages throughout her life. She was whip smart and exceptional, born to be superior, a master of the universe. But her gender, her appearance, and her basic ambivalence about what she really wanted from her life compromised her worldview and her choices.

David Savran, in a substantive 1997 interview with Wasserstein just before *An American Daughter* premiered on Broadway, asked, "At this point, as we all know, the American theatre is in pretty bad shape. Do you think theatre will survive?" To which Wasserstein replied,

> It really worries me. There will always be panels asking: "Is Broadway Dying?" And as long as there's a panel, there'll always be these "Women in Theatre" panels. Paula [Vogel] and I will grow old together. I'll see this woman once every two or three years on these "women" panels. As long as it happens, you know there's theatre, and you know there are women in theatre, and that's all fine.[13]

Would that Wasserstein were still here, growing old in the theater. She kept her final illness secret for as long as possible; even her closest friends didn't know how sick she'd become before she fell into a coma and eventually died. But hints of her choice are embedded in *Third*. When Laurie calls her friend Nancy's oncologist without permission, Nancy is furious. Laurie objects, "Nancy, you need somebody with a clear head to sort this out for you," but Nancy retorts, "Laurie, I'm sick and I deserve the privilege of my privacy!"[14]

Wondering how Wasserstein's work might have changed had she had more time to work as a playwright, her cherished friend Christopher Durang remarked that her last play, unlike many of her earlier ones, was entirely "made up; she didn't base it on anything. She wrote a very good character that came out of her head, [while] her early plays were things she had experienced or witnessed. . . . So I wonder if she would have done more of that . . . if she would have told more stories that were more fiction or triggered by events in society."[15] Even in

Third, Wasserstein wonders, through her characters, what a person does with a chance at a "next act." When Nancy finds out her cancer is in remission, she tells Laurie, "When my doctor told me he thought things were turning around, I made a resolution. If I'm getting a chance to actually live the third part of my life, I have to try to do it differently. Besides, personally it was too much work hating everything." Laurie responds, "But it makes absolutely no sense in the third part of your life to suddenly start liking everything."[16] Laurie fights to adopt a new ethic, struggling out of the rhetoric that guided her for so long. But the notion of a third act to one's life resonates. Although the play appears to be named after the character whose actions compel Laurie toward her own growth, Wasserstein also might have meant it as a hopeful gesture toward the new understandings and resolutions that come with a play's (and a life's) third act. Sadly, the playwright herself didn't get a chance to find out.

And yet Wasserstein's work always rings with a certain, persistent hope. In her conversation with Savran, the playwright admitted that she found "hope in community," and when he pointed out that "music functions in your plays to keep alive that hopefulness, because it seems so utopian," Wasserstein agreed: "I actually think [music] works to keep me alive. . . . Frankly, when I'm working I listen to music a lot because it wakes me up again. I also think that through the music you very much get a sense of time."[17] The musical interludes that punctuate Wasserstein's plays—especially her more episodic works, like *The Heidi Chronicles*—evoke sentimentality but also vivid, often embodied memories for spectators of a certain age. Her work, as Tamsen Wolff suggests in her elegiac assessment, "manages to present a nearly anachronistic example of how to reject cynicism, remain hopeful, and yet retain a witty ironic edge."[18]

For many critics, the jury remained out on Wasserstein throughout her career. She was funny but "indulgent," and when her "hilarity threatens to become gag-writing, she blunts it with compassion."[19] Another wrote, "No matter how sober her intent, Wasserstein the philosopher is continually undone by Wasserstein the gagmeister."[20] Scholar Stephen Whitfield suggested, "What is missing in Wasserstein's work, and keeps it too close to merely clever entertainment, is menace—the spooky, subterranean impulses that threaten to tear apart the skein of everyday existence." He added, "Sophisticated audiences need to ruminate over more than lively repartee."[21]

Kevin Kelly, the *Boston Globe* critic who never liked Wasserstein's plays and whose reviews of her work were typically disparaging, wrote upon seeing *The Sisters Rosensweig*, "Wasserstein refuses to probe. She eludes sadness, disappointment, disillusion as though they're to be avoided rather than dramatized. She chooses to laugh in the dark rather than light the way."[22]

And her former Yale professor, Robert Brustein, who saved his approval of Wasserstein's work for just before she died, said of *Sisters Rosensweig* and his pupil's work in general, "I had hoped, after *The Heidi Chronicles*, that my very gifted former student was shaking her witticism habit. *The Sisters Rosensweig* has a lot of charm, but it is a regression. I guess it's hard, in the precarious circus of American theater, to give up your trapeze. But, oh, Wendy Wasserstein, after you've picked up all your awards, won't you throw away your safety net?"[23]

Ironically, feminist critics weren't more generous to Wasserstein (myself included) than the mainstream newspapers' mostly white male brigade. As she noted herself in numerous essays and interviews, her popularity and visibility made her prey to the outsized expectations of those who had never before had an opportunity to see themselves onstage so publicly. Wasserstein could never meet such a high bar. When *The Heidi Chronicles* garnered such popular success, many feminists (in the theater field and outside) claimed that it distorted the movement's aims and its success in setting the terms of equality for women. Feminist critics expressed outrage at Wasserstein's nerve and pointed out how partial was her telling of a history that included many more than the white, upper-middle-class, college-educated characters the play embraced. Critics reviled her for placing disappointment with feminism at the center of Heidi's self-indulgent malaise and were infuriated by what they saw as Wasserstein's willingness to privilege gay men's fight against the HIV/AIDS pandemic over women's bid for equality and social justice. Many found the play's ending—and what seemed Wasserstein's facile solution to Heidi's problems in (easily, magically) adopting a baby from Panama—utterly distasteful and condescending to those for whom single-parent adoption was neither an economic possibility nor a feasible option for new kinship structures.[24]

The profoundly gendered nature of her critical reception, however, followed Wasserstein throughout her career. She told Savran that when people asked her what she thought of the critics, she said, "If it's one guy or another guy, one guy will like it, the other won't. It would be very nice if there were women doing that particular job in the theatre [that is, criticism]—that would be delightful."[25] Nancy Franklin, whose profile of Wasserstein remains one of the best ever, said, "While a sense of humor in a man is universally regarded as a good thing, a sense of humor in a woman is often thought of as a handicap—an unnatural growth that obscures rather than reveals her femininity. It often leads to popularity, but only rarely does it lead to intimacy."[26] But as Wasserstein herself no doubt would have said, who expected intimacy from Neil Simon? Or George S. Kaufman or Arthur Miller, for that matter? The gendered presumptions about women playwrights hounded Wasserstein and continue to hold women theater artists hostage.

In 1997 Wasserstein wrote only obliquely about Hillary Clinton's situation as a powerful woman with political aspirations. I can only wonder what the playwright would have made of her run for the 2016 presidential nomination and what new indignations Wasserstein would have observed being brought to the private costs of women in public life. During the first backlash against Hillary Clinton, as her husband rose to political power, Wasserstein parsed the moment, taking spectators behind the scenes into the private lives of female public figures, using thinly veiled fictions to suggest the humanity of those the press denounced. We need Wasserstein's righteous outrage still. While during her life I might have wanted to hear her unleash a more pointed and philosophical critique, in the decade or so since her death I feel the loss of the gentler criticisms her plays did provide. Wasserstein knew the score. That she couched her own view of women's lives—with all their costs and benefits, even for those of her characters who could metaphorically afford accountants to help them plan—in popular comic forms kept her from being taken seriously enough. From this vantage point, the comedy remains funny, and sometimes wistful; the insights seem more poignant and true; and the loss of Wasserstein's voice and presence as a remarkable woman in theater that much more difficult to bear.

Wendy Wasserstein: A Timeline

- October 18, 1950, Wendy Wasserstein is born in Brooklyn, New York, to Polish immigrant parents, Morris W. Wasserstein (a textile manufacturer) and Lola (a dancer). Wasserstein is the youngest of five siblings (Sandra Meyer, Abner, Georgette Levis, and Bruce).
- 1962, Wasserstein's family moves to Manhattan's Upper East Side; Wasserstein regularly attends Broadway matinees.
- 1963–67, Wasserstein attends the Calhoun School in New York.
- 1967–71, Wasserstein attends Mount Holyoke College; she graduates with a bachelor of arts in history.
- 1973, Wasserstein receives an MA in creative writing from City College of the City University of New York; she studied with playwright Israel Horovitz and novelist Joseph Heller.
- 1973, Wasserstein's first professional drama, *Any Woman Can't*, is produced by Playwrights Horizons.
- 1973, Wasserstein is accepted to the Yale School of Drama.
- 1975, *Uncommon Women and Others* is produced as her thesis production at Yale.
- 1976, Wasserstein earns a Master of Fine Arts from Yale School of Drama.
- November 21, 1977, *Uncommon Women and Others* premieres off Broadway at the Phoenix Theatre (Marymount Manhattan Stage).
- 1978, *Uncommon Women and Others* receives national attention as part of the Public Broadcasting Service's televised series *Theatre in America*, presented by PBS *Great Performances*.

- May 28, 1981, *Isn't It Romantic* premieres at Phoenix Theatre (Marymount Manhattan Stage).
- 1983, *Tender Offer* is produced as part of the Ensemble Studio Theatre's Marathon of One-Act Plays in New York.
- 1983, Wasserstein is awarded the John Simon Guggenheim Memorial Foundation Fellowship.
- 1983, Wasserstein is awarded a National Endowment for the Arts Fellowship.
- December 15, 1983, a revised version of *Isn't It Romantic* opens at Playwrights Horizons.
- 1985, Wasserstein is awarded the Mary Lyon Award from Mount Holyoke College.
- 1986, *Miami* is produced at Playwrights Horizons in New York; Wasserstein wrote the libretto for this musical comedy.
- April 6, 1988, *The Heidi Chronicles* premieres at Seattle Repertory Theatre.
- December 11, 1988, *The Heidi Chronicles* moves to Playwrights Horizons.
- 1988, Wasserstein wins the Hull-Warriner Award from the Dramatists Guild of America for *The Heidi Chronicles*.
- 1988–89, Wasserstein wins the Susan Smith Blackburn Prize for *The Heidi Chronicles*.
- March 9, 1989, *The Heidi Chronicles* opens on Broadway at the Plymouth Theatre.
- 1989, Wasserstein wins the Pulitzer Prize for Drama, the Tony Award for Best Play (she was the first woman to receive this award), the New York Drama Critics' Circle Award for Best Play, the Outer Critics Circle Award for Best Broadway Play, and the Drama Desk Award for Outstanding Play for *The Heidi Chronicles*.
- 1990, she receives a doctor of humane letters from Mount Holyoke College.
- 1990, Wasserstein publishes her essay collection, *Bachelor Girls*.
- October 22, 1992, *The Sisters Rosensweig* opens at the Mitzi E. Newhouse Theater at Lincoln Center.
- March 18, 1993, *The Sisters Rosensweig* opens on Broadway at the Ethel Barrymore Theatre.

- 1993, Wasserstein wins the Outer Critics Circle Award for Best Broadway Play for *The Sisters Rosensweig*.
- 1993, Wasserstein receives the William Inge Theatre Festival Distinguished Achievement in the American Theatre Award.
- 1996, Wasserstein publishes a children's book, *Pamela's First Musical*.
- April 13, 1997, *An American Daughter* opens on Broadway at the Cort Theatre.
- September 12, 1999, Wasserstein gives birth to her daughter, Lucy Jane Wasserstein.
- 2001, Wasserstein publishes her essay collection, *Shiksa Goddess (or, How I Spent My Forties)*.
- October 24, 2005, *Third* opens at the Mitzi E. Newhouse Theater at Lincoln Center.
- January 30, 2006, Wendy Wasserstein dies of lymphoma at the age of fifty-five.
- April 2006, her novel *Elements of Style* is published posthumously by Alfred A. Knopf.

Notes

Chapter 1

1. For full details of Wasserstein's life story, see Julie Salamon's authorized biography, *Wendy and the Lost Boys: The Uncommon Life of Wendy Wasserstein* (New York: Penguin Press, 2011).

2. For a discussion of how history becomes content in Wasserstein's work, see Charlotte Canning, "Feminists Perform Their Past: Constructing History in *The Heidi Chronicles* and *The Break of Day*," in *Women, Theatre and Performance: New Histories, New Historiographies*, ed. Maggie B. Gale and Vivien Gardner (New York: Palgrave, 2000), 163–79.

3. Laurin Porter, "Contemporary Playwrights/Traditional Forms," in *The Cambridge Companion to American Women Playwrights*, ed. Brenda Murphy (Cambridge: Cambridge University Press, 1999), 211.

4. In summer 2015, for example, the Manhattan Theatre Club was forced to change its 2015–16 season after an outcry on social media following its announcement of an entire season of works by white male playwrights. See "Internet Outcry over Diversity Leads Manhattan Theater Club to Announce Season Details Early," *New York Times*, http://www.nytimes.com/2015/08/22/theater/after-outcry-over-diversity-manhattan-theater-club-is-making-a-change.html

5. See *Report on the Status of Women: A Limited Engagement?* prepared for the New York State Council on the Arts Theatre Program by Susan Jonas and Suzanne Bennett, January 2002, http://www.womenarts.org/advocacy/WomenCountNYSCAReport.htm

6. See Patricia Cohen, "Rethinking Gender Bias in Theater," *New York Times*, June 23, 2009, http://www.nytimes.com/2009/06/24/theater/24play.html?_r=0, which describes the initial presentation of Sands's report in some detail.

7. See Sumru Erkut and Ineke Ceder, "Women's Leadership in Resident Theatres: Summary of Results and Recommendations," draft report, com-

missioned by Carey Perloff and Ellen Richard, American Conservatory Theater, produced by Wellesley Center for Women, Wellesley College, August 22, 2016, http://howlround.com/women-s-leadership-research-results-and-recommendations?#_=_

8. See www.5050in2020.org; the organization is now defunct.

9. Olivia Clement, "Jessie Mueller, Lupita Nyong'o and Danai Gurira Step Out for the Lilly Awards Tonight," *Playbill*, May 23, 2016, http://www.playbill.com/article/jessie-mueller-lupita-nyong-39-0-and-danai-gurira-step-out-for-the-lilly-39-s-tonight, describes the 2016 event.

10. See www.thekilroys.org. The "about" page of the website notes, "The Kilroys are a gang of playwrights and producers in LA who are done talking about gender parity and are taking action. We mobilize others in our field and leverage our own power to support one another. . . . We are Zakiyyah Alexander, Bekah Brunstetter, Sheila Callaghan, Carla Ching, Annah Feinberg, Sarah Gubbins, Laura Jacqmin, Joy Meads, Kelly Miller, Meg Miroshnik, Daria Polatin, Tanya Saracho, and Marisa Wegrzyn."

11. See http://www.athe.org/group/WTP for information about the Women and Theatre Program and its Jane Chambers Playwriting Award and www.theatrewomen.org for information about the League of Professional Theatre Women.

12. Esther Cohen, "Uncommon Woman: An Interview with Wendy Wasserstein," *Women's Studies* 15 (1988): 265.

13. Ibid., 263, 264.

14. Carrie Richman, phone interview, August 5, 2013.

15. Salamon, *Wendy and the Lost Boys*, 239.

16. Ibid., 60.

17. Nancy Franklin, "The Time of Her Life," *New Yorker*, April 14, 1997, 64.

18. Salamon, *Wendy and the Lost Boys*, 107.

19. Ibid., 297.

20. I discuss *Any Woman Can't* fully in the conclusion.

21. Wendy Wasserstein, *The Heidi Chronicles*, in *The Heidi Chronicles and Other Plays* (San Diego: Harcourt Brace Jovanovich, 1990), 165.

22. Quoted in Laurie Winer, "Julie Salamon's 'Wendy and the Lost Boys' Is a Biography of Playwright Wendy Wasserstein," *Washington Post*, September 1, 2011.

23. Quoted in Carolyn Casey Craig, "Wendy Wasserstein: Lola's Well-Rounded Daughter," in *Women Pulitzer Playwrights: Biographical Profiles and Analyses of the Plays* (Jefferson, NC: McFarland, 2004), 189.

24. See, for example, Angelika Czekay, "'Not Having It All': Wendy Wasserstein's Uncommon Women," in *The Playwright's Muse*, ed. Joan Herrington (New York: Routledge, 2002), 18; and Gail Ciociola, *Wendy Wasserstein: Dramatizing Women, Their Choices and Their Boundaries* (Jefferson, NC: McFarland, 1998).

25. Franklin, "The Time of Her Life," 63.

26. Christopher Bigsby calls the play's infamous "I thought we were all in this together" speech a "brilliantly free-form aria, which offers an account of lives that have become lifestyles, as if all that had been needed was to redecorate the room of one's own"; see Bigsby, "Wendy Wasserstein," in *Contemporary American Playwrights* (Cambridge: Cambridge University Press, 1999), 352.

27. Qtd. in ibid., 367. Bigsby takes a similar view of *Uncommon Women and Others*, suggesting that the "real feminism [of the play] lies not in the lives of the characters but the fact of the play" (338). Wasserstein's work and career might also be compared to those of playwright Mary Chase, whose popular play *Harvey* ran on Broadway for 1,775 performances in 1945–49 and won the Pulitzer Prize in Drama in 1945. Thanks to my colleague, Judith Hamera, for pointing out this connection.

28. In 2015 Lisa Kron won the Tony Award for Best Book in a Musical, and she and Jeanine Tesori won the Tony for Best Lyrics and Music, for *Fun Home*, a musical adaptation of graphic artist Alison Bechdel's memoir. Whether or not their awards create a trend for women theater artists on Broadway remains to be seen.

29. Quoted in Bigsby, "Wendy Wasserstein," 334.

30. David Savran, "Wendy Wasserstein," in *The Playwright's Voice: American Dramatists on Memory, Writing, and the Politics of Culture*, edited by David Savran (New York: Theatre Communications Group, 1999), 301. "Gorgeous" was Wasserstein's sister Georgette's nickname, as well as the name of the comfortably wealthy, suburban matron character in *The Sisters Rosensweig*.

31. Ibid., 299. Savran notes in another context: "The small audience that attends professional theatre today, whether commercial or more experimental venues, is overwhelmingly middle or upper-middle class and decidedly liberal in its social attitudes. It also must be relatively affluent, insofar as live theatre is far more expensive than movies or cable TV." See *A Queer Sort of Materialism: Recontextualizing American Theater* (Ann Arbor: University of Michigan Press, 2003), 62.

32. Tamsen Wolff, in her consideration of Wasserstein upon her death, says, "Most of her plays are social comedies, distant cousins to the work of Philip Barry, S.N. Behrman, George S. Kaufman, and Edna Ferber, among others." "The Chronicle Review: Wendy Wasserstein (1950–2006)," *Chronicle of Higher Education* 52.24 (February 17, 2006): B13.

33. Jan Balakian, "'The Heidi Chronicles': The Big Chill of Feminism," *South Atlantic Review* 60.2 (May 1995): 99. See also her *Reading the Plays of Wendy Wasserstein* (New York: Applause Theatre & Cinema Books, 2010).

34. Franklin, "The Time of Her Life," 70.

35. Canning, "Feminists Perform Their Past," 164.

36. Charles Isherwood, "Wendy Wasserstein, Chronicler of Women's

Identity Crises, Dies," *New York Times*, January 30, 2006, www.nytimes.com/2006/01/30/theater/30cnd-wasserstein.html

37. See the *New York Times* review of the original show at http://www.nytimes.com/1984/02/03/arts/stage-whoopi-goldberg-does-the-spook-show.html, and the *Times* review of the Broadway production at http://www.nytimes.com/1984/10/25/theater/stage-whoopi-goldberg-opens.html

38. For one version of this critique, see my *The Feminist Spectator as Critic* (Ann Arbor: University of Michigan Press, 1991), especially chapter 2.

39. Savran, "Wendy Wasserstein," 298.

40. Wendy Wasserstein, *Uncommon Women and Others*, in *The Heidi Chronicles and Other Plays* (San Diego: Harcourt Brace Jovanovich, 1990), 20, 34. Subsequent references will appear parenthetically in the text.

41. Wendy Wasserstein, *The Heidi Chronicles*, in ibid., 201.

42. Wendy Wasserstein, *Third, American Theatre Magazine*, April 2006, 69–87.

43. Robert Vorlicky, "[In]Visible Alliances: Conflicting 'Chronicles' of Feminism," in Joseph A. Boone and Michael Cadden, eds., *Engendering Men: The Question of Male Feminist Criticism* (New York: Routledge, 1990), 286.

44. Gayle Austin, Review of *The Heidi Chronicles*, by Wendy Wasserstein, *Theatre Journal* 42. 1 (1990): 108.

45. On the other hand, as my colleague Tamsen Wolff notes, in 1989 the common cultural associations with single mothers were that they were on welfare or somehow lacking in their social or emotional lives.

46. See Kobena Mercer, "Black Art and the Burden of Representation," in *Welcome to the Jungle: New Positions in Black Cultural Studies* (New York: Routledge, 1994), 233–258.

47. Quoted in Savran, "Wendy Wasserstein," 303. Wasserstein said, "I remember the year *Sisters Rosensweig* was on Broadway, so was Tony Kushner's play, and so was Anna Deavere Smith. I thought, 'Three years ago, nobody would have said any of these people are Broadway writers.' They would have said to Tony, 'What, a gay fantasia?' Or this black woman doing something that's like performance art. Or this play about a fifty-four-year-old woman who falls in love?" Qtd. in ibid., 308. Wasserstein's own incredulity bears witness to the persistent novelty of anyone who's not white or male or heterosexual or all of the above succeeding on Broadway.

Chapter 2

1. Wendy Wasserstein, *Uncommon Women and Others*, in *The Heidi Chronicles and Other Plays* (San Diego: Harcourt Brace Jovanovich, 1990), 4. Subsequent references will appear parenthetically in the text.

2. In response to an essay I wrote about Wasserstein in *Theatre Journal*, my colleague Megan Shea sent me a long letter detailing her experiences di-

recting *Uncommon Women and Others* when she was a graduate student at Cornell in 2007, shortly after Wasserstein's death. The letter was full of useful and important insights, not the least of which was that the actors in her production were shocked by their characters' level of sexual experience and sophistication. Although the cast did indeed do quite a lot of research about the 1970s to set the stage for their explorations of the play and its characters, it was the change in sexual mores that seemed to strike them the most. Their surprise at how much more progressive their characters' world seemed than the actors' present circumstances in the mid-2000s got the most attention from the cast and provided, according to Shea, many opportunities for the cast to share sexual knowledge and information. I much appreciate Shea's generosity in sharing her experiences with me. Correspondence via email, April 1, 2008.

3. *Holiday* was an American travel magazine printed between 1946 and 1977. According to its website, "*Holiday* was one of the most exciting magazines in the United States. Reknowned [*sic*] for its fun layout, its challenging choice of photographers, and the aura of its writers, *Holiday* was telling about the world like no other magazine. Its strength? Sending a writer and a photographer to a singular destination, distant or nearby, and asking them to tell from their point of view without constraints of style, objectiveness or length. Nor budgetary limit. At the top of its game, the magazine had more than a million subscribers." http://www.holiday-magazine.com/magazine. php. The *New York Times* calls it "the great midcentury travel magazine"; http://www.nytimes.com/2014/03/27/fashion/holiday-a-travel-magazine-is-reborn.html

4. See Anne Koedt, *The Myth of the Vaginal Orgasm* (Somerville, MA: New England Free Press, 1970).

5. Adrienne Rich, "Compulsory Heterosexuality and Lesbian Existence (1980)," in *Blood, Bread, and Poetry: Selected Prose 1979–1985* (repr., New York: W.W. Norton, 1994), 23–75.

6. Gail Ciociola, *Wendy Wasserstein: Dramatizing Women, Their Choices and Their Boundaries* (Jefferson, NC: McFarland, 1998), 18.

7. See Elin Diamond, "Brechtian Theory/Feminist Theory: Toward a Gestic Feminist Criticism," *TDR* 32.1 (Spring 1988): 82–94, an argument recapitulated and extended in her book *Unmaking Mimesis: Essays on Feminism and Theatre* (New York: Routledge, 1997).

8. Lyrics from the song "Get an Ugly Girl to Marry You," by Harry Belafonte.

9. Harold Clurman, review of *Uncommon Women and Others*, by Wendy Wasserstein, directed by Steven Robman, Phoenix Theatre, New York, *Nation*, December 17, 1977.

10. Edmund Newton, "'Women' One Can't Forget," review of *Uncommon Women and Others*, by Wendy Wasserstein, directed by Steven Robman, Phoenix Theatre, New York, *New York Post*, November 22, 1977.

11. John Beaufort, "A Wry Reunion," review of *Uncommon Women and Others*, by Wendy Wasserstein, directed by Steven Robman, Phoenix Theatre, New York, *Christian Science Monitor*, November 30, 1977.

12. Richard Eder, "Dramatic Wit and Wisdom Unite in *Uncommon Women and Others*," review of *Uncommon Women and Others*, by Wendy Wasserstein, directed by Steven Robman, Phoenix Theatre, New York, *New York Times*, November 22, 1977.

13. Douglas Watt, "Holyoke Hen Sessions," review of *Uncommon Women and Others*, by Wendy Wasserstein, directed by Steven Robman, Phoenix Theatre, New York, *New York Daily News*, November 22, 1977.

Chapter 3

1. Cuervo says in an interview that her family is "Spanish." Beth Herstein, "Interview with Alma Cuervo, *Road Show*," Talkin' Broadway, http://www.talkinbroadway.com/rialto/past/2008/111808.html

2. Wendy Wasserstein, *Isn't It Romantic*, in *The Heidi Chronicles and Other Plays* (San Diego: Harcourt Brace Jovanovich, 1990), 88. Subsequent references will appear parenthetically in the text.

3. As Jennifer Szalai reports in her 2015 *New York Times* essay "The Complicated Origins of 'Having It All,'" Gurley Brown bent to her editors' will but said, "'Having it all' sounds so [expletive] cliché to me." January 2, 2015, http://www.nytimes.com/2015/01/04/magazine/the-complicated-origins-of-having-it-all.html?_r=0. Szalai continues, "And there you have it—we somehow took a puffed-up corporate come-on, one that made Brown herself chafe more than 30 years ago, and twisted it in the collective memory into a false promise of feminism. The built-in vapidity, the vagueness with which 'having it all' specifies everything and therefore nothing, allows us to talk as if we know everything we need to know about working mothers while saying nothing substantive about the particular challenges they face. To say that women expect to 'have it all' is to trivialize issues like parental leave, equal pay and safe, affordable child care; it makes women sound like entitled, narcissistic battle-axes while also casting them as fools."

4. In her assessment of Gurley Brown, after the writer's death, *The Guardian*'s Sali Hughes said, "What Gurley Brown arguably intended was for us to *want* more, to not have to choose between having a family and retaining our own identities, or between caring for our families and providing for ourselves. 'Don't use men to get what you want in life—get it for yourself,' she often said. And she never suggested women use anything but hard graft to make it. 'Nearly every glamorous, wealthy, successful career woman you might envy now started out as some kind of schlepp.'" "Helen Gurley Brown: How to Have It All," August 14, 2012, http://www.theguardian.com/lifeand-style/2012/aug/14/helen-gurley-brown-cosmopolitan-sex

5. Anne-Marie Slaughter, "Why Women Still Can't Have it All," *Atlantic*, July/August 2012, 85–90, 92–94, 96–98, 100–102, http://www.theatlantic.com/magazine/archive/2012/07/why-women-still-cant-have-it-all/309020/. See also Slaughter's *Unfinished Business: Women Men Work Family* (New York: Random House, 2015), the book-length version of her argument. See also Debora Spar, *Wonder Women: Sex, Power, and the Quest for Perfection* (New York: Sarah Crichton Books/Farrar, Straus and Giroux, 2013), a book by the president of Barnard College that treads similar terrain; and Arianna Huffington, *Thrive: The Third Metric to Redefining Success and Creating a Life of Well-Being, Wisdom, and Wonder* (New York: Harmony Books/Random House, 2014). That these books were published around the same time demonstrates the persistence of the "having it all" mythology for white, upper-middle-class, highly educated American women.

6. Janie's final tap dance might also refer to Barbara Gordon's bestseller *I'm Dancing as Fast as I Can* (New York: Harper and Row, 1979), her memoir about her addiction to Valium, despite being a successful television producer. The memoir became a cautionary tale at the time for women eager for career success.

7. Or that she's a human being at all, since, as Katie Welsh points out, bearing children, for women, is a key measure of their worth. In Wasserstein's *An American Daughter*, Welsh recalls, the successful African American doctor, Judith, feels herself less than fully human because she hasn't had children.

8. Douglas Watt, "'Isn't It Romantic'—Sometimes," review of *Isn't It Romantic*, by Wendy Wasserstein, directed by Gerald Gutierrez, Playwrights Horizons, New York, *New York Daily News*, December 16, 1983.

9. Clive Barnes, "'Isn't It Romantic'—and It's Funny, Too," review of *Isn't It Romantic*, by Wendy Wasserstein, directed by Gerald Gutierrez, Playwrights Horizons, New York, *New York Post*, December 16, 1983.

10. Richard Corliss, "Broadway's Big Endearment," review of *Isn't It Romantic*, by Wendy Wasserstein, directed by Gerald Gutierrez, Playwrights Horizons, New York, *Time*, December 26, 1983.

11. Elliott Sirkin, review of *Isn't It Romantic*, by Wendy Wasserstein, directed by Gerald Gutierrez, Playwrights Horizons, New York, *Nation*, February 18, 1984.

12. Ibid.

13. Mel Gussow, review of *Isn't It Romantic*, by Wendy Wasserstein, directed by Steven Robman, Phoenix Theatre, New York, *New York Times*, June 15, 1981, C11.

Chapter 4

1. Susan Faludi, *Backlash: The Undeclared War Against American Women* (New York: Crown, 1991).

2. I was also the only lesbian on the panel (of people who were also all white). In an illuminating moment of Freudian slippage, one of my fellow panelists—a white, heterosexual male scholar—called me "Fran" by mistake, trading my name for that of the "fuzzy lesbian physicist" who makes her appearance in the consciousness-raising scene. Fran became famous for telling Heidi, after Heidi admits she's a humanist, not a feminist, "You either shave your legs or you don't."

3. In 2015, *Fun Home*, a musical based on Alison Bechdel's graphic novel of the same name, was a finalist for the Pulitzer Prize and won a Tony for Best Musical. Lisa Kron wrote the book and lyrics and Jeanine Tesori wrote the music for the adaptation.

4. Heidi was named after Wasserstein's friend, the set designer Heidi Ettinger, who was the first woman to graduate from Yale School of Drama with a degree in design. See Julie Salamon, *Wendy and the Lost Boys: The Uncommon Life of Wendy Wasserstein* (New York: Penguin Press, 2011), 248.

5. Wendy Wasserstein, *The Heidi Chronicles*, in *The Heidi Chronicles and Other Plays* (San Diego: Harcourt Brace Jovanovich, 1990), 160. Subsequent references will appear parenthetically in the text.

6. On this point, see Anna North's *New York Times* op-ed "Should Literature Be Relatable?," August 5, 2014, http://op-talk.blogs.nytimes.com/2014/08/05/should-literature-be-relatable/; and Rebecca Mead, "The Scourge of 'Relatability,'" *New Yorker*, August 1, 2014, http://www.newyorker.com/culture/cultural-comment/scourge-relatability

7. This line was attributed to playwright Christopher Durang, who apparently made a similar remark to Wasserstein in one of her first classes as a playwriting student at the Yale School of Drama. See Salamon, *Wendy and the Lost Boys*, 120–21, and my discussion in chapter 1.

8. As scholar Tamsen Wolff remarked in her thoughtful reflection on Wasserstein's work when the playwright died in 2006, "In her plays and essays, Wasserstein regularly documents the need for all kinds of alliances, no matter how complicated. Biological families—mostly mothers—pose particular problems for their daughters. . . . As her female characters grapple with their mothers, friends frequently constitute family, with particular bonds existing between gay men and straight women. . . . In all cases, she plumbs both the potential for intimacy and for abandonment." "The Chronicle Review: Wendy Wasserstein (1950–2006)," *Chronicle of Higher Education*, 52.24 (February 17, 2006), B13.

9. Carolyn Casey Craig, in her chapter on Wasserstein, quotes Wasserstein as saying, "I'm a single woman and my friends are really my family. . . . My nurturing has always come from my friends." Craig says, "In fact, it's the scene between Peter and Heidi, at the hospital ward, that holds the heart of the play, as Wasserstein calls it: 'That's the heart of the play, really. And actually, I found it through the writing of the play; it wasn't what I set out to write. When I set out to write the play, I thought the heart of it was Heidi's

speech to the girls' school. But in fact, Peter saying "our friends are our family" is, in summary, the heart of it.'" "Wendy Wasserstein: Lola's Well-Rounded Daughter," in *Women Pulitzer Playwrights: Biographical Profiles and Analyses of the Plays* (Jefferson, NC: McFarland, 2004), 205.

10. As Wasserstein said in an interview with Mervyn Rothstein for the *New York Times* Arts & Leisure section shortly before *The Heidi Chronicles* opened on Broadway, "In my generation what we did was we spent our time finding ourselves. And a lot of us are still spending our time finding ourselves. A lot of us—even those married and with children—still sit around and think, 'What am I going to do when I grow up'?" Rothstein, "After the Revolution, What? The Daughters of Feminism," *New York Times*, December 11, 1988, Arts & Leisure, 28.

11. Salamon reports that Wasserstein went with a friend to a consciousness-raising group organized by Tillie Olsen at Amherst: "[The friend] brought Wendy along. Most of the other fifteen or twenty women who came to the lunch were faculty wives, women who had Ph.D.'s but not jobs. Wendy didn't talk much, but she was listening, with startling acuity." *Wendy and the Lost Boys*, 90. As Salamon notes, Wasserstein recapitulated this scene in *The Heidi Chronicles*.

12. Critics remarked on her use of cartoonish gestures to portray feminism. William Henry, in *Time*, called the plot an "unconscious cartoon of feminist dialectic"; Howard Kissel, in the *New York Daily News*, said, "Wasserstein is particularly strong at satirizing the excesses of the militant years: There is a hilarious 'consciousness-raising' scene . . . and an equally funny demonstration for 'Women in Art.'" William Henry, "Way Stations," review of *The Heidi Chronicles*, by Wendy Wasserstein, directed by Daniel Sullivan, Plymouth Theatre, New York, *Time*, March 20, 1989; Howard Kissel, "'Heidi' Lights up Broadway," review of *The Heidi Chronicles*, by Wendy Wasserstein, directed by Daniel Sullivan, Plymouth Theatre, New York, *New York Daily News*, March 10, 1989.

13. Alisa Solomon, "feminism-something," *Village Voice*, December 20, 1988, 123.

14. Ibid.

15. Ibid, 124.

16. Jill Dolan, *Presence and Desire: Essays on Gender, Sexuality, Performance* (Ann Arbor: University of Michigan Press, 1993), 49. For a full discussion of the play and thoughts on a revisionist production of it I directed at the University of Wisconsin–Madison, see 50–59.

17. Gina Gionfriddo's *Rapture, Blister, Burn* (2012) comes to mind, but her play charts a different moment in American feminism through the experiences of a very different—though still white, upper-middle-class, and well-educated—woman, who is also a professor. The play was a finalist for the 2012 Pulitzer Prize for Drama. Gionfriddo, *Rapture, Blister, Burn* (New York: Dramatists Play Service, 2014).

18. Carey Purcell, "A Woman's World: Pam MacKinnon on the Decision to Restore Wasserstein's Cut Dialogue to *The Heidi Chronicles*," *Playbill*, February 28, 2015, http://www.playbill.com/news/article/a-womans-world-pam-mackinnon-on-the-decision-to-restore-wassersteins-cut-dialogue-to-the-heidi-chronicles-342388

19. Alisa Solomon, "Why 'The Heidi Chronicles' Failed to Find a New Audience," *Nation*, April 24, 2015, http://www.thenation.com/article/why-heidi-chronicles-failed-find-new-audience/. Solomon refers to Sheryl Sandberg's book *Lean In: Women, Work, and the Will to Lead* (New York: Alfred A. Knopf, 2013), which some feminist commentators saw as an assimilationist, conservative analysis of gender roles in business and industry.

20. Charles Isherwood, review of *The Heidi Chronicles*, by Wendy Wasserstein, directed by Pam MacKinnon, Music Box Theatre, New York, *New York Times*, March 19, 2015.

21. Chris Jones, "Elisabeth Moss a Good Fit for 'Heidi Chronicles' on Broadway," review of *The Heidi Chronicles*, by Wendy Wasserstein, directed by Pam MacKinnon, Music Box Theatre, New York, *Chicago Tribune*, March 19, 2015.

22. Jeremy Gerard, "Elisabeth Moss' '60s Peggy Olson is '80s 'Heidi,'" review of *The Heidi Chronicles*, by Wendy Wasserstein, directed by Pam MacKinnon, Music Box Theatre, New York, *Deadline*, March 19, 2015.

23. David Finkle, "Wendy Wasserstein's 'Heidi Chronicles' in A+ Revival," review of *The Heidi Chronicles*, by Wendy Wasserstein, directed by Pam MacKinnon, Music Box Theatre, New York, *Huffington Post*, March 19, 2015.

24. Jesse Oxfeld, "How Wendy Wasserstein and Heidi Holland Remade the World," review of *The Heidi Chronicles*, by Wendy Wasserstein, directed by Pam MacKinnon, Music Box Theatre, New York, *Jewish Daily Forward*, March 19, 2015.

25. For a discussion of Norman's play and its comparison to *Death of a Salesman*, see my chapter on its reception in *The Feminist Spectator as Critic* (Ann Arbor: University of Michigan Press, 1991).

26. Melissa Maerz, "Elisabeth Moss and Jason Biggs in *The Heidi Chronicles*," review of *The Heidi Chronicles*, by Wendy Wasserstein, directed by Pam MacKinnon, Music Box Theatre, New York, *Entertainment Weekly*, March 19, 2015.

27. Ibid., italics in the original.

28. Joan Scott, "Fifty Years of Academic Feminism," Meredith Miller Memorial Lecture, April 22, 2015, McCormick Hall, Princeton University.

29. Wasserstein qtd. in Rothstein, "After the Revolution, What?," 28.

30. Michael Paulson and Jennifer Schluesser, "*The Heidi Chronicles* Is Trailed by Questions of Feminism and Legacy," *New York Times*, April 23, 2015, C1, http://www.nytimes.com/2015/04/23/theater/the-heidi-chronicles-is-trailed-by-questions-of-feminism-and-legacy.html?_r=1

Chapter 5

1. Wendy Wasserstein, *The Sisters Rosensweig* (New York: Harcourt Brace Jovanovich, 1993), xi. Subsequent references will appear parenthetically in the text.

2. Kevin Kelly, "Wasserstein's Clever 'Sisters Rosensweig,'" review of *The Sisters Rosensweig*, by Wendy Wasserstein, directed by Daniel Sullivan, Ethel Barrymore Theatre, New York, *Boston Globe*, April 1, 1993, living section.

3. Ibid.

4. Mel Gussow, "Wasserstein: Comedy, Character, Reflection," review of *The Sisters Rosensweig*, by Wendy Wasserstein, directed by Daniel Sullivan, Mitzi E. Newhouse Theater, New York, *New York Times*, October 23, 1992, C3.

5. Ibid.

Chapter 6

1. Wendy Wasserstein, *An American Daughter* (New York: Harcourt Brace, 1998), 7. Subsequent references will appear parenthetically in the text.

2. Gail Ciociola, *Wendy Wasserstein: Dramatizing Women, Their Choices and Their Boundaries* (Jefferson, NC: McFarland, 1998), 123.

3. David Sheward, review of *An American Daughter*, by Wendy Wasserstein, directed by Daniel Sullivan, Cort Theatre, New York, *Back Stage*, April 18, 1997, 60.

4. Judith was also Wasserstein's stand-in here, as by then the playwright, too, was undergoing fertility treatments.

5. Rachel Shteir, in "From the Front Page to the Broadway Stage: Wendy Wasserstein Finds Her Muse in Washington Politics," suggests that the non-Jewish heroine defeats the play's force and Wasserstein's trademark style: "Like Neil Simon," Shteir writes, "she is funniest when she's riffing on the tormented war of wills that erupts between Jewish parents and their children. There is not enough of this kind of scene in *An American Daughter*. Ms. Wasserstein seems to have lost her way in abandoning the spunky Jewish heroines . . . for a humorless descendent of WASP scions." *Forward*, April 25, 1997, 9.

6. In the Williamstown Theatre Festival 2016 revival, directed by Evan Cabnet, which I discuss below, this line was removed from the script.

7. Ben Brantley, "In the Hostile Glare of Washington, the Media Define and Defy," review of *An American Daughter*, by Wendy Wasserstein, directed by Daniel Sullivan, Cort Theatre, New York, *New York Times*, April 14, 1997, C11.

8. Ibid.

9. Ibid.

10. Clive Barnes, "No Hitting below the Beltway," review of *An American Daughter*, by Wendy Wasserstein, directed by Daniel Sullivan, Cort Theatre, New York, *New York Post*, April 14, 1997.

11. Howard Kissel, "Political Play Fails to Capitol-ize: Wasserstein's 'Daughter' Is Topical but Character Issue Sinks D.C. Tale," review of *An American Daughter*, by Wendy Wasserstein, directed by Daniel Sullivan, Cort Theatre, New York, *New York Daily News*, April 14, 1997.

12. Ibid.

13. Wendy Wasserstein, *The Heidi Chronicles and Other Plays* (San Diego: Harcourt Brace Jovanovich, 1990), 211.

14. In his *New York Times* review of the Williamstown production, Charles Isherwood remarked, "I hardly need underscore the timeliness of the revival, with Mrs. Clinton again making headlines and sending her foes into a lather. The singular kinds of scrutiny that women in the public sphere face; the challenges of raising a family . . . while pursuing a high-profile career; the anguish that some women experience when they put off raising a family until it may be too late. . . . All remain subjects of serious moment today. Yet, despite mostly fine work from the actors . . . the characters' relationships to one another are too thinly sketched to ring true." "Review: Women's Hard Choices, Cutting Deep at Williamstown Festival," *New York Times*, August 18, 2016, http://www.nytimes.com/2016/08/19/theater/review-womens-hard-choices-cutting-deep-at-williamstown-festival.html

Chapter 7

1. *Third's* look at an openly menopausal woman mirrored television's interest in similarly middle-aged yet compelling female characters around the same time Wasserstein wrote and produced her play. Examples of such popular cultural representations include Kyra Sedgwick's tour-de-force turn as Brenda in *The Closer* (U.S., TNT, 2005–12); Holly Hunter's sexy romp on *Saving Grace* (U.S., TNT, 2007–10); Glenn Close's tough-as-nails, menopausal power-monger in *Damages* (U.S., TNT, 2007–10, DirecTV, 2010–12); Mary Louise Parker's weary cynic in *Weeds* (U.S., Showtime, 2005–12); and slightly later, Edie Falco's drug-addicted but openhearted ER nurse on *Nurse Jackie* (U.S., Showtime, 2009–15). By 2016, of course, the middle-aged woman protagonist had become even more of a popular culture staple. See, for only several examples, *The Fall* (Ireland, RTÉ One, 2013–), *Happy Valley* (United Kingdom, BBC One, 2014–16), *Broadchurch* (United Kingdom, ITV, 2013–), and *Getting On* (U.S., HBO, 2013–15), all of which boast white, middle-class, professional working women as the center of their narratives. For similar African American leading characters, see also *Scandal*, the Shonda Rhimes television series starring Kerry Washington as Olivia Pope, a political fixer

who, although not quite middle-aged, is old enough to be mature and power-ful (U.S., ABC, 2012–) and *How to Get Away with Murder* (U.S. ABC, 2014–), which stars Emmy Award–winning actor Viola Davis as a middle-aged lawyer overseeing a cadre of corrupt, willing protégés while pursuing her own sexual and career gratifications.

2. Wasserstein was already ill with lymphoma when the play was in re-hearsals, but she saw it through previews and opening night before she died in 2006.

3. Wendy Wasserstein, *Third* (New York: Dramatists Play Service, 2008). Subsequent references will appear parenthetically in the text.

4. For writing about the various "waves" of feminism and their ideo-logical differences, see, for just a few examples of a large and varied literature, Andi Zeisler, *We Were Feminists Once: From Riot Grrrl to CoverGirl, the Buying and Selling of a Political Movement* (New York: Public Affairs, 2016); and Susan Douglas, *Enlightened Sexism: The Seductive Message That Femi-nism's Work Is Done* (New York: Times Books, 2010).

5. Frank Scheck, "Prof Unsure of Her Class," review of *Third*, by Wendy Wasserstein, directed by Daniel Sullivan, Mitzi E. Newhouse Theater, New York, *New York Post*, October 25, 2005, 46.

6. In their very first scene together, Scoop predicts of Heidi, "You'll be one of those true believers who didn't understand it was all just a phase." Wendy Wasserstein, *The Heidi Chronicles*, in *The Heidi Chronicles and Other Plays* (San Diego: Harcourt Brace Jovanovich, 1990), 173. By the play's last scene, Scoop affirms his prescience, telling Heidi, "So I was right all along. You were a true believer" (247).

7. Obviously, Wasserstein knew how Jewishness inflected her work. Christopher Bigsby reports that she "has also expressed suspicion that the success of *The Heidi Chronicles* may have in part been due to the fact that the central character was a Gentile girl from Chicago. It wasn't about Wendy with the hips from New York, even if Wendy with the hips from New York had the same emotional life." Qtd. in Christopher Bigsby, "Wendy Wasser-stein," in *Contemporary American Playwrights* (Cambridge: Cambridge University Press, 2000), 332.

8. As Jan Balakian wrote of *The Sisters Rosensweig*, it is a play "of the sort Wasserstein saw as a girl in New York, one that makes us laugh a little, sigh a little, and go home feeling that despite life's confusion and pain, things will somehow work out"; see Jan Balakian, "Wendy Wasserstein: A Feminist Voice from the Seventies to the Present," in *The Cambridge Companion to American Women Playwrights*, ed. Brenda Murphy (Cambridge: Cambridge University Press, 1999), 224. The same structure of feeling is provoked by *Third*.

9. The production was particularly disappointing since Mileaf had re-cently been hailed as an up-and-coming woman director; see, for example, Randy Gener, "Maria Mileaf: Earth Mother," *Theatre Communications*

Group, http://www.tcg.org/publications/at/Oct07/mileaf.cfm. For an in-depth analysis of the production, see my November 8, 2007, blog post, "Performance Contexts: Wendy Wasserstein's *Third* in Los Angeles," *Feminist Spectator*, http://feministspectator.princeton.edu

10. Lahti's work in the Wasserstein opus also includes her performance as Lyssa Dent Hughes in the television film of *An American Daughter* (U.S., Lifetime, 2000), for which she received a Golden Globe nomination.

11. The fact that Nancy falls in love with a rabbi at the play's end meant that in this production, as in *An American Daughter*, the African American female performer bore the burden of all and any ethnicity in the play, including Jewishness.

12. Charles McNulty, reviewing the Geffen production, found annoying "Laurie's habit of reeling off academic brand names (Harvard, Swarthmore, Oxford) to establish her rarefied milieu. . . . This sort of fetishizing elitism runs throughout Wasserstein's work and is of a piece with her tendency to opt for humorous caricatures over subtler shadings." "'Third' Is, Sadly, Only Second-Rate Wasserstein," review of *Third*, by Wendy Wasserstein, directed by Maria Mileaf, Geffen Playhouse, Los Angeles, *Los Angeles Times*, September 21, 2007, www.articles.latimes.com/print/2007/sep/21/entertainment/et-third21

13. Linda Lowen, "Profs vs. Jocks: Hangar Theatre's 'Third' Mines Campus Politics, Mid-Life Crisis," review of *Third*, by Wendy Wasserstein, directed by Michael Barakiva, Hangar Theatre, Ithaca, New York, Syracuse.com, July 23, 2016, www.syracuse.com/entertainment/index.ssf/2016/07/hangar_theatre_third_review.html; James MacKillop, "First Place Finish for 'Third,'" review of *Third*, by Wendy Wasserstein, directed by Michael Barakiva, Hangar Theatre, Ithaca, New York, *Syracuse New Times*, July 27, 2016, www.syracusenewtimes.com/first-place-finish-for-third/

14. Nancy Worssam, "'Third' by Wendy Wasserstein at Arts West," *Arts Stage—Seattle Rage* (blog), March 8, 2014, http://artsstage-seattlerage.com/2014/third-by-wendy-wasserstein-at-arts-west/

15. Thomas Jenkins, "'Third' Doesn't Make the Grade," review of *Third*, by Wendy Wasserstein, directed by Catherine Babbitt, San Pedro Playhouse's Cellar Theater, San Antonio, *San Antonio Current*, September 3, 2008, www.sacurrent.com/sanantonio/third-doesn't-make-the-grade/Content?oid=2284199

16. Steve Cohen, "PTC's 'Third,'" review of *Third*, by Wendy Wasserstein, directed by Mary B. Robinson, Philadelphia Theatre Company, Philadelphia, *Broad Street Review*, March 29, 2008, www.broadstreetreview.com/dance/PTCs_Third_2nd_review

17. Tim Dunleavy, "*Third*," review of *Third*, by Wendy Wasserstein, directed by Mary B. Robinson, Philadelphia Theatre Company, Philadelphia, *Talkin' Broadway*, March 31, 2008, www.talkinbroadway.com/page/regional/philly/phil74.html

18. Hugh Hunter, "First-Rate Production of 'Third,'" review of *Third*, by Wendy Wasserstein, directed by Robert Bauer, The Drama Group, Philadelphia, *Chestnut Hill Local*, March 25, 2011, http://www.chestnuthilllocal.com/2011/03/25/first-rate-production-of-%E2%80%98third%E2%80%99/

19. Michael Sommers, "Finding Cracks in a Perfect Life: A Review of 'Third' in Red Bank," review of *Third*, by Wendy Wasserstein, directed by Michael Cumpsty, Two River Theater, Red Bank, New Jersey, *New York Times*, June 13, 2014, www.nytimes.com/2014/06/15/nyregion/a-review-of-third-in-red-bank

20. Judith Reynolds, "Aiming for Higher Education: Merely Players Stage Provocative 'Third,'" review of *Third*, by Wendy Wasserstein, directed by Mona Wood Patterson, Merely Players, Durango, Colorado, *Durango Herald*, November 15, 2011, www.durangoherald.com/article/20111115/ARTS01/711159986/

21. McNulty, "'Third' Is, Sadly, Only Second-Rate Wasserstein."

22. Bob Verini, review of *Third*, by Wendy Wasserstein, directed by Maria Mileaf, Geffen Playhouse, Los Angeles, *Variety*, September 20, 2007, www.variety.com/2007/legit/markets-festivals/third-2-1200556152/

23. See David Savran, ed., *The Playwright's Voice: American Dramatists on Memory, Writing, and the Politics of Culture* (New York: Theatre Communications Group, 1999), 307.

24. Angelika Czekay, "Interview with Wendy Wasserstein," in *The Playwright's Muse*, ed. Joan Herrington (New York: Routledge, 2002), 50.

25. Scheck, "Prof Unsure of Her Class."

26. Ibid.

27. Michael Feingold, "Wasserstein's Sourly Wistful, Autumnal Comedy of Academia Sounds a Minor," review of *Third*, by Wendy Wasserstein, directed by Daniel Sullivan, Mitzi E. Newhouse Theater, New York, *Village Voice*, October 25, 2005.

28. John Lahr, "Reversal of Fortune: A New 'Odd Couple' and an Old Formula," review of *Third*, by Wendy Wasserstein, directed by Daniel Sullivan, Mitzi E. Newhouse Theater, New York, *New Yorker*, November 7, 2005.

29. Ibid.

Conclusion

1. Lily Tomlin opened *Search for Signs of Intelligent Life in the Universe*, her one-woman show, written by her partner, Jane Wagner, on Broadway September 26, 1985. It ran until October 5, 1986. For a discussion of its world-making potential, see chapter 3 of my *Utopia in Performance: Finding Hope at the Theatre* (Ann Arbor: University of Michigan Press, 2005), 63–88.

2. For a round-up of work by Theresa Rebeck, see www.theresarebeck.

com, and for Gina Gionfriddo, see her *New York Times* essay on the resemblances between *Rapture, Blister, Burn* and *The Heidi Chronicles*, a thoughtful meditation on single motherhood, feminism, and theater. "All Hail 'Heidi': Beyond Feminism but Still a Dream," *New York Times*, June 7, 2012, http://www.nytimes.com/2012/06/10/theater/gina-gionfriddo-on-rapture-blister-burn-and-wasserstein.html?_r=0

3. See the *Eclipsed* website, http://www.eclipsedbroadway.com/, for information about the closed production.

4. See Andrew Gans and Olivia Clement, "Producers Hope to Bring Paula Vogel's *Indecent* to Broadway," *Playbill*, August 25, 2016, http://www.playbill.com/article/producers-hope-to-bring-paula-vogels-indecent-to-broadway

5. Her insights into the community of which she both was and wasn't a part were crowned by her posthumously published novel, *Elements of Style* (New York: Knopf, 2006) I discuss the novel later in the conclusion.

6. Christopher Bigsby, "Wendy Wasserstein," in *Contemporary American Playwrights* (Cambridge: Cambridge University Press, 1999), 367.

7. Nancy Franklin, "The Time of Her Life," *New Yorker*, April 14, 1997, 64.

8. See *Transparent* (U.S., Amazon, 2014–), http://www.imdb.com/title/tt3502262/?ref_=nv_sr_1; and *Orange Is the New Black* (U.S., Netflix, 2013–), http://www.imdb.com/title/tt2372162/?ref_=nv_sr_1

9. Joshua Harmon's play *Bad Jews* (2012) is a terrific, knowing look at a striving family of cousins in New York with very different relationships to Judaism and their family's traumatic past. But it is too early to tell if the young playwright's work will focus on his ethnicity. In fact, the play that followed *Bad Jews*, called *Significant Other* (2015), concerns a single gay man with women friends who are all about to be married. See Alexis Soloski's *New York Times* feature about Harmon, "With 'Significant Other,' Joshua Harmon Happily Writes about the Unhappy," June 14, 2015, http://www.nytimes.com/2015/06/14/theater/with-significant-other-joshua-harmon-happily-writes-about-the-unhappy.html?_r=0

10. Julie Salamon quotes reporter Judith Miller, who noted the "tremendous amount" of publicity surrounding Wasserstein near the opening of *The Sisters Rosensweig* and suggested, "Part of the explanation may be that she is very much a local hero, or heroine—a New York gal. There's an Upper West Side sensibility in all her work, a sensibility shared by the traditional New York theatergoing audience—male and female alike. She's a local girl made good on the local stage, which happens to be in New York, as are many of the talk shows on which she has promoted herself and her work. Not for nothing does Ms. Wasserstein hail from a family of entrepreneurs." Judith Miller, "Theater: The Secret Wendy Wasserstein," *New York Times*, October 18, 1992, qtd. in Salamon, *Wendy and the Lost Boys: The Uncommon Life of Wendy Wasserstein* (New York: Penguin Press, 2011), 299.

11. As Tamsen Wolff notes, "Wasserstein's later work reveals a growing concern about economic injustice. . . . Even so, she refuses cynicism in her essays on politics and arts advocacy, embracing instead a determined, wry faith." "The Chronicle Review: Wendy Wasserstein (1950–2006)," *Chronicle of Higher Education* 52.24 (February 17, 2006): B13.

12. Wendy Wasserstein, *Any Woman Can't,* unpublished manuscript, 1971. I'm grateful to Robert N. Sandberg for making this script available to me. Subsequent references will appear parenthetically in the text.

13. David Savran, "Wendy Wasserstein," in *The Playwright's Voice: American Dramatists on Memory, Writing, and the Politics of Culture,* edited by David Savran (New York: Theatre Communications Group, 1999), 308.

14. Wendy Wasserstein, *Third* (New York: Dramatists Play Service, 2008), 16.

15. Christopher Durang, telephone interview by the author, July 26, 2013.

16. Wasserstein, *Third,* 39–40.

17. Savran, "Wendy Wasserstein," 306.

18. Wolff, "Chronicle Review."

19. Richard Eder, "Dramatic Wit and Wisdom Unite in *Uncommon Women and Others,*" review of *Uncommon Women and Others,* by Wendy Wasserstein, directed by Steven Robman, Phoenix Theatre, New York, *New York Times,* November 22, 1977, 42.

20. Stefan Kanfer, "Past Imperfect," review of *Uncommon Women and Others,* by Wendy Wasserstein, directed by Carole Rothman, Lucille Lortel Theatre, New York, *New Leader* 77.11 (November 7, 1994): 22–23.

21. Stephen J. Whitfield, "Wendy Wasserstein and the Crisis of (Jewish) Identity," in *Daughters of Valor: Contemporary Jewish American Women Writers,* ed. Jay L. Halio and Ben Siegel (Cranbury, NJ: Associate University Presses, 1997), 226–46.

22. Kevin Kelly, "Wasserstein's Clever 'Sisters Rosensweig,'" *Boston Globe,* April 1, 1993, 61.

23. Robert Brustein, "The Sisters Rosensweig," review of *The Sisters Rosensweig,* by Wendy Wasserstein, directed by Daniel Sullivan, Mitzi E. Newhouse Theater, New York, *New Republic,* December 7, 1992, 34.

24. See my own harsh critique in Jill Dolan, *Presence and Desire: Essays on Gender, Sexuality, Performance* (Ann Arbor: University of Michigan Press, 1993), 50–59; and my reconsideration in my own obituary for Wasserstein, "Wendy Wasserstein, in Memoriam," *Feminist Spectator,* January 30, 2006, http://feministspectator.princeton.edu/2006/01/30/wendy-wasserstein-in-memoriam/; as well as in my essay "Feminist Performance Criticism and the Popular: Reviewing Wendy Wasserstein," *Theatre Journal* 60.3 (October 2008): 433–57.

25. Savran, "Wendy Wasserstein," 309.

26. Franklin, "The Time of Her Life," 62.

Bibliography

Wendy Wasserstein's Plays and Other Writings

An American Daughter. New York: Harcourt Brace, 1998.
"Annals of Motherhood: Complications." *New Yorker,* February 21, 2000. http://www.newyorker.com/magazine/2000/02/21/complications
"Any Woman Can't." Unpublished manuscript, 1971.
Elements of Style. New York: Knopf, 2006.
The Heidi Chronicles and Other Plays. San Diego: Harcourt Brace Jovanovich, 1990.
Shiksa Goddess (or, How I Spent My Forties). New York: Vintage Books, 2002.
The Sisters Rosensweig. New York: Harcourt Brace Jovanovich, 1993.
Sloth: The Seven Deadly Sins. New York: Oxford University Press, 2005.
Third. American Theatre Magazine, April 2006, 69–87.
Third. New York: Dramatists Play Service, 2008.

Interviews

Durang, Christopher. Interview by author. Phone. July 6, 2013.
Richman, Carrie. Interview by author. Phone. August 5, 2013.

Books and Essays about Wendy Wasserstein

Balakian, Jan. "'The Heidi Chronicles': The Big Chill of Feminism." *South Atlantic Review* 60.2 (May 1995): 93–101.
Balakian, Jan. *Reading the Plays of Wendy Wasserstein.* New York: Applause Theatre & Cinema Books, 2010.
Balakian, Jan. "Two Interviews with Wendy Wasserstein." *Journal of American Drama and Theatre* 9.2 (Spring 1997): 58–84.

Balakian, Jan. "Wendy Wasserstein: A Feminist Voice from the Seventies to the Present." In *The Cambridge Companion to American Women Playwrights*, edited by Brenda Murphy, 213–232. Cambridge: Cambridge University Press, 1999.

Bigsby, Christopher. "Wendy Wasserstein." In *Contemporary American Playwrights*, 330–68. Cambridge: Cambridge University Press, 1999.

Canning, Charlotte. "Feminist Performance as Feminist Historiography." *Theatre Survey* 45.2 (November 2004): 227–33.

Canning, Charlotte. "Feminists Perform Their Past: Constructing History in *The Heidi Chronicles* and *The Break of Day*." In *Women, Theatre and Performance: New Histories, New Historiographies*, edited by Maggie B. Gale and Vivien Gardner, 163–79. New York: Palgrave, 2000.

Carlson, Susan L. "Communities 1937 and 1977: Clare Boothe and Wendy Wasserstein." In *Modern American Drama: The Female Canon*, edited by June Schleuter, 207–17. Madison, NJ: Fairleigh Dickinson University Press, 1996.

Chirico, Miriam M. "Female Laughter and Comic Possibilities: *Uncommon Women and Others*." In *Wendy Wasserstein: A Casebook*, edited by Claudia Barnett, 81–105. New York: Garland, 1999.

Ciociola, Gail. *Wendy Wasserstein: Dramatizing Women, Their Choices, and Their Boundaries*. Jefferson, NC: McFarland, 1998.

Coen, Stephanie. "A World, One's Life." *American Theatre* 14.7 (September 1, 1997): 24.

Cohen, Esther. "Uncommon Woman: An Interview with Wendy Wasserstein." *Women's Studies* 15 (1988): 257–70.

Cohen, Sarah Blacher. "Wendy Wasserstein: Isn't It Romantic." In *Making a Scene: The Contemporary Drama of Jewish American Women*, edited by Sarah Blacher Cohen, 18–70. Syracuse, NY: Syracuse University Press, 1997.

Craig, Carolyn Casey. "Wendy Wasserstein: Lola's Well-Rounded Daughter." In *Women Pulitzer Playwrights: Biographical Profiles and Analyses of the Plays*, 184–206. Jefferson, NC: McFarland, 2004.

Czekay, Angelika. "'Interview with Wendy Wasserstein: Interview Conducted by Angelika Czekay in February 2001." In *The Playwright's Muse*, edited by Joan Herrington, 45–52. New York: Routledge, 2002.

Czekay, Angelika. "'Not Having It All': Wendy Wasserstein's Uncommon Women." In *The Playwright's Muse*, edited by Joan Herrington, 17–44. New York: Routledge, 2002.

Dolan, Jill. "Feminist Performance Criticism and the Popular: Reviewing Wendy Wasserstein." *Theatre Journal* 60.3 (October 2008): 433–57.

Dolan, Jill. "Performance Contexts: Wendy Wasserstein's *Third* in Los Angeles." *Feminist Spectator*, November 8, 2007. http://feministspectator.princeton.edu

Dolan, Jill. "Wendy Wasserstein, in Memoriam." *Feminist Spectator,* January 30, 2006. http://feministspectator.princeton.edu

Douthit, Lue Morgan. "Reconsidering the Feminism of 'Heidi': A Look at the Comic Structure in *The Heidi Chronicles." Text & Presentation: The Journal of the Comparative Drama Conference* 14 (1993): 11–19.

Frank, Glenda. "The Struggle to Affirm: The Image of Jewish-Americans on Stage." In *Staging Difference: Cultural Pluralism in American Theatre and Drama,* edited by Marc Maufort, 245–57. New York: Peter Lang, 1995.

Franklin, Nancy. "The Time of Her Life." *New Yorker,* April 14, 1997, 62–71.

Gener, Randy. "Liberal Doubts: An Interview with André Bishop about the Playwright [Wendy Wasserstein]." *American Theatre,* April 2006, 70–71.

Greene, Alexis. *Wasserstein in an Hour.* Hanover, NH: In an Hour Books, Smith and Kraus, 2012.

Isherwood, Charles. "Wendy Wasserstein, Chronicler of Women's Identity Crises, Dies." *New York Times,* January 30, 2006. www.nytimes.com/2006/01/30/theater/30cnd-wasserstein.html

Jones, Chris. "Wendy Wasserstein, 1950–2006." *Chicago Tribune,* January 31, 2006. http://articles.chicagotribune.com/2006–01–31/news/0601310160_1_baby-boomer-women-well-to-do-women-play

Keyssar, Helene. "Drama and the Dialogic Imagination: *The Heidi Chronicles* and *Fefu and Her Friends." Modern Drama* 34.1 (1991): 88–106.

Mandl, Bette. "Feminism, Postfeminism, and *The Heidi Chronicles." Studies in the Humanities* 17.2 (December 1990): 120–28.

Salamon, Julie. *Wendy and the Lost Boys: The Uncommon Life of Wendy Wasserstein.* New York: Penguin Press, 2011.

Savran, David. "Wendy Wasserstein." In *The Playwright's Voice: American Dramatists on Memory, Writing, and the Politics of Culture,* edited by David Savran, 289–310. New York: Theatre Communications Group, 1999.

Wasserstein, Wendy. "Wendy Wasserstein." In *The Playwright's Art: Conversations with Contemporary American Dramatists,* edited by Jackson R. Bryer, 257–76. New Brunswick, NJ: Rutgers University Press, 1995.

Watermeier, Daniel J. "The Search for Self: Attachment, Loss, and Recovery in *The Heidi Chronicles.*" In *Staging Difference: Cultural Pluralism in American Theatre and Drama,* edited by Marc Maufort, 351–62. New York: Peter Lang, 1995.

Weales, Gerald. "Prize Problems: Chronicles & Cocktail Hour." *Commonweal,* May 5, 1989, 279–80.

Whitfield, Stephen J. "Wendy Wasserstein and the Crisis of (Jewish) Identity." In *Daughters of Valor: Contemporary Jewish American Women Writers,* edited by Jay L. Halio and Ben Siegel, 226–46. Cranbury, NJ: Associated University Presses, 1997.

Wolff, Tamsen. "The Chronicle Review: Wendy Wasserstein (1950–2006)." *Chronicle of Higher Education* 52.24 (February 17, 2006): B13.

Reviews of Salamon's Wendy and the Lost Boys

Als, Hilton. "Critic's Notebook: Talk Therapy." Review of *Wendy and the Lost Boys: The Uncommon Life of Wendy Wasserstein*, by Julie Salamon. *New Yorker*, September 12, 2011. http://www.newyorker.com/magazine/2011/09/12/talk-therapy

Berson, Misha. "Author Brings Wendy Wasserstein's Complexities, Gifts to Light." Review of *Wendy and the Lost Boys: The Uncommon Life of Wendy Wasserstein*, by Julie Salamon. *Seattle Times*, August 27, 2011. http://www.popmatters.com/article/146985-author-brings-wendy-wassersteins-complexities-gifts-to-light/

Brawarsky, Sandee. "Understanding Wendy." Review of *Wendy and the Lost Boys: The Uncommon Life of Wendy Wasserstein*, by Julie Salamon. *Jewish Woman Magazine*, August 2011. http://www.jwi.org/Page.aspx?pid=2971#sthash.QLyW0oS6.dpbs

Brockes, Emma. "And Now, Wendy Gets Her Chronicles." Review of *Wendy and the Lost Boys: The Uncommon Life of Wendy Wasserstein*, by Julie Salamon. *New York Times*, August 18, 2011, C1.

Clum, John M. "*Wendy and the Lost Boys: The Uncommon Life of Wendy Wasserstein*, and *Reading the Plays of Wendy Wasserstein* (review)." *Theatre Journal* 64.4 (December 2012): 626–27.

Collins-Hughes, Laura. "Playwright's Biography Sets Scenes but Fails to Explore." Review of *Wendy and the Lost Boys: The Uncommon Life of Wendy Wasserstein*, by Julie Salamon. *Boston Globe*, August 26, 2011, G9.

Connelly, Sherryl. "'Wendy and the Lost Boys: The Uncommon Life of Wendy Wasserstein' Follows Strong Female Lede." Review of *Wendy and the Lost Boys: The Uncommon Life of Wendy Wasserstein*, by Julie Salamon. *New York Daily News*, August 22, 2011. http://www.nydailynews.com/life-style/wendy-lost-boys-uncommon-life-wendy-wasserstein-strong-female-lede-article-1.947443

"Girl Guide: A New York Playwright Who Gave Voice to the Ambivalence of Her Generation." Review of *Wendy and the Lost Boys: The Uncommon Life of Wendy Wasserstein*, by Julie Salamon. *Economist*, August 13, 2011. http://www.economist.com/node/21525819

Isherwood, Charles. "Theater Talkback: I Could Read a Book." Review of *Wendy and the Lost Boys: The Uncommon Life of Wendy Wasserstein*, by Julie Salamon. *New York Times*, October 21, 2011. http://artsbeat.blogs.nytimes.com/2011/10/21/theater-talkback-i-could-read-a-book/?_r=0

McCabe, Vinton Rafe. Review of *Wendy and the Lost Boys: The Uncommon Life of Wendy Wasserstein*, by Julie Salamon. *New York Journal of Books*, August 18, 2011. http://www.nyjournalofbooks.com/book-review/wendy-and-lost-boys-uncommon-life-wendy-wasserstein

McNulty, Charles. Review of *Wendy and the Lost Boys: The Uncommon Life of Wendy Wasserstein*, by Julie Salamon. *Los Angeles Times*, September 4, 2011. http://articles.latimes.com/2011/sep/04/entertainment/la-ca-julie-salamon-20110904

O'Grady, Megan. "Uncommon Woman: A New Biography Chronicles the Life and Work of Playwright Wendy Wasserstein." Review of *Wendy and the Lost Boys: The Uncommon Life of Wendy Wasserstein*, by Julie Salamon. *Vogue Daily*, August 16, 2011. http://www.vogue.com/873816/uncommon-woman-bra-new-biography-chronicles-the-life-and-work-of-playwright-wendy-wasserstein/

Prose, Francine. "The Wendy Chronicles: What Wendy Wasserstein Wrought." Review of *Wendy and the Lost Boys: The Uncommon Life of Wendy Wasserstein*, by Julie Salamon. *New York Times*, August 28, 2011, Sunday Book Review, BR13.

Salamon, Julie. "What Wendy Knew." *Daily Beast*, August 30, 2011. http://www.thedailybeast.com/articles/2011/08/30/wendy-wasserstein-biographer-on-why-she-s-a-role-model.html

Weber, Katharine. "Wendy Wasserstein in Neverland." Review of *Wendy and the Lost Boys: The Uncommon Life of Wendy Wasserstein*, by Julie Salamon. *Moment* 36.4 (July/August 2011): 68–69.

Weiss, Hedy. "Wendy Wasserstein's Life No Open Book." Review of *Wendy and the Lost Boys: The Uncommon Life of Wendy Wasserstein*, by Julie Salamon. *Chicago Sun Times*, August 25, 2011. www.suntimes.com/entertainment/books/7225227–421/wassersteins-life-no-open-book.html

Winer, Laurie. "Julie Salamon's 'Wendy and the Lost Boys' Is a Biography of Playwright Wendy Wasserstein." Review of *Wendy and the Lost Boys: The Uncommon Life of Wendy Wasserstein*, by Julie Salamon. *Washington Post*, September 1, 2011. http://www.washingtonpost.com/entertainment/books/julie-salamons-wendy-and-the-lost-boys-is-a-biography-of-playwright-wendy-wasserstein/2011/08/02/gIQAaM80uJ_story.html

Reviews of Original and Revival Productions

Uncommon Women and Others (Phoenix Theatre, November 21, 1977)

Beaufort, John. "A Wry Reunion." Review of *Uncommon Women and Others*, by Wendy Wasserstein, directed by Steven Robman, Phoenix Theatre, New York. *Christian Science Monitor*, November 30, 1977. In *New York*

Theater Critics' Reviews Off Broadway Supplement IV, vol. 38, no. 22, edited by Joan Marlowe and Betty Blake, 140. New York: Critics' Theatre Reviews, 1977.

Clurman, Harold. Review of *Uncommon Women and Others*, by Wendy Wasserstein, directed by Steven Robman, Phoenix Theatre, New York. *Nation*, December 17, 1977, 667.

Eder, Richard. "Dramatic Wit and Wisdom Unite in *Uncommon Women and Others*." Review of *Uncommon Women and Others*, by Wendy Wasserstein, directed by Steven Robman, Phoenix Theatre, New York. *New York Times*, November 22, 1977, 42.

Newton, Edmund. "'Women' One Can't Forget." Review of *Uncommon Women and Others*, by Wendy Wasserstein, directed by Steven Robman, Phoenix Theatre, New York. *New York Post*, November 22, 1977. In *New York Theater Critics' Reviews Off Broadway Supplement IV*, vol. 38, no. 22, edited by Joan Marlowe and Betty Blake, 140. New York: Critics' Theatre Reviews, 1977.

Watt, Douglas. "Holyoke Hen Sessions." Review of *Uncommon Women and Others*, by Wendy Wasserstein, directed by Steven Robman, Phoenix Theatre, New York. *New York Daily News*, November 22, 1977. In *New York Theater Critics' Reviews Off Broadway Supplement IV*, vol. 38, no. 22, edited by Joan Marlowe and Betty Blake, 139. New York: Critics' Theatre Reviews, 1977.

Uncommon Women and Others, 1994 Revival (Lucille Lortel Theatre, October 26, 1994)

Kanfer, Stefan. "Past Imperfect." Review of *Uncommon Women and Others*, by Wendy Wasserstein, directed by Carole Rothman, Lucille Lortel Theatre, New York. *New Leader* 77.11 (November 7, 1994): 22–23.

Isn't It Romantic (Phoenix Theatre, May 28, 1981)

Gussow, Mel. Review of *Isn't it Romantic*, by Wendy Wasserstein, directed by Steven Robman, Phoenix Theatre, New York. *New York Times*, June 15, 1981, C11.

Isn't It Romantic (Playwrights Horizons, December 15, 1983)

Barnes, Clive. "'Isn't It Romantic'—and It's Funny, Too." Review of *Isn't It Romantic*, by Wendy Wasserstein, directed by Gerald Gutierrez, Playwrights Horizons, New York. *New York Post*, December 16, 1983. In *New York Theater Critics' Reviews*, vol. 44, no. 18, edited by Joan Marlowe and Betty Blake, 70. New York: Critics' Theatre Reviews, 1983.

Corliss, Richard. "Broadway's Big Endearment." Review of *Isn't It Romantic*, by Wendy Wasserstein, directed by Gerald Gutierrez, Playwrights Horizons, New York. *Time*, December 26, 1983. In *New York Theater Critics' Reviews*, vol. 44, no. 18, edited by Joan Marlowe and Betty Blake, 70–71. New York: Critics' Theatre Reviews, 1983.

Kissel, Howard. Review of *Isn't It Romantic*, by Wendy Wasserstein, directed by Gerald Gutierrez, Playwrights Horizons, New York. *Women's Wear Daily*, December 16, 1983. In *New York Theater Critics' Reviews*, vol. 44, no. 18, edited by Joan Marlowe and Betty Blake, 69. New York: Critics' Theatre Reviews, 1983.

Sirkin, Elliott. Review of *Isn't It Romantic*, by Wendy Wasserstein, directed by Gerald Gutierrez, Playwrights Horizons, New York. *Nation*, February 18, 1984: 202–03.

Watt, Douglas. "'Isn't It Romantic'—Sometimes." Review of *Isn't It Romantic*, by Wendy Wasserstein, directed by Gerald Gutierrez, Playwrights Horizons, New York. *New York Daily News*, December 16, 1983. In *New York Theater Critics' Reviews*, vol. 44, no. 18, edited by Joan Marlowe and Betty Blake, 69–70. New York: Critics' Theatre Reviews, 1983.

The Heidi Chronicles (Playwrights Horizons, December 11, 1988)

Barnes, Clive. "Hello, I'm the Me Generation." Review of *The Heidi Chronicles*, by Wendy Wasserstein, directed by Daniel Sullivan, Playwrights Horizons, New York. *New York Post*, December 12, 1988. In *New York Theater Critics' Reviews*, vol. 50, no. 5, edited by Joan Marlowe and Betty Blake, 332–33. New York: Critics' Theatre Reviews, 1989.

Beaufort, John. "Bright Facades and Serious Insights." Review of *The Heidi Chronicles*, by Wendy Wasserstein, directed by Daniel Sullivan, Playwrights Horizons, New York. *Christian Monitor*, December 16, 1988. In *New York Theater Critics' Reviews*, vol. 50, no. 5, edited by Joan Marlowe and Betty Blake, 334–35. New York: Critics' Theatre Reviews, 1989.

Gold, Sylviane. "Circle Pins to Power Lunches." Review of *The Heidi Chronicles*, by Wendy Wasserstein, directed by Daniel Sullivan, Playwrights Horizons, New York. *Wall Street Journal*, December 16, 1988. In *New York Theater Critics' Reviews*, vol. 50, no. 5, edited by Joan Marlowe and Betty Blake, 331–32. New York: Critics' Theatre Reviews, 1989.

Gussow, Mel. "A Modern-Day Heffalump in Search of Herself." Review of *The Heidi Chronicles*, by Wendy Wasserstein, directed by Daniel Sullivan, Playwrights Horizons, New York. *New York Times*, December 12, 1988, C13.

Kissel, Howard. "'Heidi' Grows Up, with Grace." Review of *The Heidi Chronicles*, by Wendy Wasserstein, directed by Daniel Sullivan, Playwrights Horizons, New York. *New York Daily News*, December 12, 1988.

In *New York Theater Critics' Reviews*, vol. 50, no. 5, edited by Joan Marlowe and Betty Blake, 331. New York: Critics' Theatre Reviews, 1989.

Rothstein, Mervyn. "After the Revolution, What? The Daughters of Feminism." *New York Times*, December 11, 1988, Arts & Leisure, H1, 28.

Solomon, Alisa. "feminism-something." *Village Voice*, December 20, 1988, 123.

Watt, Doug. "This 'Heidi' Is Quite a Character—Second Thoughts on First Nights." Review of *The Heidi Chronicles*, by Wendy Wasserstein, directed by Daniel Sullivan, Playwrights Horizons, New York. *New York Daily News*, December 23, 1988. In *New York Theater Critics' Reviews*, vol. 50, no. 5, edited by Joan Marlowe and Betty Blake, 331. New York: Critics' Theatre Reviews, 1989.

Winer, Linda. "Real People with Tough Questions." *New York Newsday*, December 12, 1988. Review of *The Heidi Chronicles*, by Wendy Wasserstein, directed by Daniel Sullivan, Playwrights Horizons, New York. In *New York Theater Critics' Reviews*, vol. 50, no. 5, edited by Joan Marlowe and Betty Blake, 333–34. New York: Critics' Theatre Reviews, 1989.

The Heidi Chronicles (Broadway, March 9, 1989)

Austin, Gayle. "Theatre Review: *The Heidi Chronicles*." Review of *The Heidi Chronicles*, by Wendy Wasserstein, directed by Daniel Sullivan, Plymouth Theatre, New York. *Theatre Journal* 42.1 (March 1990): 107–8.

Henry, William A. "Way Stations: *The Heidi Chronicles* by Wendy Wasserstein." Review of *The Heidi Chronicles*, by Wendy Wasserstein, directed by Daniel Sullivan, Plymouth Theatre, New York. *Time*, March 20, 1989. In *New York Theater Critics' Reviews*, vol. 50, no. 5, edited by Joan Marlowe and Betty Blake, 337. New York: Critics' Theatre Reviews, 1989.

Kelly, Kevin. "AIDS Treated Too Often as a Subplot." *Boston Globe*, April 16, 1989, B39.

Kelly, Kevin. "*Heidi* Has Shine, Not Depth." Review of *The Heidi Chronicles*, by Wendy Wasserstein, directed by Daniel Sullivan, Plymouth Theatre, New York. *Boston Globe*, April 6, 1989, 73.

Kissel, Howard. "'Heidi' Lights up Broadway." Review of *The Heidi Chronicles*, by Wendy Wasserstein, directed by Daniel Sullivan, Plymouth Theatre, New York. *New York Daily News*, March 10, 1989. In *New York Theater Critics' Reviews*, vol. 50, no. 5, edited by Joan Marlowe and Betty Blake, 335. New York: Critics' Theatre Reviews, 1989.

McGuigan, Cathleen. "The Uncommon Wendy Wasserstein Goes to Broadway." Review of *The Heidi Chronicles*, by Wendy Wasserstein, directed by Daniel Sullivan, Plymouth Theatre, New York. *Newsweek*, March 20, 1989. In *New York Theater Critics' Reviews*, vol. 50, no. 5, edited by Joan Marlowe and Betty Blake, 336. New York: Critics' Theatre Reviews, 1989.

Richards, David. "The Life and Loves of 'Heidi': On Broadway, Wasserstein's

Baby Boomer 'Chronicles.'" Review of *The Heidi Chronicles*, by Wendy Wasserstein, directed by Daniel Sullivan, Plymouth Theatre, New York. *Washington Post*, March 14, 1989, E1.

Span, Paula. "Uncommon Wendy and Her Broadway 'Chronicles': Playwright Wasserstein & The Long Road Uptown." *Washington Post*, March 12, 1989, G1.

Stearns, David Patrick. "Lively, Liberated 'Heidi.'" Review of *The Heidi Chronicles*, by Wendy Wasserstein, directed by Daniel Sullivan, Plymouth Theatre, New York. *USA Today*, March 10, 1989. In *New York Theater Critics' Reviews*, vol. 50, no. 5, edited by Joan Marlowe and Betty Blake, 335–36. New York: Critics' Theatre Reviews, 1989.

The Heidi Chronicles, 2015 Revival (Broadway, March 19, 2015)

Finkle, David. "Wendy Wasserstein's 'Heidi Chronicles' in A+ Revival." Review of *The Heidi Chronicles*, by Wendy Wasserstein, directed by Pam MacKinnon, Music Box Theatre, New York. *Huffington Post*, March 19, 2015. http://www.huffingtonpost.com/david-finkle/first-nighter-wendy-wasserstein-heidi-chronicles_b_6906898.html

Gerard, Jeremy. "Elisabeth Moss' '60s Peggy Olson is '80s 'Heidi.'" Review of *The Heidi Chronicles*, by Wendy Wasserstein, directed by Pam MacKinnon, Music Box Theatre, New York. *Deadline*, March 19, 2015. http://deadline.com/2015/03/elisabeth-moss-heidi-chronicles-review-broadway-1201395185/

Isherwood, Charles. Review of *The Heidi Chronicles*, by Wendy Wasserstein, directed by Pam MacKinnon, Music Box Theatre, New York. *New York Times*, March 19, 2015. http://www.nytimes.com/2015/03/20/theater/review-the-heidi-chronicles-with-elisabeth-moss-opens-on-broadway.html?_r=0

Jones, Chris. "Elisabeth Moss a Good Fit for 'Heidi Chronicles' on Broadway." Review of *The Heidi Chronicles*, by Wendy Wasserstein, directed by Pam MacKinnon, Music Box Theatre, New York. *Chicago Tribune*, March 19, 2015. http://www.chicagotribune.com/entertainment/theater/broadway/sc-heidi-chronicles-broadway-review-20150319-column.html

Maerz, Melissa. "Elisabeth Moss and Jason Biggs in *The Heidi Chronicles*." Review of *The Heidi Chronicles*, by Wendy Wasserstein, directed by Pam MacKinnon, Music Box Theatre, New York. *Entertainment Weekly*, March 19, 2015. http://www.ew.com/article/2015/03/19/elisabeth-moss-and-jason-biggs-heidi-chronicles-ew-review

Oxfeld, Jesse. "How Wendy Wasserstein and Heidi Holland Remade the World." Review of *The Heidi Chronicles*, by Wendy Wasserstein, directed by Pam MacKinnon, Music Box Theatre, New York. *Jewish Daily Forward*, March 19, 2015. http://forward.com/culture/216972/how-wendy-wasserstein-and-heidi-holland-remade-the/

Paulson, Michael, and Jennifer Schluesser. "*The Heidi Chronicles* Is Trailed by Questions of Feminism and Legacy." *New York Times*, April 23, 2015. http://www.nytimes.com/2015/04/23/theater/the-heidi-chronicles-is-trailed-by-questions-of-feminism-and-legacy.html?_r=1

Purcell, Carey. "A Woman's World: Pam MacKinnon on the Decision to Restore Wasserstein's Cut Dialogue to *The Heidi Chronicles*." *Playbill*, February 28, 2015. http://www.playbill.com/news/article/a-womans-world-pam-mackinnon-on-the-decision-to-restore-wassersteins-cut-dialogue-to-the-heidi-chronicles-342388

Solomon, Alisa. "Why 'The Heidi Chronicles' Failed to Find a New Audience." *Nation*, April 24, 2015. http://www.thenation.com/article/why-heidi-chronicles-failed-find-new-audience/

The Sisters Rosensweig (Mitzi E. Newhouse Theater at Lincoln Center, October 22, 1992)

Brustein, Robert. "The Sisters Rosensweig." Review of *The Sisters Rosensweig*, by Wendy Wasserstein, directed by Daniel Sullivan, Mitzi E. Newhouse Theater, New York. *New Republic*, December 7, 1992. In *New York Theater Critics' Reviews*, vol. 54, no. 4, edited by Norma Adler et al., 78–79. New York: Critics' Theatre Reviews, 1993.

Gussow, Mel. "Wasserstein: Comedy, Character, Reflection." Review of *The Sisters Rosensweig*, by Wendy Wasserstein, directed by Daniel Sullivan, Mitzi E. Newhouse Theater, New York. *New York Times*, October 23, 1992, C3.

The Sisters Rosensweig (Broadway, March 18, 1993)

Kelly, Kevin. "Wasserstein's Clever 'Sisters Rosensweig.'" Review of *The Sisters Rosensweig*, by Wendy Wasserstein, directed by Daniel Sullivan, Ethel Barrymore Theatre, New York. *Boston Globe*, April 1, 1993, Living section, 61.

An American Daughter (Broadway, April 13, 1997)

Barnes, Clive. "No Hitting below the Beltway." Review of *An American Daughter*, by Wendy Wasserstein, directed by Daniel Sullivan, Cort Theatre, New York. *New York Post*, April 14, 1997, 35.

Brantley, Ben. "In the Hostile Glare of Washington, the Media Define and Defy." Review of *An American Daughter*, by Wendy Wasserstein, directed by Daniel Sullivan, Cort Theatre, New York. *New York Times*, April 14, 1997, C11. http://www.nytimes.com/1997/04/14/theater/in-the-hostile-glare-of-washington-the-media-define-and-defy.html

Kissel, Howard. "Political Play Fails to Capitol-ize: Wasserstein's 'Daughter'

Is Topical but Character Issue Sinks D.C. Tale." Review of *An American Daughter*, by Wendy Wasserstein, directed by Daniel Sullivan, Cort Theatre, New York. *New York Daily News*, April 14, 1997. http://www.ny-dailynews.com/archives/nydn-features/political-play-fails-capitol-ize-wasserstein-daughter-topical-character-issue-sinks-tale-article-1.751339

Sheward, David. Review of *An American Daughter*, by Wendy Wasserstein, directed by Daniel Sullivan, Cort Theatre, New York. *Back Stage*, April 18, 1997, 60.

Shteir, Rachel. "From the Front Page to the Broadway Stage: Wendy Wasserstein Finds Her Muse in Washington Politics." *Forward*, April 25, 1997, 9.

An American Daughter (Williamstown Theatre Festival, August 6, 2016)

Isherwood, Charles. "Women's Hard Choices, Cutting Deep at Williamstown Festival." Review of *An American Daughter*, by Wendy Wasserstein, directed by Evan Cabnet, Williamstown Theatre Festival, Williamstown, Massachusetts. *New York Times*, August 18, 2016. http://www.nytimes.com/2016/08/19/theater/review-womens-hard-choices-cutting-deep-at-williamstown-festival.html

Third (Mitzi E. Newhouse Theater at Lincoln Center, October 24, 2005)

Feingold, Michael. "Wasserstein's Sourly Wistful, Autumnal Comedy of Academia Sounds a Minor." Review of *Third*, by Wendy Wasserstein, directed by Daniel Sullivan, Mitzi E. Newhouse Theater, New York. *Village Voice*, October 25, 2005. http://www.villagevoice.com/arts/wassersteins-sourly-wistful-autumnal-comedy-of-academia-sounds-a-minor-7137011

Lahr, John. "Reversal of Fortune: A New 'Odd Couple' and an Old Formula." Review of *Third*, by Wendy Wasserstein, directed by Daniel Sullivan, Mitzi E. Newhouse Theater, New York. *New Yorker*, November 7, 2005, 144–45.

Scheck, Frank. "Prof Unsure of Her Class." Review of *Third*, by Wendy Wasserstein, directed by Daniel Sullivan, Mitzi E. Newhouse Theater, New York. *New York Post*, October 25, 2005, 46.

Third (Other Productions)

Cohen, Steve. "PTC's 'Third.'" Review of *Third*, by Wendy Wasserstein, directed by Mary B. Robinson, Philadelphia Theatre Company, Philadelphia. *Broad Street Review*, March 29, 2008. www.broadstreetreview.com/dance/PTCs_Third_2nd_review

Dunleavy, Tim. *"Third."* Review of *Third*, by Wendy Wasserstein, directed by Mary B. Robinson, Philadelphia Theatre Company, Philadelphia. *Talkin' Broadway*, March 31, 2008. www.talkinbroadway.com/page/regional/philly/phil74.html

Hunter, Hugh. "First-Rate Production of 'Third.'" Review of *Third*, by Wendy Wasserstein, directed by Robert Bauer, The Drama Group, Philadelphia. *Chestnut Hill Local*, March 25, 2011. http://www.chestnuthilllocal.com/2011/03/25/first-rate-production-of-%E2%80%98third%E2%80%99/

Jenkins, Thomas. "'Third' Doesn't Make the Grade." Review of *Third*, by Wendy Wasserstein, directed by Catherine Babbitt, San Pedro Playhouse's Cellar Theater, San Antonio. *San Antonio Current*, September 3, 2008. www.sacurrent.com/sanantonio/third-doesn't-make-the-grade/Content?oid=2284199

Lowen, Linda. "Profs vs. Jocks: Hangar Theatre's 'Third' Mines Campus Politics, Mid-Life Crisis." Review of *Third*, by Wendy Wasserstein, directed by Michael Barakiva, Hangar Theatre, Ithaca, New York. Syracuse.com, July 23, 2016. www.syracuse.com/entertainment/index.ssf/2016/07/hangar_theatre_third_review.html

MacKillop, James. "First Place Finish for 'Third.'" Review of *Third*, by Wendy Wasserstein, directed by Michael Barakiva, Hangar Theatre, Ithaca, New York. *Syracuse New Times*, July 27, 2016. http://www.syracusenewtimes.com/first-place-finish-for-third/

McNulty, Charles. "'Third' Is, Sadly, Only Second-Rate Wasserstein." Review of *Third*, by Wendy Wasserstein, directed by Maria Mileaf, Geffen Playhouse, Los Angeles. *Los Angeles Times*, September 21, 2007. www.articles.latimes.com/print/2007/sep/21/entertainment/et-third21

Reynolds, Judith. "Aiming for Higher Education: Merely Players Stage Provocative 'Third.'" Review of *Third*, by Wendy Wasserstein, directed by Mona Wood Patterson, Merely Players, Durango, Colorado. *Durango Herald*, November 15, 2011. www.durangoherald.com/article/20111115/ARTS01/711159986/

Sommers, Michael. "Finding Cracks in a Perfect Life: A Review of 'Third' in Red Bank." Review of *Third*, by Wendy Wasserstein, directed by Michael Cumpsty, Two River Theater, Red Bank, New Jersey. *New York Times*, June 13, 2014. www.nytimes.com/2014/06/15/nyregion/a-review-of-third-in-red-bank

Verini, Bob. Review of *Third*, by Wendy Wasserstein, directed by Maria Mileaf, Geffen Playhouse, Los Angeles. *Variety*, September 20, 2007. www.variety.com/2007/legit/markets festivals/third-2–1200556152/

Worssam, Nancy. "'Third' by Wendy Wasserstein at Arts West." Review of *Third*, by Wendy Wasserstein, directed by Peggy Gannon, Arts West, Seattle. *Arts Stage—Seattle Rage* (blog). March 8, 2014. http://artsstage-seattlerage.com/2014/third-by-wendy-wasserstein-at-arts-west/

Secondary Sources

Abramovitch, Seth. "Helen Gurley Brown on Money, Sex and Having It All." August 13, 2012. http://www.hollywoodreporter.com/news/helen-gurley-brown-money-sex-quotes-quotations-361417

Alter, Charlotte. "Kirsten Gillibrand on Why She Hates the Phrase 'Having It All.' *Time*, October 1, 2014. http://time.com/3453839/kirsten-gillibrand-have-it-all/

Andreach, Robert J. *Understanding Beth Henley*. Columbia: University of South Carolina Press, 2006.

Association for Theatre in Higher Education. "Women & Theatre Program." http://www.athe.org/group/WTP

Bachrach, Judy. "When It Comes to 'Having It All' Helen Gurley Brown Wrote the Book—with a Little Inspiration from Her Dear David." *People*, November 1, 1982. www.people.com/people/archive/article/0,,20083447,00.html

Berman, Eliza. "Life Before 'Having It All': Portrait of a Working Girl in 1940." *Time*, May 14, 2015. http://time.com/3828274/working-girl-1940/.

Bial, Henry. *Acting Jewish: Negotiating Ethnicity on the American Stage and Screen*. Ann Arbor: University of Michigan Press, 2005.

Carlson, Gretchen. "My Take On Having It All." *Fox News*, June 23, 2015. www.foxnews.com/opinion/2015/06/23/my-take-on-having-it-all.html

Chinoy, Helen Krich, and Linda Walsh Jenkins. *Women in American Theatre*. 3rd ed. New York: Theatre Communications Group, 2006.

Clement, Olivia. "Jessie Mueller, Lupita Nyong'o and Danai Gurira Step Out for the Lilly Awards Tonight." *Playbill*, May 23, 2016. http://www.playbill.com/article/jessie-mueller-lupita-nyong-39-0-and-danai-gurira-step-out-for-the-lilly-39-s-tonight

Cohen, Patricia. "Rethinking Gender Bias in Theater." *New York Times*, June 23, 2009. http://www.nytimes.com/2009/06/24/theater/24play.html?_r=0

Collins-Hughes, Laura. "Internet Outcry over Diversity Leads Manhattan Theater Club to Announce Season Details Early." *New York Times*, August 20, 2015. http://www.nytimes.com/2015/08/22/theater/after-outcry-over-diversity-manhattan-theater-club-is-making-a-change.html

Diamond, Elin. "Brechtian Theory/Feminist Theory: Toward a Gestic Feminist Criticism." *TDR* 32.1 (Spring 1988): 82–94.

Diamond, Elin. *Unmaking Mimesis: Essays on Feminism and Theatre*. New York: Routledge, 1997.

Dines, Gail. "'Having It All' Looks Very Different for Women Stuck in Low-Paid Jobs." *Guardian*, June 25, 2012. http://www.theguardian.com/commentisfree/2012/jun/25/having-it-all-women-anne-marie-slaughter

Dolan, Jill. *The Feminist Spectator as Critic.* Ann Arbor: University of Michigan Press, 1991.

Dolan, Jill. *The Feminist Spectator in Action: Feminist Criticism for the Stage and Screen.* Basingstoke: Palgrave Macmillan, 2013.

Dolan, Jill. *Presence and Desire: Essays on Gender, Sexuality, Performance.* Ann Arbor: University of Michigan Press, 1993.

Dolan, Jill. *Utopia in Performance: Finding Hope at the Theatre.* Ann Arbor: University of Michigan Press, 2005.

Douglas, Susan. *Enlightened Sexism: The Seductive Message That Feminism's Work Is Done.* New York: Times Books, 2010.

Erkut, Sumru, and Ineke Ceder, "Women's Leadership in Resident Theatres: Summary of Results and Recommendations." Draft report, Wellesley Center for Women, Wellesley College, August 22, 2016. http://howlround.com/women-s-leadership-research-results-and-recommendations?#_=_

Fairchild, Caroline. "Three Things Women Leaders Say about 'Having It All.'" *Fortune,* January 5, 2015. http://fortune.com/2015/01/05/3-things-women-leaders-say-about-having-it-all/

Faludi, Susan. *Backlash: The Undeclared War against American Women.* New York: Crown, 1991.

50/50 in 2020. www.5050in2020.org

Fischer, Molly. "When Will We Stop Talking about 'Having It All'?" *New York Magazine,* August 7, 2013. http://www.nymag.com/thecut/2013/08/when-will-we-stop-talking-about-having-it-all.html

Flores, Yolanda. *The Drama of Gender: Theater by Women of the Americas.* New York: Peter Lang, 2000.

Gener, Randy. "Maria Mileaf: Earth Mother." Theatre Communications Group. http://www.tcg.org/publications/at/Oct07/mileaf.cfm

Gionfriddo, Gina. "All Hail 'Heidi': Beyond Feminism but Still a Dream." *New York Times,* June 7, 2012. http://www.nytimes.com/2012/06/10/theater/gina-gionfriddo-on-rapture-blister-burn-and-wasserstein.html?_r=0

Gionfriddo, Gina. *Rapture, Blister, Burn.* New York: Dramatists Play Service, 2014.

Goodman, Lizbeth. *Contemporary Feminist Theatres.* London: Routledge, 1993.

Gordon, Barbara. *I'm Dancing as Fast as I Can.* New York: Harper and Row, 1979.

Gussow, Mel. "Whoopi Goldberg Does 'The Spook Show.'" Review of *Spook Show,* by Whoopi Goldberg, Dance Theater Workshop, New York. *New York Times,* February 3, 1984. http://www.nytimes.com/1984/02/03/arts/stage-whoopi-goldberg-does-the-spook-show.html

Hart, Lynda, ed. *Making a Spectacle: Feminist Essays on Contemporary Women's Theater.* Ann Arbor: University of Michigan Press, 1999.

"Having It All, and Then Some: Why the Best-Educated Women Are Opting for More Children." *Economist*, May 23, 2015. http://www.economist.com/node/21651833

Hewlett, Sylvia Ann. "Executive Women and the Myth of Having It All." *Harvard Business Review*, April 2002. http://hbr.org/2002/04/executive-women-and-the-myth-of-having-it-all

Holledge, Julie, and Joanne Tompkins. *Women's Intercultural Performance*. London: Routledge, 2000.

Hollows, Joanne, and Rachel Moseley, eds. *Feminism in Popular Culture*. New York: Berg, 2006.

Huffington, Arianna. *Thrive: The Third Metric to Redefining Success and Creating a Life of Well-Being, Wisdom, and Wonder*. New York: Harmony Books/Random House, 2014.

Hughes, Sali. "Helen Gurley Brown: How to Have It All." *Guardian*, August 14, 2012. www.theguardian.com/lifeandstyle/2012/aug/14/helen-gurley-brown-cosmopolitan-sex.

Jonas, Susan, and Suzanne Bennett. *Report on the Status of Women: A Limited Engagement?* New York State Council on the Arts Theatre Program, January 2002. http://www.womenarts.org/nysca-report-2002

Keyssar, Helene, ed. *Feminist Theatre and Theory*. New York: St. Martin's Press, 1996.

The Kilroys. "The Kilroys: We Make Trouble and Plays." www.thekilroys.org

Koedt, Anne. *The Myth of the Vaginal Orgasm*. Somerville, MA: New England Free Press, 1970.

Kornbluth, Jesse. "The Queen of the Mouseburgers." *New York Magazine*, September 27, 1982.

Laughlin, Karen, and Catherine Schuler, eds. *Theatre and Feminist Aesthetics*. Teaneck, NJ: Fairleigh Dickinson University Press, 1995.

League of Professional Theatre Women. www.theatrewomen.org

McRobbie, Angela. "Post-feminism and Popular Culture: Bridget Jones and the New Gender Regime." In *Media and Cultural Theory*, edited by James Curran and David Morley, 59–69. London: Routledge, 2006.

Mead, Rebecca. "The Scourge of 'Relatability.'" *New Yorker*, August 1, 2014. http://www.newyorker.com/culture/cultural-comment/scourge-relatability

Mercer, Kobena. "Black Art and the Burden of Representation." In *Welcome to the Jungle: New Positions in Black Cultural Studies*, 233–58. New York: Routledge, 1994.

Murphy, Brenda, ed. *The Cambridge Companion to American Women Playwrights*. Cambridge: Cambridge University Press, 1999.

North, Anna. "Should Literature Be Relatable?" *Op-Talk* (blog). *New York Times*, August 5, 2014. http://op-talk.blogs.nytimes.com/2014/08/05/should-literature-be-relatable/

Porter, Laurin. "Contemporary Playwrights/Traditional Forms." In *The Cambridge Companion to American Women Playwrights*, edited by Brenda Murphy, 195–212. Cambridge: Cambridge University Press, 1999.

Rich, Adrienne. "Compulsory Heterosexuality and Lesbian Existence (1980)." In *Blood, Bread, and Poetry: Selected Prose 1979–1985*, by Adrienne Rich, 23–75. 1986. Reprint, New York: W. W. Norton, 1994.

Rich, Frank. "'Whoopi Goldberg' Opens." Review of *Whoopi Goldberg*, by Whoopi Goldberg, supervised by Mike Nichols, Lyceum Theater, New York. *New York Times*, October 25, 1984. http://www.nytimes.com/1984/10/25/theater/stage-whoopi-goldberg-opens.html

Sandberg, Sheryl. *Lean In: Women, Work, and the Will to Lead.* New York: Alfred A. Knopf, 2013.

Savran, David, ed. *The Playwright's Voice: American Dramatists on Memory, Writing, and the Politics of Culture.* New York: Theatre Communications Group, 1999.

Savran, David. *A Queer Sort of Materialism: Recontextualizing American Theater.* Ann Arbor: University of Michigan Press, 2003.

Schlueter, June. Introduction to *Modern American Drama: The Female Canon*, edited by June Schlueter, 11–23. Madison, NJ: Fairleigh Dickinson University Press, 1990.

Schroeder, Patricia R. "American Drama, Feminist Discourse, and Dramatic Form: A Defense of Critical Pluralism." In *Theatre and Feminist Aesthetics*, edited by Karen Laughlin and Catherine Schuler, 66–81. Madison, NJ: Fairleigh Dickinson University Press, 1995.

Scott, Joan. "Fifty Years of Academic Feminism." Meredith Miller Memorial Lecture, McCormick Hall, Princeton University, Princeton, NJ, April 22, 2015.

Slaughter, Anne-Marie. *Unfinished Business: Women Men Work Family.* New York: Random House, 2015.

Slaughter, Anne-Marie. "Why Women Still Can't Have It All." *Atlantic*, July/August 2012. www.theatlantic.com/magazine/archive/2012/07/why-women-still-cant-have-it-all/309020/

Soloski, Alexis. "With 'Significant Other,' Joshua Harmon Happily Writes about the Unhappy." *New York Times*, June 14, 2015. http://www.nytimes.com/2015/06/14/theater/with-significant-other-joshua-harmon-happily-writes-about-the-unhappy.html?_r=0

Spar, Debora L. *Wonder Women: Sex, Power, and the Quest for Perfection.* New York: Sarah Crichton Books/Farrar, Straus and Giroux, 2013.

Szalai, Jennifer. "The Complicated Origins of 'Having It All.'" *New York Times*, January 2, 2015. http://www.nytimes.com/2015/01/04/magazine/the-complicated-origins-of-having-it-all.html?_r=0

Thurman, Judith. "Owning Your Desire: Remembering Helen Gurley Brown." *New Yorker*, August 15, 2012. www.newyorker.com/books/page-turner/owning-your-desire-remembering-helen-gurley-brown

Vorlicky, Robert. "[In]Visible Alliances: Conflicting 'Chronicles' of Feminism." In *Engendering Men: The Question of Male Feminist Criticism*,

edited by Joseph A. Boone and Michael Cadden, 275–90. New York: Routledge, 1990.

Zeisler, Andi. *We Were Feminists Once: From Riot Grrrl to CoverGirl, the
Buying and Selling of a Political Movement*. New York: Public Affairs,
2016.

Index

Trump, Donald: misogyny of, 116–17
Turner, Ike and Tina, 138
Two River Theater (Red Bank), 129

Uncommon Women and Others (1977), 1, 13, 19, 21, 41–42, 45, 52–54, 58, 61, 63, 83, 120, 147, 154n2; 2007 Cornell performance, 154n2; representation of women, 9–10, 12, 15–16, 23–39, 44, 50, 128–29, 153n27

The Vagina Monologues (1996, Ensler), 15
Variety, 130
Verini, Bob, 130
Village Voice, 72, 131
Vineyard Theatre (New York), 134
Vogel, Paula, x, 16, 142; *Indecent* (2017), 134
Vorlicky, Robert, 18

Wagner, Jane: *Search for Signs of Intelligent Life in the Universe* (1985), 14, 133, 165n1
Washburn, Anne, xi
Washington, Kerry: *Scandal* (2012–), 162n1
Wasserstein, Abner, 7, 147
Wasserstein, Bruce, 6–8, 140, 147
Wasserstein, George, 7
Wasserstein, Georgette. *See* Levis, Georgette Wasserstein
Wasserstein, Lola, 2, 6–7, 17, 41, 147

Wasserstein, Lucy Jane, 2, 5, 149
Wasserstein, Morris, 6–7, 147
Wasserstein, Sandra. *See* Meyer, Sandra Wasserstein
Watt, Douglas, 38, 54
Weaver, Lois, 14. *See also* Split Britches
Weeds (2005–2012), 162n1
Wegrzyn, Marisa, 152n10
Wellesley Center for Women, 4
Welsh, Katie, 157n7
Westside Theatre (New York), 15
Whitfield, Stephen, 143
Wiest, Dianne, 119
Wiig, Kristen: *Bridesmaids* (2011), 32
William Inge Theatre Festival Distinguished Achievement in the American Theatre Award, 149
Williamstown Theatre Festival (Williamstown), 112–17, 161n6, 162n14
Wolff, Tamsen, 143, 153n32, 154n45, 158n8, 167n11
Women's Experimental Theatre, ix
Women's Project and Productions Theatre (New York), 4
Wood, Kimba, 11, 100–102, 108
Woolf, Virginia, 27, 34–35

Yale School of Drama, 1, 7–9, 12–13, 23–24, 37, 138, 141, 144, 147, 158n4, 158n7

Zaks, Jerry, 52

Printed and bound by CPI Group (UK) Ltd, Croydon, CR0 4YY

09/06/2025

14685634-0001